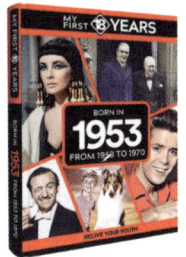
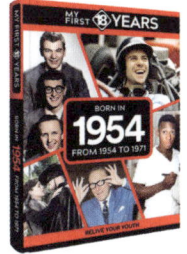

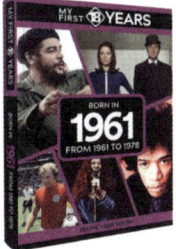
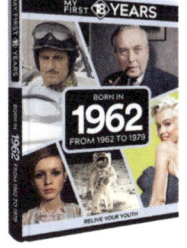
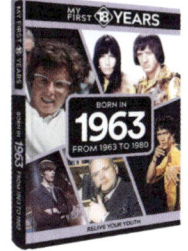
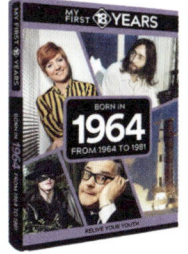

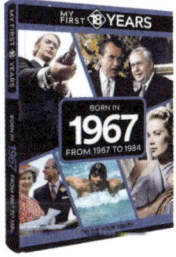

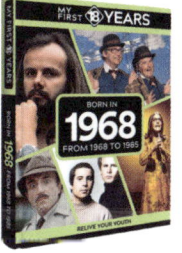

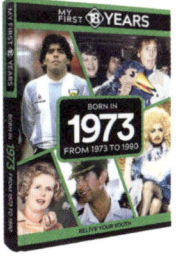
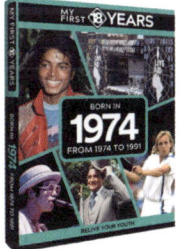
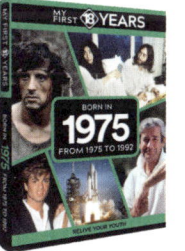

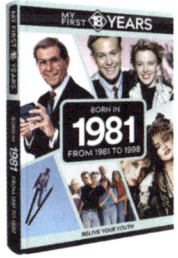
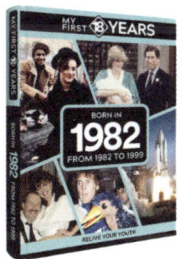
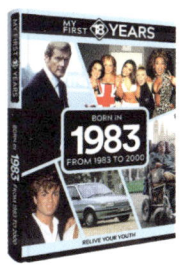
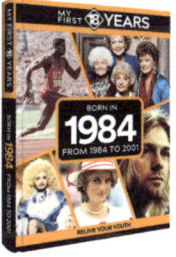

# MY FIRST 18 YEARS

**BORN IN**
# 1970
**FROM 1970 TO 1987**

© 2024 TDM Publishing. Rights reserved.

*My First 18 Years* is a brand of TDM Publishing.
The image, brand and logos are protected and owned by TDM Publishing.

www.mijneerste18jaar.nl
info@mijneerste18jaar.nl

*My First 18 Years* idea and concept: Thars Duijnstee.
Research and text: Lucinda Gosling, Stephen Barnard, Jeffrey Roozeboom, Katherine Alcock.
Composition and image editing: Jeffrey Roozeboom.
Design: Ferry Geutjes, Boudewijn van der Plas, Jeffrey Roozeboom.
Proofreading: Alison Griffiths.

Every effort has been made to trace the rights holders of all images. If you believe an image has been incorrectly credited, please contact the publisher.

No part of this publication may be reproduced, stored in or introduced to an automated data-file, or made public, in any form or by electronic, digital, mechanical, photocopying, recording or any other means, without the prior written consent of the publisher.

Photos: Sound & Vision, National Archives, Getty images, Mary Evans Picture Library, Shutterstock, BNNVARA, AVROTROS, Veronica, KRO-NCRV, KIPPA, *Mijn eerste 18 jaar* archives.

In writing this series, the authors drew from the following sources: view from 1963-1999, NTS / NOS Annual Review, nueens.nl, vandaagindegeschiedenis.nl, beleven.org, IMDb, Wikipedia, Eye Filmmuseum, Rollingstone.com, image & sound, National Archives, Onthisday.com, Parlement.com, *Complete Book of UK Hit Singles, First Hits 1949-1959* (Boxtree Books), Billboard Books, *Reader's Digest* Music series 1950s-1970s, British Library Newspaper Archive, rogerebert.com

Thanks to: Spotify, Rick Versteeg, Rik Booltink.

The Top 10 list for each year is compiled by Stephen Barnard and is a personal selection of best-selling hits, radio favourites and lesser-known tracks that reflect the popular artists and styles of each year. Some are universally regarded classics, others will be less remembered yet are equally emblematic of the tastes of that year. Each list should provoke many 'Ah yes!' moments, particularly those almost forgotten treasures that are rarely heard even as 'golden oldies' yet tickled the ears in their day.

How to use Spotify playlists:

1. Open Spotify.
2. Click search (the magnifying glass in the image).
3. Click scan (the camera in the picture).
4. Point your camera at the Spotify code in the book.
5. After that, you can play the selected list.

ISBN 978 94 9331 779 6
NUR: 400

# 1970 — MY FIRST 18 YEARS

## SPORT

### World Cup, Mexico '70
England travel to the World Cup in Mexico as defending champions, and kids around the country get busy collecting bubblegum and Panini cards and Esso medallions featuring their England heroes. England's first ever World Cup song, 'Back Home' proves prophetic and they are indeed back home sooner than anticipated after being knocked out in the quarter-finals by West Germany. In the group play-offs, they are also beaten by a magnificent Brazilian side who go on to win the tournament.

### Commonwealth Games
The British Commonwealth Games are held from the 16th to 25th July in Edinburgh. England come second in the medal table, behind Australia, with a good haul of medals in track and field.

### £200K move for Martin
Martin Peters becomes the first £200,000 footballer when he makes a move from West Ham to Tottenham Hotspur. The investment proves worthwhile for the North Londoners on 21st March, when he scores on his first appearance for his new team against Coventry City.

### A vintage year for Jacklin
1970 is a year to remember for Tony Jacklin who receives an OBE in the New Year honours list, then goes on to win the US Open at Hazaltine, Minnesota. Away from the golf course, he even records an album of American songbook standards, *Tony Jacklin Swings Into*.

### Dominance on Court
Australian Margaret Court wins all four Grand Slam tennis tournaments.

### England vs. Rest of the World

The South Africa cricket team are scheduled to play England this summer but mounting pressure over apartheid leads to a cancellation of their tour. With no international fixtures for England's 1970 cricket season, a Rest of the World team is formed, captained by Gary Sobers (photo). The World XI win the test match series 4-1 but Ray Illingworth's England side put in an impressive performance against a team featuring the cream of the world's cricketers.

---

**18 JAN 1970** — The grave of Karl Marx in Highgate Cemetery is vandalised and daubed with swastikas.

**11 FEB 1970** — Plans are announced to decentralise the NHS by creating ninety separate regional health authorities.

**6 MAR 1970** — A rabies outbreak in Newmarket, Suffolk leads to a ban on imported animals to the UK.

# 1970

## DOMESTIC NEWS

### Northern Ireland
In June there are riots in Derry over the arrest of MP Bernadette Devlin, imprisoned for incitement to riot during the Battle of the Bogside in 1969, and in July three civilians and a journalist are killed by the British Army in clashes with the Irish Republican Army in Belfast. On 23rd July, Irish Nationalists throw two cans of CS or 'tear' gas into the House of Commons chamber, leading to an evacuation and one MP being hospitalised.

### Thalidomide scandal
*23rd March 1970* The courts award nearly £370,000 to eighteen victims of the thalidomide scandal. Thalidomide, which was marketed as an anti-nausea drug to treat morning sickness in pregnant women, caused birth defects in some 10-20,000 children worldwide.

### Goodbye Minor – hello Range Rover!
*18th April 1970* British Leyland announce beloved classic the Morris Minor, in production since 1948, is to be discontinued. As fans say goodbye to the Minor, a new success is on the books for Leyland with the launch of the Range Rover in June. The new vehicle proves popular as a sleeker, more urban version of the classic Land Rover.

### Virgin gets going
*February 1970* Richard Branson launches his first Virgin Group business. The Virgin brand begins with a mail-order business offering popular records at a discount. The business' first store will open in 1971, before other products and businesses are added under the Virgin name.

### Bridge disasters
*23rd May 1970* Two bridges are heavily damaged within two weeks, as a fire in the Britannia Bridge over the Menai Strait is followed by the collapse of the Cleddau Bridge in Pembrokeshire. The fire in the Britannia Bridge is caused by schoolboys playing in the structure, whilst the collapse at Cleddau occurs during construction and results in the deaths of four workers.

DO YOU REMEMBER THIS?
Reel-to-reel tape recorder

BRITANNIA BRIDGE, MENAI STRAITS

### 4 APR 1970
Gay Trip wins the Grand National at Aintree.

### 19 MAY 1970
Government agrees to bail out Rolls Royce to the tune of £20 million as it struggles with cost of developing new aero-engines.

### 27 JUN 1970
The Bath Festival of Blues and Progressive Festival takes place and includes a headline set by Led Zeppelin.

# 1970

### Babes in the wood
*17th June 1970* The nation is horrified as the bodies of two children, Susan Blatchford and Gary Hanlon, are found in woodland at Sewardstone, Essex, 78 days after the friends disappeared on a walk. What happened to the children remains a mystery for over twenty years, until their murderer, Ronald Jebson, finally confesses in 1998.

### Docks strike
*15th July 1970* Dock workers across the United Kingdom go on strike, calling for an increase in wages of £11 a week. A state of emergency is declared as the strikes get underway, with the army standing ready to protect food imports. The strike is finally settled on the 30th, with an agreed increase in pay of 7%.

### Mangrove marches
*9th August 1970* Members of the black community in Notting Hill march to the local police station in protest at the frequent raids conducted on the Mangrove, a Caribbean restaurant that served as an important meeting place for black activists. Violence breaks out, and nine protesters are arrested and charged with incitement to riot. All are acquitted of incitement in a trial that sheds light on allegations of racism and brutality within the police force.

### Dawson's Field hijacks
*6th September 1970* As hijackings become part of the methodology of what are terrorists to some and freedom fighters to others, the Popular Front for the Liberation of Palestine (PFLP) hijack four passenger aircraft and force two of them to land at Dawson's Field, an airstrip in Jordan, where they are joined by a third a few days later. During intense negotiations, most of the hostages are released while the hijackers blow up the empty planes. While the Jordanian military move against Palestinian groups in the kingdom, the remaining hostages, all British, are released in exchange for captured hijackers.

### Goodbye to narrowboat freight
*15th October 1970* An era draws to a close, as the last narrowboats to carry commercial freight on UK canals deliver their final load of coal from Atherstone to West London. This delivery brings to an end a way of life and transport in existence since the eighteenth century.

### 8 JUL 1970
Painter Dame Laura Knight dies at the age of 92.

### 24 AUG 1970
A section of Windscale power station is sealed off due to a suspected radiation leak.

### 12 SEP 1970
Residents complain of noise following first landing of Concorde at Heathrow.

# 1970

### Iceland stores open
*18th November 1970* Malcolm Walker opens his very first Iceland store in Oswestry, Shropshire. Iceland specialises in frozen food, initially loose items, later launching its own-label packaged food in 1977. It quickly becomes a staple of the British high street, providing cheap dinners to price-conscious shoppers.

### In the Navy
Prince Charles graduates from the University of Cambridge with a 2:2 in History and joins the Royal Navy.

## FOREIGN NEWS

## ROYALTY & POLITICS

### Surprise at the polls
A General Election takes place on 18th June, the first where people aged 18 or over can vote following the lowering of the age of majority from 21 to 18 in the Representation of the People Act the previous year. After six years of a Labour government and against expectations, Edward Heath's Conservatives win a surprise victory.

### Margaret Thatcher, milk snatcher
Free school milk in secondary schools is abolished by Ted Heath's Conservative government. The proposal is passed on to Secretary of State for Education Margaret Thatcher who argues the savings can be used to improve school buildings. Rather than abolishing all school milk, she reaches a compromise. Milk is no longer provided in secondary schools, but nursery and primary school children continue to receive a ½ pint of milk each day, dished out by whichever pupil is given the weighty responsibility of being 'milk monitor'.

### East and West meet
*19th March 1970* For the first time since the division of Germany after the Second World War, West and East German leaders meet in person. West German Chancellor Willy Brandt is received warmly by East German Deputy Prime Minister Willi Stoph, heralding a normalisation of relations between the two countries. On a visit to Poland in December, Brandt is applauded when he unexpectedly kneels at the memorial to the uprising in the Warsaw ghetto in 1944.

### Coup in Japan
*25th November 1970* An attempted coup in Japan by right-wing militia leader Yukio Mishima fails. After making a public address, he commits *seppuku* - ritual suicide.

**19 OCT 1970**
BP announce they have found oil in British waters of the North Sea 110 mile east of Aberdeen.

**27 NOV 1970**
The Gay Liberation Front stage their first demonstration in London.

**15 DEC 1970**
MPs vote for an Industrial Relations Court in a bid to curb strikes.

# 1970

### 'Houston, we have a problem'
*11th April 1970* Apollo 13 launches to take men to the Moon for the third time. Two days after launch, the oxygen tank explodes. Captain Jim Lovell reports the issue with the words 'Okay, Houston, we've had a problem here'. The Moon landing is aborted and all efforts are focused on improvising a way to get the three astronauts safely back to Earth. This involves sending the craft into Moon orbit, shutting down the command module's systems to conserve its resources for re-entry and transferring the crew to the lunar module, which acts as a lifeboat. They splash down on 17th April at 18:07pm UK time. The men are safe, their rescue as breathtaking and ingenious as the original Moon landing itself.

### Earth Day
*22nd April 1970* The first Earth Day is celebrated to show support for protecting the globe's threatened environments. More than 20 million take part in peaceful protests across the US, beginning what becomes an annual global event that is still marked a half century later.

## ENTERTAINMENT

### Divorced, beheaded, died
The BBC stakes its position as an expert creator of quality period dramas with *The Six Wives of Henry VIII*, which begins on 1st January with Annette Crosbie playing the first of the spouses, Catherine of Aragon. Keith Mitchell turns in an Emmy Award-winning performance as the complex Tudor king and has to age throughout the series, transforming from cultured, athletic young prince to bloated, bitter middle-aged monarch. Lavish costumes and Tudor music all enhance the authentic period atmosphere.

### Nasser and de Gaulle
Two of the post-war world's most controversial politicians are no more. In September the death of General Gamal Abdel Nasser of Egypt changes the dynamic in the Middle East, as the outwardly more western-minded Anwar Sadat (photo) takes over as President. In November, the last of the Second World War leaders, former French President Charles de Gaulle, dies suddenly at the age of 80.

# 1970

### Who changes colour
Doctor Who regenerates for the second time on 3rd January and emerges in the form of Jon Pertwee. This new version of the Doctor has the air of a flamboyant Victorian dandy, with his velvet frock coats, frilly jabots and dramatic capes, much of which is harvested from Pertwee's own wardrobe. The transformation also coincides with the sci-fi drama being shown in colour for the first time.

### The Railway Children
*The Railway Children*, which is released on 21st December, tells the story of the three Waterbury children. When their beloved father is wrongly imprisoned, their mother (Dinah Sheridan) is obliged to leave behind a comfortable middle-class existence in suburban London and move to a modest cottage in Yorkshire. The film and its success has easily eclipsed E. Nesbit's original 1905 novel and includes a final scene guaranteed to ensure there isn't a dry eye in the cinema.

### Words and Pictures
*Words and Pictures*, the BBC Schools programme dedicated to helping children learn to read phonetically through animations and stories, is first broadcast on 17th October.

### Britain's fittest pit their wits
What will become Britain's longest-running sports quiz begins on BBC1 on 5th January. *A Question of Sport* is hosted by David Vine with boxer Henry Cooper and Welsh rugby international Cliff Morgan as team captains. The very first guests to share their sporting knowledge are footballers George Best and Tom Finney, cricketer Ray Illingworth and track and field athlete Lillian Board.

### Side-splitting
*The Banana Splits Adventure Hour* has been on American TV for two years before it is first shown in the UK on 20th February. Coming from the Hanna-Barbera stable, *The Banana Splits* features comedy sketches and cartoons, all topped off with an ear-worm of a theme tune. It's fast-paced and action-packed so it's no surprise that one of its directors, Richard Donner, goes on to make several Hollywood blockbusters including *The Goonies* and the *Lethal Weapon* series.

# 1970

**Scooby Dooby Doo**
September sees the introduction of two new cartoon characters in the UK. On the 17th, *Scooby-Doo, Where Are You!* is shown on BBC1. Scooby is a dim but lovable Great Dane who accompanies a gang of teens who drive around in the Mystery Machine solving spooky crimes. Two days after Scooby's debut, slinky, rose-tinted sophisti-cat *The Pink Panther* prowls nonchalantly onto screens, accompanied by Henry Mancini's famous creeping saxophone theme tune.

**Cat-napped**
*The Aristocats*, the last Disney Studios film to be approved by Walt Disney himself before his death in 1966, is released in cinemas on 27th December.

**Sing and bear it**
Although he doesn't look a day over 10, Rupert Bear is already 50 years old when he stars in *The Adventures of Rupert Bear* on ITV this year. Now, Rupert, who lives with his mother and father in Nutwood, is brought to life as a string puppet along with his friends Bill Badger, Podge the Pig, Pong Ping the Pekingese and a host of other characters. Just thirteen episodes of *The Adventures of Rupert Bear* are initially made (the first airs on 28th October) but the series is such a success, it eventually runs for six years and 156 episodes.

**The Street reaches 1,000th episode**
*Coronation Street* celebrates its 1,000th episode on 19th August but on 30th June, actor Arthur Leslie, who plays Rovers Return landlord Jack Walker, dies suddenly of a heart attack, obliging the Street's writers to come up with a storyline to explain his absence (it is decided Jack would suffer the same fate off-screen). Key characters departing for whatever reason is a recurring issue in a long-running soap but as the novelist John Braine concludes in a piece he writes in a special 1,000th episode issue of the *TV Times*, 'the most important character in the Street is the Street itself. No matter who comes and goes, the Street remains.'

**Scouting for jobs**
With the advent of decimalisation, the Scout Association decide to change the name of their annual Bob-A-Job Week to the less snappy-sounding Scout Job Week.

**Goodie, Goodie yum-yum**
Cambridge Footlights alumni Tim Brooke-Taylor, Graeme Garden and Bill Oddie aka *The Goodies* are let loose on TV screens on 8th November. Cycling around on their 'trandem' their cartoonish humour has huge, cross-generational appeal. Viewers can't get enough of sketches like Kitten Kong (using chroma-key, green screen technology), Bill practising the ancient martial art of 'Ecky Thump' and their catalogue of silly songs including stone-cold classic, '*The Funky Gibbon*'.

# 1970

## Page 3 provocation
Editor of the *Sun* newspaper, Larry Lamb, starts publishing a daily photograph of a topless glamour model on page 3, a controversial move that helps to double the newspaper's circulation to 2.5 million within a year. Page 3 understandably provokes protests against the sexualisation of women in what is marketed as a 'family newspaper' but it will be 45 years before the *Sun* removes Page 3 girls from its printed paper in 2015 after increasing pressure from campaigners. By 2017, topless models also disappear from its web site.

## Scent of the seventies
The fragrance Aqua Manda's musky blend of mandarin, coriander, jasmine and aromatic herbs pervades every party, club and disco in the land. With its distinctive orange floral packaging and reasonable price point, Aqua Manda is the undisputed smell of the seventies.

## Creedence opt out
*26th March 1970* Woodstock, the film of the 1970 music festival, goes on global release. Missing from the movie is a group who performed there but vetoed their inclusion in the film - Creedence Clearwater Revival. Originally from San Francisco and one of the top groups on the planet right now, Creedence's music is barnstorming rock'n'roll that conjures up a southern landscape of swamps, riverboats and highways in piledrivers like *Proud Mary* and *Up Around the Bend*.

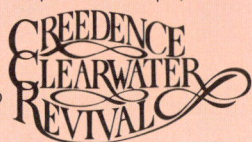

## Butch Cassidy and the Sundance Kid
Paul Newman and Robert Redford make a pair of devastatingly handsome Wild West outlaws in *Butch Cassidy and the Sundance Kid*, which arrives in UK cinemas on 6th February. The inclusion of the Burt Bacharach song *Raindrops Keep Falling on my Head* is controversial yet the track, which is used to accompany the famous bicycle scene in the film, goes on to become a huge hit reaching No. 1 in the US Billboard chart.

## The Beatles split
*10th April 1970* Paul McCartney has left the Beatles. The band's dissolution is finalised in the courts at the end of the year. The *Let it Be* album is a mixed epitaph, disliked by Paul for the production sheen added by John's buddy Phil Spector. Paul is first to release a solo album with *McCartney*, while Ringo makes an LP of swing era songs as a present for his mum. John records as the Plastic Ono Band but it is a rejuvenated George who wins the most plaudits with the Spector-produced *All Things Must Pass*.

# MUSIC

## Jackson Five
*25th April 1970* At No. 1 in the US with *ABC* are the Jackson Five, the soul-singing siblings discovered by Diana Ross. Originally from Gary, Indiana, the group are as dazzling to watch as they are to listen or dance to - much of which is down to twelve-year-old Michael's precociously emotive voice and stage presence.

# 1970

## Simon says
*28th February 1970* As news breaks that Simon and Garfunkel have parted company, their sonic masterpiece *Bridge over Troubled Water* begins its hold on the single and LP charts in the US and UK. Its soul-searching introspection has touched a real chord with America's post-Woodstock generation.

## 'Four dead in Ohio'
*4th May 1970* Crosby, Stills, Nash and Young are America's supergroup of the moment. Formed by members of the Byrds (David Crosby), Buffalo Springfield (Steve Stills, Neil Young) and the Hollies (Graham Nash), their music is homespun but spiky - especially the impassioned *Ohio*, one of the most political songs ever to reach the US Top 40. It is Young's response to the shooting by National Guardsmen of four protesting students at Kent State University.

## Everything's all Wight
*26th - 31st August 1970* The second Isle of Wight Festival attracts 500,000 people. The most glowing reviews go to Emerson, Lake and Palmer, the supergroup playing live for only the second time. The most lingering memory is of Jimi Hendrix making what will be his very last live performance.

## Hendrix is dead
*18th September 1970* Jimi Hendrix dies in London aged 27 after taking an overdose of barbiturates and choking on his own vomit. The coroner returns an open verdict. As demonstrated indelibly by his *Are You Experienced* and *Electric Ladyland* albums, Hendrix was simply the most imaginative, most technically adept and most instinctively creative guitarist of his generation.

## Just a word
*3rd June 1970* Making a 6,000-mile round trip today to re-record just one word of his song *Lola* is Ray Davies of the Kinks. BBC Radio won't play the track unless its reference to Coca-Cola is changed. So Ray flies to London, enters a recording studio and sings 'cherry cola' instead, then hotfoots it back to the US. It's surprising that the BBC is prepared to play it at all, given that Lola is a transvestite.

## Janis is dead
*4th October 1970* Still reeling from the death of Jimi Hendrix, the rock world is shaken by the death of Janis Joplin at the same age of 27. The greatest white female blues voice of her time, her death is attributed to a heroin overdose. She had only been solo for a year, having stuck with the San Francisco band Big Brother and the Holding Company longer than she needed to.

# 1970

### Singer-songwriters on the rise
Singer-songwriters are the flavour of the year, many of them recording for the hippest California record label, Warner Reprise. Some have been around for a while - James Taylor recorded for Apple in London, Joni Mitchell made her first LP in 1968, and Van Morrison has his roots in the UK beat boom - but the introspective nature of their songs suits the new decade's sombre mood. Taylor's *Sweet Baby James* outsells them all but August sees a young UK singer-pianist make his live US debut at the Troubadour in Los Angeles. His name is Elton John.

### Eric becomes Derek
*15th June 1970* Having joined Delaney and Bonnie Bramlett's touring band to expunge the excesses of his Cream and Blind Faith days, Eric Clapton forms Derek and the Dominoes with the Bramletts' rhythm section. The revitalised Clapton plays in a subtler, more concise and low-key style typified by *Layla*, a love song to George Harrison's wife Patti, who he will marry after their divorce.

### MY FIRST 18 YEARS TOP 10 — 1970

1. **Layla** Derek and the Dominoes
2. **Big Yellow Taxi** Joni Mitchell
3. **Fire and Rain** James Taylor
4. **Mama Told Me Not to Come** Three Dog Night
5. **Spirit in the Sky** Norman Greenbaum
6. **Tears of a Clown** Smokey Robinson
7. **Woodstock** Matthews Southern Comfort
8. **I Hear You Knockin'** Dave Edmunds
9. **Let it Be** The Beatles
10. **Abraham, Martin and John** Marvin Gaye

### Happy families
*23rd September 1970* From Screen Gems, makers of *The Monkees*, comes a television music show that makes a huge star of showbiz kid David Cassidy. *The Partridge Family* is about a pop group of young siblings and their mother, played by Hollywood songstress Shirley Jones, heartthrob David's real life stepmother.

### Guitar heroes
If Jimi Hendrix defined the term 'guitar hero', other axe-playing stars are ready to take on the mantle such as Rory Gallagher of Taste, Alvin Lee of Ten Years After and Led Zeppelin's Jimmy Page. For Peter Green, the adulation is too much and he leaves Fleetwood Mac before the band makes a career-changing move to the US.

PHOTO CREDITS Copyright 2024, TDM Rights BV.
Photos: **A** Peter Robinson Empics - PA Images / **B** PA Images - Getty Images / **C** Roger Jackson - Hulton Archive - Getty Images / **D** Bettmann - Getty Images / **E** Fox Photos - Hulton Archive - Getty Images / **F** Bettmann - Getty images / **G** Bettmann - Getty Images / **H** Matt Stroshane - Getty Images / **I** Bettmann - Getty Images / **J** Ronald Grant Archive - Mary Evans / **K** Evening Standard - Hulton Archive - Getty Images / **L** Studiocanal Films Ltd - Mary Evans / **M** BBC - AF Archive - Mary Evans / **N** AF Archive - Mary Evans / **O** Ruby Spears Productions - Ronald Grant Archive - Mary Evans / **P** Disney - AF Archive - Mary Evans / **Q** AF Archive - Mary Evans / **R** The Scout Association - Mary Evans / **S** BBC - Ronald Grant - Mary Evans / **T** Sunset Boulevard - Corbis Historical - Getty Images / **U** Michael Ochs Archives - Getty Images / **V** Michael Ochs Archives - Getty Images / **W** Michael Ochs Archives - Getty Images / **X** Universal History Archive - Universal History Archive - Getty Images / **Y** GAB Archive - Redferns - Getty Images / **Z** GAB Archive - Redferns - Getty Images.

# 1971

## MY FIRST 18 YEARS

## SPORT

### Tragedy at Ibrox
66 people are killed and 200 more are injured during the 'Old Firm' match between Glasgow Rangers and Celtic at the Ibrox Stadium in Glasgow on 2nd January, due to a crush as fans exit the game. The stadium had suffered tragedy once already when a wooden stand collapsed during an international match in 1902, killing 25. The 1971 disaster is the worst in British football history to that point and leads to a rebuilding of Rangers ground.

### Arsenal win the double
Five days after becoming League champions of the 1970-1 football season Arsenal face Liverpool at Wembley on 8th May in front of a crowd of 100,000 for the FA Cup Final. They win 2-1 with goals in extra time from Eddie Kelly (helped by George Graham) and Charlie George. The win makes Arsenal only the fourth team to secure the double.

### V for victory?
Show jumping rebel Harvey Smith, son of a Yorkshire builder, loses a major title and £2000 in prize money after allegedly flicking the 'V' sign at the judges at the British Show Jumping Derby with horse Mattie Brown on 15th August. Smith protests he was making a 'V for victory' gesture. Notorious for clashing with judges and officials, Smith is a great favourite with the public and after two days his disqualification is reversed.

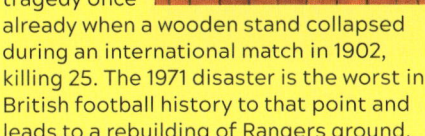

## DOMESTIC NEWS

### Northern Ireland
Troubles in Northern Ireland continue with violent riots throughout the year. In August, hundreds of people are arrested by British forces and are interred in Long Kesh prison, where they are held without trial. Known as 'Operation Demetrius', this policy leads to the Ballymurphy Massacre, where eleven people are killed by British forces. The autumn sees a fourteen-year-old girl, Annette McGavigan, killed when caught in crossfire, and two women shot dead at a checkpoint in Belfast. The worst incident of the Troubles so far occurs on 4th December, when a bomb destroys McGurk's bar in Belfast killing fifteen.

### The lion roars
The British Lions rugby tour of New Zealand between 12th May and 14th August sees them play in four Test series against the mighty All Blacks. The British side, captained by John Dawes and comprised of the best players from the England, Ireland, Wales and Scotland teams, win two, lose one and draw in a final, nail-biting match to secure a historic Test series win.

**15 JAN 1971**
George Harrison releases his first solo single *My Sweet Lord*.

**6 FEB 1971**
Apollo 14 astronaut Alan Shepard hits a golf ball on the moon during a two-day moonwalk.

**8 MAR 1971**
Brian Faulkner becomes Prime Minister of Northern Ireland.

# 1971

### Divorce Reform
*1st January 1971* The year begins with changes to divorce laws in the UK, allowing couples to divorce if they have been living separately for two years. For the first time divorce can be granted on the grounds that the relationship has irretrievably broken down, with no need for one partner to be proven at fault.

### Seabed treaty
*11th February 1971* Countries including the UK, USA and Soviet Union sign the Seabed Arms Control Treaty which agrees to outlaw the use of nuclear weapons on the ocean floors. The treaty covers the seabed within 12 miles of the coast and seeks to prevent the escalation of nuclear tensions.

### Postal workers strike
*20th January 1971* Postal workers go out on strike for the first time in their history, demanding a better pay deal. The strike lasts seven weeks and sees a variety of alternatives spring up in the space left by the Post Office.

### Decimalisation day
*15th February 1971* The UK and the Republic of Ireland complete the switch to a decimal currency. Pounds are now worth 100 pence, replacing the 'old money' system of 20 shillings to the pound and 12 pence to the shilling. Initially people can still pay in old money, but they receive their change in the new currency. As of September, the old penny and threepence are no longer legal tender.

### Angry Brigade bombs
*12th January 1971* The home of the Secretary of State for Employment, Robert Carr, is bombed along with his offices at the Department of Education. Responsibility is claimed by a left-wing group calling themselves the 'Angry Brigade'. Before the year is out, they will have struck the Biba store in Kensington, London, and the Post Office Tower.

## 15 APR 1971
City of London announces plans for the building of the Barbican Centre.

## 11 MAY 1971
Closure of 62-year-old paper, *The Daily Sketch*.

## 19 JUN 1971
Viewing figures show talent show Opportunity Knocks is the country's most popular TV programme.

# 1971

## Industrial Relations Act protests
**1st March 1971** The proposed Industrial Relations Act prompts huge protests in London where between 120,000 and 250,000 people join 'kill the bill' strikes across the capital. The Act will ensure that only registered trade unions have negotiating power, something workers fear will lead to restrictions upon industrial action. Despite this, the bill is passed and receives royal assent in September.

## Spaghetti Junction opens
**10th November 1971** The infamous Gravelly Hill Interchange or 'Spaghetti Junction' opens for the first time. Initially featuring 10 routes, including the A38, A5127, and M6, it later expands to 12 in 1972.

## ROYALTY & POLITICS

## UK to join EEC
The House of Commons approves the UK's entry into Europe by a majority of 112 votes on 28th October. In his speech to the Commons, Anthony Barber, Chancellor of the Exchequer says, 'We shall join the Six as a proud and powerful country, able and ready to make its full contribution.'

## Royal winner
After winning the individual medal at the world 3-day eventing championship at Burghley, aged 21, Princess Anne is voted BBC Sports Personality of the Year.

## Paisley forms DUP
Protestant minister, hardline Unionist and MP for North Antrim Ian Paisley founds the Democratic Unionist Party (DUP).

## Queen gets a big pay rise
Parliament debates an increase to the Civil List from £475,000 to £980,000. The Commons Select Committee, which makes the recommendation, justifies the increase of more than 100% stating, 'there is little further scope for economies in the Royal Household'.

**6 JUL 1971** Crash helmets are to become compulsory for motorcyclists.

**27-28 AUG 1971** Clashes break out between police and Hell's Angels at Weeley Festival in Essex.

**3 SEP 1971** Qatar gains independence from the United Kingdom.

# 1971

## FOREIGN NEWS

**Idi the cruel**
*25th January 1971* General Idi Amin Dada seizes power in Uganda when President Milton Obote makes a trip abroad. The former boxing champion is welcomed at first but soon establishes a destructive dictatorship which earns him the nickname 'Slaughterer of Africa'. During his reign, Amin has 300,000 opponents eliminated.

**The first email**
In the US, 23 computers located at various universities are now connected to the ARPANET, the forerunner of the internet. Computer programmer Ray Tomlinson sends the first message over the network from one computer to another. He comes up with the @ sign to distinguish the domain and the recipient. The medium we know as email is born.

**Starbucks starts**
*30th March 1971* The first branch of coffee shop giant Starbucks opens in Seattle, Washington, as a store selling varities of coffee beans.

**First space station**
*19th April 1971* Salyut 1, the world's first space station, is launched by the Soviet Union. The first crew of cosmonauts is unable to dock while the second crew are also forced to abort after 23 days aboard in June. When their craft, Soyuz 11, returns to Earth, all three cosmonauts are found dead from an air supply leak. The decision to abandon the station is taken in October.

**Pentagon Papers**
*30th June 1971* The US Supreme Court rules that the *New York Times* can publish the Pentagon Papers, overruling objections from the Nixon administration. The Papers are classified studies made for the Department of Defense which reveal the double-dealing and secret machinations that brought the US to war in Vietnam. The revelations strengthen opposition to the war still further in a year in which Australia and New Zealand withdraw their troops from Vietnam, the US resumes bombing of North Vietnam and the conflict spreads to Laos.

**Bangladesh goes alone**
*31st May 1971* Four months after the devastating Cyclone Bhola, the former East Pakistan - now Bangladesh - declares its independence from Pakistan, which brutally crushes the rebellion and creates two million refugees. After Pakistan declares war on India in December, India invades Bangladesh with Bengali rebel support. Pakistan surrenders on 15th December.

## 1 OCT 1971
The CAT scan is first used in patient diagnosis in Wimbledon.

## 28 NOV 1971
51-year-old farmer, Ray Covine, uncovers an immigrant smuggling operation on his farm near Huntingdon.

## 30 DEC 1971
Sean Connery returns for the final time as Bond in Diamonds are Forever.

# 1971

## ENTERTAINMENT

**Twin towers topped out**
*19th July 1971* The topping out of the South Tower of the new World Trade Center in New York takes place, following the topping-out ceremony for the North Tower six months earlier.

**Greenpeace launches**
*14th October 1971* Greenpeace is founded in Vancouver, Canada, to campaign actively against US plans for nuclear tests in Alaska. As the organization grows its action-based but non-violent opposition to causes such as large-scale whaling, seal hunting and the dumping of nuclear waste at sea brings it into direct conflict with governments.

Chocolate cigarettes

**Top deck**
The first episode of *Here Come the Double Deckers* is shown on BBC1 on 15th January. A comedy adventure series with a brilliant theme tune, it features a gang of kids - Scooper, Tiger, Brains, Sticks, Doughnut, Spring and Billie - whose HQ is an abandoned double-decker bus in a London junkyard. The Double Deckers get into various scrapes every episode, and most of us wonder where on earth their parents are.

**Clackers really knacker**
Possibly the worst idea for a toy ever, 'clackers', consisting of two hard acrylic balls on string, are all the rage during the summer of 1971. After several accidents, many schools ban them as a serious hazard.

# 1971

### Kids get a *Look-In*
*Look-in* is launched as a junior version of the *TV Times*. Jam-packed with comic strips, interviews and pull-out posters focused on ITV's programmes, it also features pop music, cool hobbies like skateboarding and a regular column from radio DJ Ed Stewart called, 'Stewpot's Newsdesk'. Through most of the 1970s, *Look-in* covers are illustrated by Arnaldo Putzo, who also designs posters for films like *Get Carter* and the *Carry On* series.

### Elizabeth R
The success of *The Six Wives of Henry VIII* in 1970 encourages the BBC to tackle the story of his daughter next; the first of six 75-minute episodes is shown on 17th February. *Elizabeth R* has Glenda Jackson in imperious form, playing the queen from a fifteen-year-old princess to the aging Gloriana.

### A shocking end
Valerie Barlow (Anne Reid) and husband Ken (William Roache) are preparing to leave the Street for a new life in Jamaica in *Coronation Street*'s 27th January edition when she is electrocuted by a faulty hairdryer and killed instantly.

### Music for musos
On 21st September, the thinking person's music show, *The Old Grey Whistle Test* airs for the first time. This is the place to hear non-chart music and album tracks through live performances in a pared-back studio setting. *The Old Grey Whistle Test* boasts some special moments in music from Roxy Music in their glam rock pomp performing *Ladytron* to David Bowie on the eve of his 1972 Ziggy Stardust tour, rattling through a blistering performance of *Queen Bitch*.

### *Playaway* on Saturday
*Playaway* starts on 20th November and becomes a Saturday afternoon refuge for kids away from sports-dominated weekend TV schedules during the 1970s. A older sibling of the weekday programme *Playschool*, its lively variety show format includes songs, bad jokes, sketches, and general tomfoolery. Along with more familiar Playschool alumni like Brian Cant and Floella Benjamin (photo), Jeremy Irons and Tony Robinson both do time as Playaway presenters.

# 1971

## Comedy sitcoms on-screen
Several popular British TV sitcoms capitalise on their success and get a big-screen upgrade this year with *Dad's Army*, *Up Pompeii* and *On the Buses* all made into full-length feature films.

## Upstairs, Downstairs
*Upstairs, Downstairs*, the long-running drama about the aristocratic Bellamy family of 165 Eaton Place, SW1 and their retinue of servants below stairs, is the surprise hit drama of the decade. Originally the idea of actresses Eileen Atkins and Jean Marsh (who would play parlourmaid Rose Buck in the series), the first episode of this period drama is buried by ITV in the ignominious 10:15pm slot on Sunday 10th October, but audience figures quickly increase, eventually soaring to 18 million. Through five series, the lives of the Bellamys and their employees are interwoven with world events such as the suffragette movement and the sinking of the *Titanic*, in a dramatic formula that would be successfully revived four decades later in *Downton Abbey*.

## Save us from Sesame Street
British kids have enjoyed American cartoons and comedy series since the 1950s but are introduced to a very different kind of transatlantic offering this year in a show that provokes significant controversy in advance of its broadcast on 29th March on HTV. *Sesame Street* is populated by a cast of brightly coloured puppets (many created by Jim Henson) whose daily lives form the basis of didactic teaching methods. The BBC refuses to air it since it seems specifically tailored to educating American children; ITV does so reluctantly on the understanding it 'should not be construed as endorsement of *Sesame Street* to British children'. The hand wringing of educationalists means little to parents and children, who love characters like Big Bird, Eric and Ernie and The Count (who, you've guessed it, counts!) and find novelty in exotic Americanisms such as trash, zip code and cookies - as gobbled up by Cookie Monster.

## And it's goodnight from him
*The Two Ronnies* appear on BBC1 on 10th April in a show that will run for the next sixteen years. With many sketches based on Ronnie Barker's fondness for word play (and others playfully mocking Ronnie Corbett's short stature), their partnership produces comedy gold from a brain-teasing *Mastermind* spoof to hardware store confusion in 'Four Candles'.

# 1971

## A ticklish tale
The first six books in the *Mr. Men* series by advertising executive and frustrated cartoonist Roger Hargreaves are published on 10th August. The very first character is *Mr. Tickle*, whose unfeasibly long arms cause all sorts of mischief. *Mr. Men* is an instant success and becomes a cartoon series in 1974 (narrated by Arthur Lowe). Hargreaves goes on to create 46 *Mr. Men* and 33 *Little Miss* characters in total. In 2004, his widow sells the rights to *Mr. Men* to Chorion for a cool £28 million.

### Beatrix Potter ballet
*The Tales of Beatrix Potter*, a ballet film featuring various characters created by Potter, danced by the Royal Ballet to choreography by Sir Frederick Ashton, is released in cinemas 30th June. Wayne Sleep dances the part of Squirrel Nutkin; Ashton himself plays Mrs. Tiggywinkle. The costumes by Christine Edzard form an exhibition on board the *QE2* liner this year.

### Very persuasive
The pairing of Tony Curtis and Roger Moore as millionaire playboys from different sides of the tracks in *The Persuaders* is intentionally incongruous, with Curtis as the rough and ready New Yorker Danny Wilde, and Moore playing to type as the posh and polished British nobleman, Lord Brett Sinclair. Sporting equally wide sideburns and ties, *The Persuaders* embark on a series of escapades with the help of fast cars, John Barry's seventies synth soundtrack and glamorous co-stars like Susan George, Imogen Hassall and Joan Collins. Curtis, aged 46, personally performs all of his stunts.

### On-screen Gangster
A grim and gloomy Newcastle-upon-Tyne is the setting for *Get Carter*, released 10th March, featuring Michael Caine as a brutal London gangster returning to his roots to seek revenge among the Geordie criminal underworld.

## MUSIC

### Balm for the soul
*10th February 1971* After divorce from Gerry Goffin, re-marriage and a move to the Californian hills, top 60s songwriter Carole King is back with an album full of homeliness and good feeling. Including her own versions of *I Feel the Earth Move, You've Got a Friend* and *A Natural Woman*, *Tapestry* is musical balm for the soul in dark times. Over 25 million sales prove it.

### Stones get sticky
*12th May 1971* Negative headlines surround Mick Jagger's *très chic* wedding to Nicaraguan socialite Bianca Pérez-Mora Macías in St Tropez. The Stones are getting stick in the music press for becoming tax exiles in the south of France but they are on top form with the *Sticky Fingers* album, the first Stones release on their very own record label. Its cover has a real working zip - the work of Andy Warhol's Factory and a nightmare for record store owners the world over.

# 1971

### Glastonbury
*20th - 24th June 1971* Worthy Farm owner Michael Eavis times the first Glastonbury Festival proper - after a small event under a different name a year earlier - to coincide with the summer solstice. The line-up includes Traffic, Fairport Convention, a pre-Ziggy Stardust David Bowie and a diehard of 1970s festivals, Hawkwind.

### Blue days
*22nd June 1971* Joni Mitchell releases *Blue*, the outcome of a year of travelling after her relationship with Graham Nash breaks up. A searingly honest and self-revealing LP, it will dazzle and inspire scores of artists over the next 50 years.

### Marvin's mission
*21st May 1971* Motown superstar Marvin Gaye releases the album *What's Going On*, a huge shift from the punchy dance-driven tracks he is known for. Largely inactive since the death of his singing partner Tammi Terrell and his failing marriage to Berry Gordy's sister Anna, Marvin has set a series of socially conscious songs to a looser, expansive sound. Motown owner Gordy thinks it's commercial suicide but hands him a new deal allowing him creative freedom - at one million dollars, the most lucrative deal yet secured by a black recording artist.

### Satchmo passes on
*6th July 1971* Louis Armstrong, the cornet-playing father of Dixieland jazz, dies at the age of 71.

### Concerts for Bangladesh
*1st August 1971* George Harrison organises two Concerts for Bangladesh at Madison Square Garden, New York. Joining him on stage are Eric Clapton, Bob Dylan and sitar virtuoso Ravi Shankar. The concerts and subsequent album raise around $12 million for victims of the Bangladesh catastrophe.

Rotary dial telephone

### T. Rextasy!
Singing songs about hobbits and goblins in a quavering voice, Marc Bolan of *Tyrannosaurus Rex* was an icon of late 1960s progressive rock. Now former male model Marc has truncated the band's name to T. Rex and is ditching the hippie gear for an androgynous glittery look and a much younger (and female) audience.

### Gene Vincent RIP
*12th October 1971* Be Bop a Lula legend Gene Vincent dies in California aged 36. Although plagued by a leg injury aggravated by the car crash that killed his friend Eddie Cochran in 1961, he epitomised the rough and greasy sound and look of classic rock'n'roll.

# 1971

### The club of 27
*3rd July 1971* Jim Morrison, charismatic leader of California band the Doors, is found dead in his bathtub at his apartment in Paris aged 27. The rest of the group try to carry on but disband at the end of 1972.

### Zappa attacked
*10th December 1971* Frank Zappa, musical iconoclast and satirist of the pretentious and worthy, receives life-changing injuries when he is pulled off stage by a fan at the Rainbow Theatre, Finsbury Park.

### Lennon leaves UK
*3rd September 1971* John Lennon leaves the UK for New York with wife Yoko. He will never return. After exploring his primal therapy treatment in *John Lennon and the Plastic Ono Band*, he makes the mellower *Imagine* but can't resist a scoff at Paul McCartney on the track *How Do You Sleep*. He and Yoko end the year by wishing everyone *Happy Xmas (War is Over)* in a Christmas single.

## MY FIRST 18 YEARS TOP 10 — 1971

1. **Maggie May** Rod Stewart
2. **Help Me Make it Through …** Kris Kristofferson
3. **Theme from Shaft** Isaac Hayes
4. **My Sweet Lord** George Harrison
5. **Sweet Caroline** Neil Diamond
6. **Gypsies, Tramps and Thieves** Cher
7. **Family Affair** Sly and the Family Stone
8. **Just My Imagination** The Temptations
9. **Coz I Luv You** Slade
10. **I'm Still Waiting** Diana Ross

### Hello ELO
*October 1971* As the Move call it a day with a final concert tour, Roy Wood and Jeff Lynne launch the Electric Light Orchestra (ELO) with a musical blueprint inspired by the Beatles' cello-laden *I Am the Walrus*. Within a year Wood leaves to form Wizzard and Lynne takes ELO to the next level with plans for a full string section and spectacular stage effects.

---

PHOTO CREDITS Copyright 2024, TDM Rights BV.
Photos: A Lynne Cameron - PA Images - Getty Images / B De bergamont - Shutterstock / C PA Images - Getty Images / D Dave Rendle - / E Mirrorpix - Getty Images / F Mirrorpix - Getty Images / G William Vanderson - ulton Archive - Getty Images / H Keystone - Hulton Archive - Getty Images / I Bettmann - Getty Images / J Bettmann - Getty Images / K Ronald Grant Archive - Mary Evans / L Mondadori Portfolio Editorial - Getty Images / M John Madden - Hulton Archive - Getty Images / N Watal Asanuma Shinko Music - ulton Archive - Getty Images / O Mirrorpix - Getty Images / P Studiocanal Films Ltd - Mary Evans / Q AF Archive - Mary Evans / R PA Images - Getty Images / S David Cairns - Hulton Archive - Getty Images / T Ronald Grant Archive - Mary Evans / U Estate of Keith Morris - Redferns - Getty Images / V Jim Britt - Michael Ochs Archives - Getty Images / W Ullstein Bild - Getty Images / X Keystone - Hulton Archive - Getty Images / Y Hulton Archive - Getty Images.

# 1972

 **SPORT**

### A league of their own
The Great Britain rugby league team arrive for the World Cup in France as the underdogs, but confound expectations and win the tournament. Great Britain is captained by Clive Sullivan, the first black player to captain a British team at any sport.

### Pawns or kings?
*11th July 1972* It's the Cold War in miniature: seemingly invincible world chess champion Boris Spassky of the Soviet Union versus mercurial US champion Bobby Fischer in neutral Reykjavik, Iceland. After 21 games, with Fischer leading, Spassky concedes. The final score is 12 ½ to 8 ½. Fischer becomes the first American world chess champion.

### Golden girl
33 year old Mary Peters from Belfast is Britain's Olympic champion in Munich when she triumphs over her rival, the West German Heide Rosendahl, to clinch the gold medal in the pentathlon. Peters wins by just 10 points, setting a world record in the process.

Platform shoe

### Gymnastic wonder
Belarussian gymnast Olga Korbut rewrites the rule book by performing unprecedented moves at the Olympics; a back flip on the beam and what becomes known as the 'Korbut flip' on the asymmetric bars. Korbut's gobsmacking performance is hugely influential and within two years, three million British girls are members of gymnastic clubs.

### Women on the ball
It is a freezing afternoon on 18th November, when England and Scotland play the first ever women's football international in the UK at Ravenscraig Stadium, Greenock. England come from 2-0 down to win 3-2.

---

**13 JAN 1972**
Royal Navy officer David Bingham is sentenced to 21 years in prison after selling defence secrets to the Soviet Union to pay family debts.

**16 FEB 1972**
Nine-hour blackouts imposed across the country and householders asked to heat only one room as miners' pay dispute continues.

**31 MAR 1972**
A revival of the anti-nuclear Aldermaston marches of the 1950s and 1960s takes place, but with just 600 participants.

# 1972

## DOMESTIC NEWS

### Miners and dockers strike
*9th January 1972* Members of the National Union of Mineworkers go out on strike for seven weeks, with the fuel shortages and a cold snap leading to the Prime Minister declaring a national state of emergency as blackouts grip the nation. The strike ends in February with a pay agreement, but on 4th August a second state of emergency is declared after dock workers go out on strike following the trial of the Pentonville Five.

### Economic trouble
*20th January 1972* New figures demonstrate that over 1 million people are unemployed in the UK for the first time since the 1930s. The number has almost doubled in two years, casting doubt on Prime Minister Heath's handling of the economy. In November, the government freezes pay and prices in the hope of countering inflation, which falls slightly in the following months.

### Bloody Sunday
*30th January 1972* A dark day in British history as troops open fire on unarmed demonstrators in Derry, killing fourteen. The event becomes known as Bloody Sunday and precedes one of the worst years of the Troubles with 497 fatalities across numerous protests, clashes, and bombings. In February, the British Embassy in Dublin is burnt by rioters as days later mounted police charge protesters in London. Bombings in 1972 include explosions at Aldershot Barracks, 'Bloody Friday' bombings in Belfast, and the 'Claudy' bombing or 'Bloody Monday'. In March the British government introduces direct rule over Northern Ireland and enters secret negotiations with the Provisional IRA that prove fruitless.

### 27 APR 1972
Five Oxford University colleges announce plans to admit up to 100 women students in 1974.

### 22 MAY 1972
The Dominion of Ceylon becomes the Republic of Sri Lanka but remains within the British Commonwealth.

### 27 JUN 1972
The Official IRA calls a ceasefire and embarks on secret talks with the British government, but sectarian violence erupts again after two weeks.

# 1972

### Thomas Cook & Son privatised
*26th May 1972* Thomas Cook, owned by the government since 1948 as part of the British Transport Commission, is privatised. The business is purchased by a consortium including the Midland bank, which later becomes the sole controller, and continues to provide holidays to the British public well into the 21st century.

### Staines air disaster
*18th June 1972* British Airways Flight 548 crashes just outside Staines shortly after take-off from London Heathrow. All 118 people on their way to Brussels are killed, despite at least one person initially surviving the impact. It remains the deadliest air accident in UK history.

### Idi Amin expels British Asians
*4th August 1972* President of Uganda Idi Amin expels people of South Asian origin from the country in a wave of anti-Indian sentiment. Over the next three months, 27,200 of those who are British passport holders emigrate to the United Kingdom.

### School leaving age
*1st September 1972* The school leaving age in the UK is raised from 15 to 16 years old, sparking a wave of construction work across the country as schools build new classrooms to cater for the increase in student numbers.

### Battersea Fun Fair disaster
*30th May 1972* The nation is horrified when the Big Dipper rollercoaster at Battersea Fun Fair comes off its rails, killing five children and injuring thirteen. An investigation finds the ride manager and engineer guilty of manslaughter, and despite attempts to reopen with a replacement ride, the park closes in 1974.

### Gay Pride
*1st July 1972* The UK's very first Pride march takes place when 2,000 members of London's gay community take to the streets. The date selected is the nearest Saturday to the anniversary of the Stonewall riots in New York in 1969 and sees attendees protesting legislation targeting the gay community and demonstrating their pride in their sexuality.

## 28 JUL 1972
Nationwide dock strike begins and lasts until 16th August.

## 31 AUG 1972
American super swimmer Mark Spitz wins seven gold medals at the Munich Olympics, each in a record time.

## 14 SEP 1972
Death of Geoffrey Francis Fisher, former Archbishop of Canterbury who had presided over the 1953 Coronation.

# 1972

### The Second Cod War
*5th September 1972* The Second Cod War between Britain and Iceland breaks out as Iceland seeks to expand its territorial waters to 50 miles off the coast. An altercation between an Icelandic Coast Guard vessel and a British trawler, the *Peter Scott*, results in violence as the crew refuse to identify themselves and instead play *Rule Britannia!* over the radio. In November, the Foreign Secretary announces that British Navy ships will be stationed to defend trawlers in the disputed waters.

### Rise of Japanese cars
*1972* proves a popular year for Japanese cars, as Honda begins importing vehicles such as its Civic hatchback (photo). Nissan sells over 30,000 cars in Britain, more than three times the previous year's total, and Mazda and Toyota also enjoy success.

### Death of Duke of Windsor
The Queen visits her uncle the Duke of Windsor on 18th May during a state visit to France. The former king is too ill to be able to attend a tea provided by the Duchess downstairs, but the Queen spends fifteen minutes with her 'Uncle David' in his first-floor sitting-room. Just ten days later he dies of complications arising from throat cancer. He is laid to rest in the Royal Burial Ground at rogmore, Windsor on 5th June after a funeral service at St. George's Chapel.

### Tragedy for the Gloucesters
Thirty-year-old Prince William of Gloucester, elder son of the Duke and Duchess of Gloucester and cousin of the Queen, dies when his Cherokee single-engine aircraft crashes at the Goodyear International Air Trophy at Halfpenny Green near Wolverhampton on 28th August.

## ROYALTY & POLITICS

### Direct rule for Northern Ireland
*On 30th March,* the situation in Northern Ireland leads to the suspension of the Parliament of Northern Ireland which is replaced by direct rule by Westminster. William Whitelaw is appointed Secretary of State for Northern Ireland.

Rolodex

---

**23 OCT 1972**
Access credit cards – 'your flexible friend' – introduced as a rival to Barclaycard.

**NOV 1972**
The PEOPLE party is formed in Coventry, changing its name to the Ecology Party in 1975 and then the Green Party in 1985.

**6 DEC 1972**
Four members of revolutionary left-wing group The Angry Brigade are each jailed for ten years at the Old Bailey.

# 1972

## FOREIGN NEWS

### Yokoi at peace
**24th January 1972** Apparently unaware of his country's surrender at the end of the Second World War, Japanese soldier Shoichi Yokoi is discovered on the Pacific island of Guam after spending 28 years hiding in the jungle.

### Nixon on the world stage
**21st February 1972** Richard Nixon's popularity is on a high as he becomes the first US President to visit the People's Republic of China. In May, he is the first US President to visit the Soviet Union where he agrees a drastic reduction in nuclear weaponry with Soviet leader Brezhnev.

### Tricky Dicky
**17th June 1972** Five men are arrested when they break into the Democratic Party headquarters in the Watergate complex in Washington DC. Dogged *Washington Post* reporters Carl Bernstein and Bob Woodward make the link between the burglars and President Nixon's re-election campaign team and uncover a much larger plan of 'dirty tricks' to thwart the Democrat challenge. Nixon defeats Senator George McGovern in a landslide in November but is already slipping towards possible impeachment.

### War photo
**8th June 1972** After a devastating US napalm bombardment on the Vietnamese village of Trang Bàng, Nick Ut takes the most famous war photo in history. Nine-year-old girl Phan Thi Kim Phúc is running away from her bombed village, naked and crying. The desperate moment is captured by the photographer - who then takes her to hospital. When the photo appears on the front page of the *New York Times*, it prompts a further wave of revulsion against the war.

### Pocket calculator
Hewlett-Packard markets the first scientific pocket calculator, consigning the slide rule to history. The HP-35 weighs only 248 grams and measures 15 x 8.1 centimetres. It costs $395. Ultimately, 300,000 are sold.

# 1972

## Massacre at Munich
**5th - 6th September 1972** At the Olympic Games in Munich, two members of Israel's Olympic team are killed and nine kidnapped when Arab terrorist faction Black September invades the athletes' village. In an attempt by West German police to free the hostages, eleven Israelis, five terrorists and a policeman are killed. Incredibly, the Games continue.

## Andean air disaster
**13th October 1972** A Uruguayan plane carrying a rugby union team crashes into a glacier in the Andes on the border between Argentina and Chile. Only sixteen of the 45 passengers survive. They manage to stay alive in freezing conditions for 72 days by eating the flesh of their deceased fellow passengers.

## So long Apollo
**19th December 1972** With the return of Apollo 17 to Earth, the Apollo programme closes. Astronauts Gene Cernan and Harrison Schmitt are the last men to set foot on the Moon. Planning for the next crewed mission to the Moon will not begin until 2017.

## The limits to growth
A new report called *The Limits to Growth* shows that humanity's future is threatened by overpopulation, environmental pollution and depletion of raw materials. Modern phosphate-based detergents are blamed for water pollution, and aerosol cans and old refrigerators spread chlorofluorocarbons (CFCs) that cause the hole in the ozone layer.

# ENTERTAINMENT

## Fingerbobs
Quite possibly the lowest budget children's programme ever made, *Fingerbobs*, which is first shown on 14th February, features presenter Rick Jones aka Yoffy, who sits making up stories with the help of a random selection of creatures made from gloves and sugar paper - a rodent called Fingermouse, Gulliver the seagull, Scampi the sea creature and a typically slow and steady tortoise called Flash. Simple, charming, homespun fun.

## Puppy love
Andrex toilet tissue commercials featuring an adorable yellow Labrador puppy are shown for the first time this year. With guaranteed 'aah' factor, the puppy becomes the brand's enduring mascot, and helps Andrex build their market share to 30% by the end of the decade.

## And...action
On the April, *Clapperboard* begins on ITV. Presented by Chris Kelly, *Clapperboard* offers a fascinating insight into the world of film and television, past and present. It's a fount of knowledge for any budding movie buff.

# 1972

### Here is the news
*John Craven's Newsround*, explaining serious news in simple terms for kids, is broadcast on 4th April on BBC1. Craven fronts over 3,000 bulletins for *Newsround* until he leaves the programme in 1989. He also becomes resident news specialist on *Multicoloured Swap Shop* and *Saturday Superstore*.

### Cosmo girls
The first UK issue of the notoriously racy *Cosmopolitan* magazine is published in March. Alongside articles on fabulous fashion, beauty and careers, *Cosmo* delivers frank advice on sex and relationships. Over in the US, the April issue causes a sensation when it features a naked Burt Reynolds as the first male centrefold. No subject is taboo to the magazine's international editor-in-chief, Helen Gurley-Brown, whose 1962 international bestseller, *Sex and the Single Girl*, sets the tone. Cosmo readers are single career girls; ambitious, glamorous, and sexually adventurous. Can women have it all? Cosmo says 'yes'!

### Evel Knievel doll released
Ideal Toys release a six-inch action figure of American stunt motorcyclist Evel Knievel in the same year the real Evel attempts a high-publicised jump across the Snake River Canyon in Idaho (his parachute releases prematurely, ruining the stunt, but he gets away with only minor injuries).

### Watership Down
Richard Adams' epic novel about a band of rabbits risking everything to establish a new warren goes on to sell 50 million copies worldwide. The 1978 animation film is an instant classic, fuelled by the Art Garfunkel's song *Bright Eyes*.

### Pebble Mill at One
In January, the government lifts the restrictions on the numbers of hours of broadcasting and schedulers begin to look at expanding daytime programming. *Pebble Mill at One*, the magazine programme filmed in the foyer of the BBC's Pebble Mill studios in Birmingham, is first broadcast at 1pm on 2nd October and remains a fixture of daytime television until 1986.

### Give us a wave
As the 1970s becomes renowned as the decade of the disaster movie, *The Poseidon Adventure*, about an ailing ocean liner capsized by a tidal wave, vies to be the one filled with the most hysterical screaming. An ensemble cast play a small group of survivors led by Gene Hackman's maverick preacher, taking their chances and dicing with death as they navigate their way out of the topsy-turvy vessel.

### I've started so I'll finish
Hopeful quizzers take to the black chair to face questions asked by Magnus Magnusson in *Mastermind*, which is first broadcast on BBC1 late at night on 11th September (it's moved to a primetime slot the following year).

# 1972

**A British *Jesus Christ Superstar***
Andrew Lloyd-Webber and Tim Rice's biblical rock opera *Jesus Christ Superstar* opens at the Palace Theatre on 9th August with Paul Nicholas moving from *Hair* to take on the role of Jesus, Stephen Tate as Judas and Dana Gillespie playing Mary Magdalene. *Jesus Christ Superstar* began as an album before stage musical adaptations on Broadway and in Australia and by the time it opens in London, the timing, the anticipation and the buzz ensure it's a smash hit. *Jesus Christ Superstar* runs for 3,358 performances until 1980, then tours the UK from 1983.

**Retail therapy**
There's rarely a dull moment at Grace Brothers Department Store, what with Mr Humphries camping it up in his latest outrageous sales promotion costume, or Mrs Slocombe, head of the ladies' department, changing her hair colour and worrying about her pussy. The pilot episode of the retail comedy *Are You Being Served?* is broadcast on 8th September. Famed for its double entendres, a series follows in 1973, with nine more, and a 1977 feature film, produced over the next twelve years.

**The Adventures of Black Beauty**
*The Adventures of Black Beauty* begins on ITV on 27th September and although inspired by Anna Sewell's 1877 novel, the action is instead shifted forward to the turn of the twentieth century and places Beauty in the care of widower Dr. James Gordon and his two children Vicky and the very un-Edwardian-sounding Kevin. Featured in ITV's family-friendly Sunday teatime slot, the uplifting *Black Beauty* theme tune, Denis King's *Galloping Home*, becomes more famous than the series itself, ingrained in the memory of every 1970s kid.

**The Godfather**
'A bloody good story, or a good bloody story' is how Derek Malcolm describes *The Godfather* in his *Guardian* review. Francis Ford Coppola's monumental gangster film based on Mario Puzo's novel about the Corleone family is released in the UK on 24th August. Conflict over casting decisions had dogged the early stages of production, with Coppola digging in his heels to cast Marlon Brando as Vito Corleone and Al Pacino as his son and heir, Michael; Brando wins an Oscar and *The Godfather* becomes the highest-grossing film of 1972.

**Birth of Pong**
The video game revolution begins in America with the release of the Pong arcade game on 29th November. Three years later, the simple table-tennis game is adapted for play on a console connected to a television allowing early gamers to pong and ping to their heart's content from the comfort of their armchair.

# 1972

# MUSIC

### Paul spreads his Wings
*8th February 1972* Paul and Linda McCartney hit the road with their new band Wings. They make their live debut at Nottingham University when they turn up unannounced and offer to do a lunchtime gig. Tickets are just 40 pence.

### American Pie
*15th January 1972* Don McLean was inspired to write his seven minute-epic *American Pie*, now at No. 1 in the US, by the death of his idol Buddy Holly in 1959. It tells the story of rock music with biblical imagery and cloaked allusions to Dylan, the Beatles, the Rolling Stones, Janis Joplin and others.

### Far from plain
*21st January 1972* A session on John Peel's Radio 1 evening show introduces Roxy Music, who don't even have a record deal yet. The band is an art-cum-music project fronted by Bryan Ferry, whose strangled diction makes for a sneering vocal style. Musically and visually they mix Hollywood cool with futuristic sonic wizardry and costumes to match. A dazzlingly inventive debut album is followed by the single *Virginia Plain*, its rococo lyrics referencing everything from Fred Astaire movies to casinos and chic American cars.

### Heartbreak tale
*11th March 1972* At No. 1 in the UK is one of the most affecting heartbreak ballads ever, *Without You* by Harry Nilsson, who is best known for singing *Everybody's Talkin'* over the *Midnight Cowboy* credits. Written by Pete Ham and Tom Evans of Badfinger, its sales are so huge that the two young songwriters should be set up for life. Instead, disputes over royalties lead to the suicides of both men, in 1975 and 1983 respectively.

### Bowie breakthrough
*16th June 1972* After years as one of UK rock's fringe figures, David Bowie makes a huge breakthrough with *The Rise and Fall of Ziggy Stardust and the Spiders from Mars*. On the album he assumes the role of an androgynous rock star who soars to fame as the Earth awaits an apocalypse. The Bowie look and style defines glam rock at its most serious and sexually questioning, underpinned by Mick Ronson's searing guitar.

### Bagpipe blast
*15th April 1972* Over the years the record chart has featured singing nuns, chickens, dogs and even ventriloquists, but never bagpipe bands. Standing proudly at No. 1 are the Pipes and Drums and Military Band of the Royal Scots Dragoon Guards with the eighteenth-century hymn *Amazing Grace*. Its million-selling success is generally credited to (or blamed on) Radio 1 DJ Tony Blackburn. A vocal-only version by folk singer Judy Collins is also one of the year's top sellers.

# 1972

### School's Out!
**29th July 1972** As schools break for summer, never has a record release been better timed than *School's Out* by Alice Cooper. Alice and his horror movie-derived stage show, his pet snake, garage band sound and all-American sweetheart name are calculated to appal parents and delight adolescents.

## MY FIRST 18 YEARS
## TOP 10  1972

1. **Let's Stay Together** Al Green
2. **All the Young Dudes** Mott the Hoople
3. **Sylvia's Mother** Dr Hook and the Medicine Show
4. **Me and Mrs Jones** Billy Paul
5. **Starman** David Bowie
6. **Mama Weer All Crazee Now** Slade
7. **Rocket Man** Elton John
8. **Ain't No Sunshine** Michael Jackson
9. **I Can See Clearly Now** Johnny Nash
10. **Guitar Man** Bread

### Osmonds everywhere
Osmondmania grips the country. Twelve year-old Donny revives *Puppy Love* and *Too Young* and joins his Mormon brothers on a string of Top Tenners before his younger brother Jimmy - just nine years old - bags the Christmas No. 1 with *Long Haired Lover from Liverpool*. Waiting in the wings is sister Marie, soon to top the chart with *Paper Roses*.

### The Philly sound
Challenging Motown's grip on making precision-tuned radio-friendly soul music are producers Kenny Gamble and Leon Huff at the Philadelphia International label. The 'Philly sound' they have perfected matches great rhythm tracks to sweet orchestral backings on hits for Harold Melvin, Billy Paul and the O'Jays. Another Philly producer, Thom Bell, is behind the hits of the Stylistics while Barry White gives the template a twist with his vocal group Love Unlimited.

### All crazee now
While glam rock avatars T. Rex are beginning to stutter, Wolverhampton band Slade's raucous and cheeky brand of updated rock'n'roll reaches out to the guys as well as the girls. Their trademarks are hits with deliberately misspelt song titles like *Take Me Bak 'Ome* and *Mama Weer All Crazee Now*, while guitarist Dave Hill's platform boots and singer Noddy Holder's mutton-chop sideburns make the Clockwork Orange-influenced look the height of teen fashion.

PHOTO CREDITS Copyright 2024, TDM Rights BV.
Photos: **A** Picture Alliance - Getty Images / **B** David Attie - Archive Photos - Getty Images / **C** R. Viner - Hulton Archive - Getty Images / **D** Independent News and Media - Hulton Archive - Getty Images / **E** Evening Standard - Hulton Archive - Getty Images / **F** Evening Standard - Hulton Archive - Getty Images / **G** Keystone - Hulton Royals Collection - Getty Images / **H** Bettmann - Getty Images / **I** Alessandra Benedetti - Corbis News - Getty Images / **J** Express - Archive Photos - Getty Images / **K** Photo12 - Universal Images Group Editorial - Getty Images / **L** Tim Roney - Hulton Archive - Getty Images / **M** Tony Evans Timelapse Library Ltd - Hulton Archive - Getty Images / **N** D Morrison - Hulton Archive - Getty Images / **O** Studiocanal Films Ltd - Mary Evans / **P** Silver Screen Collection - Moviepix - Getty Images / **Q** Brian Cooke - Redferns - Getty Images / **R** Michael Ochs Archives - Redferns - Getty Images / **S** Hulton Archive - Getty Images / **T** George Wilkes Archive - Hulton Archive - Getty Images.

# 1973

## MY FIRST 18 YEARS

## SPORT

**Football's FA Cup Fairytale**
When Second Division side Sunderland arrive at Wembley on 5th May for their FA Cup final match against Leeds, few people fancy their chances against a tough team who are the 1972 Cup winners and have dominated First Division football over the past couple of seasons. But in one of the most spectacular examples of giant-killing football, the Black Cats win 1-0, with Ian Porterfield's goal coming in the thirty-second minute, and several outstanding saves from the Wearsiders' goalie Jimmy Montgomery to keep them ahead. When the final whistle goes and Sunderland's manager Bob Stokoe runs onto the pitch, it's a fairytale ending for a team whose fanbase is as loyal as it is large.

**Flying Scot quits at the top**
Following the death of his Tyrrell-Ford team-mate Francois Cevert in a practice race at Watkins Glen on 6th October, three-times world F1 champion, Jackie Stewart announces his retirement.

**Hunt the Shunt hits F1**
James Hunt makes his debut in Formula One racing as a driver for Hesketh; his highest position is second in the US Grand Prix. The RAC award him with the Campbell trophy at the end of the season for best British driver.

**Battle of the Sexes**
In the year the US Open pays equal prize money to male and female players, a tennis match between 55-year-old Bobby Riggs and 29-year-old Billie Jean King takes place on 20th September. Billed as the 'Battle of the Sexes' the contest had arisen due to Riggs's public declarations about the inferiority of the women's game. After a $100,000 prize is offered, King agrees to take up the challenge. Watched by a global television audience of 90 million, King wins 6-4, 6-4, 6-3, a significant point scored in King's long-running battle for equality in the sport.

**7 JAN 1973**
British Darts Organisation is founded.

**5 FEB 1973**
*The Wombles* begins on BBC1, narrated by Bernard Cribbins and with music by Mike Batt.

**27 MAR 1973**
The first women traders are admitted onto the floor of the London Stock Exchange.

# 1973

### The Sunshine Showdown
Number-one-ranked heavyweight boxer George Foreman and heavyweight champion Joe Frazier slug it out on 22nd January in Kingston, Jamaica in a bid to become WBA, WBC and The Ring champion. Foreman overpowers Frazier who hits the canvas six times in just two rounds before the match is stopped and Foreman declared the winner.

### European Economic Community
*1st January 1973* Britain enters the EEC alongside fellow new members Ireland and Denmark.

### *Everton* shelled by Iceland
*26 May 1973* British Trawler *Everton* refuses to follow instructions from the Icelandic Coast Guard and is shelled as it flees to the protection of British Navy ship HMS *Jupiter*. This latest incident in the Second Cod War precedes a number of escalations and collisions throughout the year before an agreement is signed in November bringing the conflict to an end.

## DOMESTIC NEWS

### IRA bombs England
*1973* sees the trouble in Northern Ireland spread to London and Manchester, with a series of bombings taking place across the country. Thirteen bombs are planted in the capital, ten of which detonate. These include bombs at Whitehall and the Old Bailey, and in stations such as Victoria, King's Cross and Euston, injuring over 60 people. In March, a referendum on sovereignty in Northern Ireland sees 98.9% of voters choose to remain within the UK, although turn-out for Catholics is less than 1%.

### London Bridge opens
*17th March 1973* The newly completed London Bridge, at least the fourth to stand on the site, is opened by Her Majesty the Queen. Traffic flows over the newly widened bridge, reducing the congestion that has been prevalent in the city since the old bridge was dismantled in 1968.

### Secondary banking crisis
The country's economic problems continue in 1973, as the end of the year witnesses the start of the secondary banking crisis, which would last into 1974. The sharp drop in property prices and an increase in interest rates threatens many secondary lending banks with bankruptcy.

### 8 APR 1973
Jackie Stewart wins the BRDC International Trophy at Silverstone.

### 18 MAY 1973
Soviet party leader Leonid Brezhnev visits West Germany.

### 24 JUN 1973
90-year-old Eamon de Valera, the world's oldest head of state, resigns as President of Ireland.

# 1973

**New radio stations**
8th October 1973 The London Broadcasting Company (photo David Jessel) begins broadcasting and becomes the first commercial independent radio station to operate legally within the UK. LBC's talk radio content is followed eight days later by the launch of Capital Radio, which focuses on music programming.

**Value added tax**
1st April 1973 Value added tax replaces purchase tax in the UK. Unlike its predecessor, VAT is applied at the point of sale, not at the point of manufacture, and is fixed at 10%. Purchase tax had varied based on the perceived luxuriousness of the goods in question, from 13% for small items, up to 55% for purchases such as motor vehicles.

**Oil crisis**
4th November 1973 Angered by western support for Israel in the Yom Kippur War, the Organization of the Petroleum Exporting Countries (OPEC) hits back by raising prices and reducing supplies, triggering an oil crisis with huge consequences for all western economies, forcing the introduction of petrol rationing by some and pushing up material and transport costs.

**Pizza Hut opens**
American restaurant chain Pizza Hut opens its first UK branch in Islington, London. Pizza Hut expands to offer a variety of branches, from diner-style restaurants to take-away premises, and quickly becomes a firm high street favourite.

## ROYALTY & POLITICS

**Princess Anne marries at the Abbey**
On 14th November, the same day as her brother Prince Charles turns twenty-five, Princess Anne marries Captain Mark Phillips at Westminster Abbey wearing a medieval-style gown and Queen Mary's fringe tiara.

**Queen opens Opera House of Oz**
During a tour of Australia, on 20th October, the Queen opens the Sydney Opera House.

**Tory sex scandals**
Government ministers Lord Lambton and Earl Jellicoe both resign this year after the secret service discover their associations with prostitutes. The story breaks when photographs of Lambton are sold to the papers.

**1 JUL 1973**
A merger of the British Museum Library and the National Lending Library for Science & Technology at Boston Spa, creates the British Library.

**15 AUG 1973**
Sitcom *Man About the House* starring Richard O'Sullivan begins on ITV.

**3 SEP 1973**
Death of J. R. R. Tolkien, scholarly creator of *'Lord of the Rings'*.

# 1973

## FOREIGN NEWS

### LBJ dies
*22nd January 1973* Lyndon Baines Johnson, 36th President of the US, dies at his Texas home aged 64.

### 'Peace with honour'
*27th January 1973* US President Richard Nixon signs the Paris Peace Accords. The historic agreement with the governments of North and South Vietnam ensures a temporary ceasefire, after which US troops will withdraw.

### Skylab
*14th May 1973* Skylab, the US space station, is launched. Three extended manned missions are completed aboard the station by the end of November.

### Watergate rumbles on
*16th July 1973* The revelation that President Nixon has been secretly recording conversations in the Oval Office opens a whole new avenue of investigation into the Watergate burglary and whether he knew of it or approved it. The newly convened US Senate Watergate Committee demands access to the tapes and Nixon refuses.

### Mobile calling
*3rd April 1973* Inventor Martin Cooper makes the very first cell phone call with a prototype of the Motorola DynaTAC, a 2.5lb cordless phone connected to an antenna on the roof of the hotel across the street. Cheekily, Cooper calls a major competitor to report that Motorola has succeeded in making mobile phone calls.

### Yom Kippur War
*6th October 1973* On Israel's holiest day, Yom Kippur, Egypt and Syria launch a surprise attack to recapture the territories lost in the Six-Day War in 1967. Egyptian troops cross the Suez Canal and enter the Sinai Desert as Syria retakes the Golan Heights. Israel launches a counter-offensive and pushes the Egyptians back across the Suez Canal. On 24th October, when Israeli troops are within one hundred kilometres of Cairo, the US presses Israel to sign an armistice.

### Picasso
*8th April 1973* Pablo Picasso dies at the age of 91. He was the founder of cubism and creator of masterpieces such as *Guernica*, depicting the German-Italian bombardment of the city during the Spanish Civil War.

### 17 OCT 1973
The price of oil increases by 70% leading to rocketing petrol prices and pressure on the UK economy.

### 1 NOV 1973
Final issue of the underground, counterculture magazine *Oz* is published.

### 5 DEC 1973
50mph speed limits put in place on UK roads in a bid to save fuel.

# 1973

**Dictator Pinochet**
*11th September 1973* With CIA support, General Augusto Pinochet stages a military coup against Chile's socialist President Salvador Allende. The object is to ensure that the country will not be the next domino to fall to communism. During the coup, the presidential palace is bombed and Allende is killed. Pinochet's tenure as President is vicious and uncompromising.

**Kissinger controversy**
*10th December 1973* The most surprising and controversial award in the history of the Nobel Prize is made as US Secretary of State Henry Kissinger and North Vietnamese negotiator Le Duc Tho are jointly awarded the Nobel Prize for Peace. Kissinger is widely seen as a power broker who has acted with a consistent disregard for democracy and human rights. Tho declines the prize but Kissinger accepts.

Fisher Price Tree-house

**High, wide and handsome**
It's a giddy year for architecture as dazzling new structures are unveiled in different parts of the world. The Sears Tower in Chicago becomes the world's tallest building at 442 metres. The iconic Sydney Opera House is opened by Queen Elizabeth II. In Istanbul, the Bosphorus Bridge connects Europe and Asia for the first time across the Bosphorus Strait. But the new buildings of most long-term significance are the twin towers of the new World Trade Center: construction has taken ten years and final costs are estimated at $900 million.

**ETA attacks**
*20th December 1973* Luis Carrero Blanco, General Franco's (photo) Prime Minister and right-hand man, is killed in a bomb attack by the Basque separatist movement ETA.

# 1973

## ENTERTAINMENT

### Delia's Debut
After appearing in the cookery slot on East Anglia Television's *Look East* programme, Delia Smith fronts her own BBC1 programme, *Family Fare*, which is first broadcast on 15th May. She writes several successful cookbooks this decade including 1978's best-selling *Complete Cookery Course* and is rapidly on track to become the doyenne of British food writers and television cooks.

### Teddy Edward
Based on the books by Mollie and Patrick Edward, *Teddy Edward* is a gentle tale of a toy bear and his friends, told through still photographs and narrated by Richard Baker. It begins on BBC1 on 5th January.

### Game of the Year
The game Mastermind, which pits code-maker against code-breaker, with the help of a series of coloured, plastic pegs, is announced as Game of the Year. First launched in 1970, Mastermind has huge international success selling 30 million during the decade.

### Big biba
Biba moves into the old seven-storey Derry and Tom's store in Kensington High Street. 'Big' Biba is a phenomenon, offering the complete Biba lifestyle and becoming London's second-biggest tourist attraction after the Tower of London.

### Let's do the time warp
Richard O'Brien's musical fantasy, *The Rocky Horror Show*, opens at the 63-seat performance space, Royal Court Theatre Upstairs on 19th June. Made on a shoestring budget, with costumes begged, borrowed and adapted, *The Rocky Horror Show* takes inspiration from old Hollywood sci-fi B-movies, goth horror and burlesque and blends it with a witty and knowingly camp celebration of seventies sexual fluidity. The production later moves to the King's Road Theatre where it continues until 1979. With the release of a 1975 film, *The Rocky Horror Picture Show*, this wickedly wacky musical gains a loyal, global following cementing Rocky Horror's status as a cult classic.

### Charley says…
Kids in 1973 are kept safe from daily hazards with the help of Tony and his pet cat Charley, whose feline wisdom warns against going off with strangers or playing with matches. Charley's meowed advice is in fact the voice of radio DJ Kenny Everett.

# 1973

## The Wicker Man
A folk horror about paganism and sacrifice, *The Wicker Man*, released 6th December, is British film-making at its most weird and inventive. The sacrificial target in question is Edward Woodward, playing a devoutly Christian police officer who travels to a remote Scottish island in search of a missing girl, only to discover the inhabitants are fully-fledged pagans under the patriarchal leadership of Christopher Lee's fiendish Lord Summerisle. The film's horrifying climax goes on to have a wide-ranging cultural impact.

## Wheely, wheely funny
Half man, half walking disaster, Frank Spencer, of *Some Mothers Do 'Ave 'Em*, goes to a roller disco and finds himself accidentally flying through the exit doors and dodging the traffic of Edmonton in the episode 'Fathers' Clinic' which airs on 20th December. Michael Crawford, who plays the luckless, neurotic but ultimately adorable Spencer (ably supported by Michele Dotrice as wife Betty), performs all his own stunts in the series.

## Lizzie Dripping
In East Midlands dialect, 'Lizzie Dripping' is a term for a girl with an overly active imagination and a tendency to tell fibs. Prolific children's author Helen Cresswell uses this as the premise for a children's drama serial, which begins on BBC1 on 13th March. Cresswell's main character, Penelope Arbuckle, is a typical 'Lizzie Dripping' who discovers a mischievous witch in her village. Of course, only Lizzie can see her. Tina Heath who plays Lizzie goes on to become *Blue Peter*'s tenth presenter in 1979.

## Away you go!
*We Are the Champions*, presented by Ron Pickering, begins on BBC1 on 13th June – an inter-school competition which is 70% school sports day and 30% *It's a Knock-out*. The highlight of every episode comes after the swimming races when Pickering shouts, 'Away you go!' and the kids forget their savage rivalry and dive bomb into the pool en masse. Joyful chaos.

## *Enter the Dragon*, exit Bruce Lee
On 20th July, Bruce Lee, legendary martial arts expert and actor, is found dead in his Hong Kong hotel room of cerebral edema. He is just 32. Lee's last film, *Enter the Dragon*, acquires almost mythological status when it is released a month after his death, becoming the highest-grossing martial arts film of all time.

# 1973

**Petrifying puppets**
The hallowed halls of children's TV puppetry welcome a number of strange new arrivals this year. *Pipkins* (photo) introduces attention-seeking Hartley Hare along with a motley selection of animal friends all of whom have a different regional accent. Pig is a Brummie, Mrs Penguin a Geordie and the blank-eyed, frankly petrifying Topov the Monkey is a Cockney. If the *Pipkins* posse wasn't odd enough, then over at *Hickory House*, which first broadcasts on 12th March, there is sleepy, banana-guzzling Humphrey the Cushion, and a red-nosed, obsessively houseproud kitchen mop called Dusty Mop!

**Wholegrain nostalgia**
Ridley Scott directs a TV commercial for Hovis bread that strikes a chord with nostalgic Brits. Showing a boy pushing a bike up a cobbled hill (the famously picturesque Gold Hill in Shaftesbury) to the strains of Dvorak's *New World Symphony* played with mournful tones by the Ashington Colliery Brass Band, the tune will forever more be known as 'the Hovis tune' and the advert is later voted the UK's favourite of all time in a 2006 poll.

**Pucker up**
The lip balm revolution begins when skincare company Bonne Bell develop a special balm to help protect skiers' lips. Before long the balm is sold in a range of sickly flavours for the teen market under the name Lip Smackers.

**Why Don't You?**
Why don't you just switch off television set and go out and do something less boring instead? That is the rather ironic question posed by the opening credits of *Why Don't You*, which becomes a fixture of morning telly through the school summer holidays as of 20th August 1973.

 **MUSIC**

**Guess the subject**
*January 1973* Peaking at No. 3 in the UK, Carly Simon's *You're So Vain* has everybody guessing who she has in mind. The betting is on infamous womaniser Warren Beatty but could it be Mick Jagger, who can be heard on backing vocals?

**On the dark side**
*1st March 1973* Pink Floyd release *The Dark Side of the Moon*, an album exploring the theme of madness that has taken over a year to record and fine-tune. Their most emotional work, it propels them into the big league of British bands in the US, where it spends over 730 weeks in the LP chart.

# 1973

## Tubular Bells
*25th May 1973* The first release from Richard Branson's new Virgin record label is Mike Oldfield's *Tubular Bells*. It's a mesmeric, slow-building 50-minute work featuring scores of overdubs by Oldfield playing different instruments and narration by Viv Stanshall of the Bonzo Dog Doo Dah Band. The album is not only a surprise hit, its main theme is heard in *The Exorcist*.

## Second time unlucky
*7th April 1973* Ever hopeful, Cliff Richard has another go at winning Eurovision with *Power to All Our Friends*. He comes third. Anne Marie David wins it for Luxembourg with *Wonderful Dream*.

## Join the love train!
*24th March 1973* Philadelphia soulsters the O'Jays invite the people of every nation to join hands and form a *Love Train*. The song's mentions of Egypt, Israel, Russia and China catalogue the enmities that characterise global politics in 1973. Hopelessly idealistic, *Love Train* makes the world seem just a little more jolly.

## Yellow ribbons
*21st April 1973* At No. 1 in the UK is the year's biggest-selling global hit. Dawn's *Tie A Yellow Ribbon Round The Old Oak Tree* is a story song that resonates with returning servicemen from prison camps in Vietnam who really are welcomed home by yellow ribbons.

## Rhymin' Simon
*6th May 1973* Paul Simon starts his first solo tour since splitting with Art Garfunkel to promote *There Goes Rhymin' Simon*, an album embracing gospel, reggae and doo-wop styles and including his comment on Watergate malaise, *American Tune*.

## Bowie and Reed
*3rd July 1973* David Bowie announces his retirement from live performing but his real aim is to abandon his alter ego stage creations, Ziggy Stardust and Aladdin Sane. His skills as a producer benefit Velvet Underground founder Lou Reed, whose *Transformer* takes him from cult figure to major star. Amazingly, iconic track *Walk on the Wild Side* is added to the Radio 1 playlist, despite clear references to cross-dressing, drugs and oral sex.

## Suzi Q
Under the Chinnichap banner, songwriting team Nicky Chinn and Mike Chapman and veteran producer Mickie Most deliver hit after hit for Sweet, Mud, Suzi Quatro and more. Suzi is a leather-clad, bass-playing rock'n'roller from Detroit whose sound is pared-down and punky. It's no wonder that she'll be chosen to play streetwise Leather Truscadero in the 1950s-set US TV comedy *Happy Days*.

# 1973

### Stevie feels the sunshine
**6th August 1973** Stevie Wonder lies in a coma for four days after a car accident in North Carolina but returns to live performing within weeks. Having won full creative freedom from Motown, his albums retain the soulful accessibility of earlier records but are now explorative, innovatory and deeply philosophical. When asked by an interviewer how he can write *You Are the Sunshine of My Life* when he has never seen the Sun, he explains 'but I can feel it, man'.

## MY FIRST 18 YEARS — TOP 10 — 1973

1. **Superstition** Stevie Wonder
2. **Stuck in the Middle with You** Stealers Wheel
3. **Nutbush City Limits** Ike and Tina Turner
4. **Loving and Free** Kiki Dee
5. **Like Sister and Brother** The Drifters
6. **Goodbye Yellow Brick Road** Elton John
7. **Live and Let Die** Paul McCartney and Wings
8. **Roll Away the Stone** Mott the Hoople
9. **See My Baby Jive** Wizzard
10. **Reelin' in the Years** Steely Dan

### Slade stalled
**4th July 1973** With a US tour beckoning, Slade drummer Don Powell is seriously injured in a car crash that kills his girlfriend. The band opt to stay in the UK and help him learn to play the drums again. They return to form in December with the song that Noddy Holder will call his pension because it is released year after year - *Merry Xmas Everybody*. Recorded during a New York heatwave, it brings much-needed hope and fun to a nation about to knuckle down to a three-day week.

### Golden oldies
**7th July 1973** As the Carpenters proclaim it's *Yesterday Once More*, the hits of 1973 prove their point. There are revivals and comebacks galore, by Neil Sedaka, the Drifters, Perry Como, Ike and Tina Turner and many more, while TV-advertised compilations of past hits clog the album charts and 'golden oldie' radio explodes in the US. Roy Wood's new band Wizzard bring back the Phil Spector wall of sound, 10cc recall the Beach Boys on *The Dean and I*, while David Essex stars as a would-be early 1960s rock star in the film *That'll Be The Day* and storms the chart with *Rock On*, which name-checks James Dean and blue suede shoes.

### Walrus of Love
After working for years as an arranger and producer, the rotund Barry White has become an unlikely superstar and sex icon. His every record is soaked in lush orchestrations and bass rhythms as belly-deep as his voice.

# 1974

**MY FIRST 18 YEARS**

## SPORT

### Rumble in the Jungle
The long-awaited and much-hyped fight between champion heavyweight George Foreman and Muhammad Ali takes place in Kinshasa, Zaire on 30th October. Foreman's heft and power is more than matched by Ali's clever tactics, including his dope-and-rope technique, and after eight rounds, Foreman is floored by a straight punch to the face from Ali. The fight attracts an estimated global audience of one billion and is considered one of the greatest sporting moments of all time.

### Sunday league
In 1974, Sundays are still viewed as a day of rest. But an energy crisis caused by spiralling oil costs and a strike by the National Union of Mineworkers is the catalyst for the introduction of Sunday football league matches this year. With Edward Heath's three-day week affecting the UK in the first two months of the year, energy saving measures are crucial, including daytime matches that require no floodlights. The first Sunday match is played between Millwall and Fulham at The Den at 11:30am on 20th January. Millwall wins 1-0.

Monchichi monkey

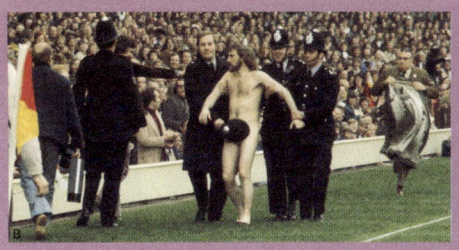

### Nude interruption
A streaker makes the front pages after he runs onto the pitch stark naked at Twickenham on 20th April during a friendly rugby international between England and France. The man had made the streak for a £10 bet after drinking several pints of lager. The police officers who catch up with him cover his genitals with a helmet before carting him off to Twickenham magistrates' court (where his £10 bet is immediately handed over as a fine for 'insulting behaviour'). He returns to the ground as one of the founding fathers of a streaking craze which continues throughout the 70s and beyond.

### 1 JAN 1974
News Year's Day becomes a public holiday for the first time.

### 1 FEB 1974
Ronnie Biggs, one of the perpetrators of the Great Train Robbery is arrested in Brazil.

### 6 MAR 1974
Miners' strike ends after a 35% wage increase is agreed and two days later, the UK returns to a five-day working week.

# 1974

### Love match
There is romance in the air at Wimbledon this year when American golden couple Jimmy Connors and Chris Evert arrive at the tournament engaged to be married. When they each win the singles title, it seems like the perfect outcome. At the Wimbledon Champions' Dinner the pair dance to 'The Girl That I Marry' but in October, they break off their engagement, deciding that tennis must come before love.

### Conteh the champion
Liverpudlian John Conteh becomes WBC World Light Heavyweight Champion after defeating Jorge Ahumada at the Empire Pool, London on 1st October. It's an excellent year for Conteh, who not only has an episode of *This Is Your Life* dedicated to him, but also wins the second series of masters of sport TV competition *Superstars*.

### Flixborough Disaster
*1st June 1974* The chemical industry reels as news breaks of an explosion at a chemical plant near the village of Flixborough, North Lincolnshire. Faulty, modified equipment leads to a large cloud of hydrogen leaking and igniting, killing 28 people and injuring 36 more. There is a national outcry over the event, which occurs as a new Health and Safety at Work Act is passed through Parliament.

## DOMESTIC NEWS

### Three-day week
*1st January 1974* Coal shortages caused by industrial action lead to a reduction in the generation of electricity, with Prime Minister Edward Heath introducing the three-day working week. Businesses are limited to three consecutive days of electricity consumption in a seven-day period. It lasts until 7th March.

### First McDonald's
*13th November 1974* Britain gets its first McDonald's restaurant, in Woolwich, southeast London. Soon the restaurant chain begins to compete with established brands like Wimpy, and the so-called 'Golden Arches' become a familiar site on British high streets.

### Oil embargo ends
*18th March 1974* The Organisation of Arab Petroleum Exporting Countries finally lift their embargo on oil exports to the United Kingdom, relieving the pressure on the fuel shortages felt across the country.

### 2 APR 1974
Tatum O'Neil, aged 10, becomes youngest recipient of an Academy Award for Best Supporting Actress.

### 6 MAY 1974
Chancellor Willy Brandt resigns amidst controversy over his aide's ties with the Stasi.

### 13 JUN 1974
Prince Charles makes his maiden speech in the House of Lords.

# 1974

**Red Lion Square**
*15th June 1974* Members of the National Front marching through London clash with counter-protesters in Red Lion Square. Individuals representing the International Marxist Group charge a police cordon separating them from the marchers, and riots break out. In the melee twenty-year-old student Kevin Gately is killed.

**Ceefax launched**
*23rd September 1974* The BBC launches Ceefax, a pun on the words 'see facts', as the first teletext service in the world. Starting with 30 pages, viewers can use their television remotes to type in a page number before viewing useful information on a variety of topics

**Economic trouble**
Economic trouble for the UK continues throughout 1974. Aside from the strikes and the three-day week implemented in January, figures launched at the beginning of the year show the country had entered its first post-war recession at the end of 1973. Inflation reaches a 34 year high of 17.2%.

**Lord Lucan disappears!**
*7th November 1974* London is rocked by the disappearance of Lord Lucan, following the murder of the children's nanny. Lucan's wife is found injured, claiming that her husband has attacked her and murdered the nanny. Lucan's car is found abandoned and stained with blood, and the peer disappears, never to be heard from again.

**The Birmingham Six**
*21st November 1974* The bombing of two pubs in Birmingham kills 21 people and is the single most deadly attack on the country since the end of the Second World War. Six Irish men are arrested almost immediately amid concerns the IRA is to blame and undergo brutal treatment at the hands of the police. Their conviction, on flawed evidence, becomes one of the country's most famous miscarriages of justice.

**The Troubles**
Trouble in Northern Ireland continues as the collapse of the Sunnydale agreement leads to the re-establishment of direct rule. 1974 sees many bombings across the country, including the M62 massacre which kills 12 people. Bombs in the summer detonate in Dublin and Monaghan planted by the Ulster Volunteer Force, and in London at the Houses of Parliament and the Tower of London by the IRA. October brings the Guildford pub bombings, killing five, and an attack on Brook's club in London. Sports Minister Denis Howell's family survive a car bomb, and the home of Edward Heath is targeted.

**3 JUL 1974**
Long-standing Leeds United coach Don Revie accepts £200,000 to become the new England manager.

**29 AUG 1974**
Hippies and police clash when the latter try to close down the illegal, Windsor Free Festival.

**14 SEP 1974**
Giant pandas Chia-Chia and Ching-Ching arrive at London Zoo, the result of a diplomatic deal with China brokered by Edward Heath.

# 1974

## ROYALTY & POLITICS

### The balance of power
Juggling several crises and locked in a battle with trade unions, a beleaguered Edward Heath calls a General Election for 28th February to secure a new mandate for his policies. His gamble backfires and he resigns, and Harold Wilson returns as Labour Prime Minister. Labour wins a second election on 11th October with a tiny majority of just three seats. It is the first time since 1910 that two general elections have been held in one year.

### Attempted kidnapping
*20th March 1974* Princess Anne narrowly escapes a kidnapping as she and husband Captain Mark Philips wrestle with attacker Ian Bail. Bail stops the Princess's car and shoots her driver and protection officer, before attempting to drag her from the vehicle. He is foiled by intervening citizens and the timely arrival of the police, despite shooting a police officer and a member of the public. No one is killed, and Bail is detained under the Mental Health Act.

### Death of the Duke of Gloucester
Henry, Duke of Gloucester, uncle to the Queen and the last surviving son of George V, dies on 10th June at his home, Barnwell Manor, following a period of ill health.

### Hover bother
During his General Election campaign, Liberal leader Jeremy Thorpe tours the coastal towns of south-west Britain via hovercraft, the transport mode of the moment.

## FOREIGN NEWS

### Worst air disaster
*3rd March 1974* The highest fatalities to date in an air disaster occur when the rear cargo hatch of a DC-10 of Turkish Airlines Flight 981 flies open over Meaux, France. The sudden pressure difference causes the hull to burst and all 340 passengers and crew are killed instantly.

### Terracotta Army
*29th March 1974* A magnificently preserved Terracotta Army of life-size figures is discovered at Xi'an in China. The sculptures date from 210-209 BC and were buried with the body of Emperor Qin Shi Huang to protect him in the afterlife. The three pits in which they are found contain more than 8,000 soldiers, 130 chariots with 520 horses, and 150 cavalry horses.

### 16 OCT 1974
Riots break out at the Maze prison in Belfast.

### 27 NOV 1974
The Prevention of Terrorism Act is passed giving police special powers when they suspect terrorism.

### 22 DEC 1974
The London home of Conservative party leader and ex-PM Edward Heath is bombed by the Provisional IRA.

# 1974

### Golf launch
**30th March 1974** A worthy successor to the immensely popular but outdated Beetle rolls off the Volkswagen production line at Wolfsburg. An affordable small family hatchback, the first Golf model sells around thirty million.

### Four billion
**1st April 1974** The US Census Bureau calculates that for the first time there are more than four billion people on the planet - a doubling of the world's population since 1930.

### Pompidou est mort, Brandt tritt zurück
**April - May 1974** Within a month, Europe loses two of its most effective political leaders. French President Georges Pompidou dies aged 62 having initiated the large-scale industrialisation of France. On 6th May, West German Chancellor Willy Brandt resigns with his secretary revealed as an East German spy and the oil crisis threatening his social reforms.

### Rubik's cube
**19th May 1974** Hungarian mathematician Ernő Rubik has a question: 'How can I make part of an object move without the whole object falling apart?' He builds a cube to answer that question and shows it to his students. Put into mass production, it becomes one of the biggest fads of the 1970s and 1980s.

### Nixon resigns
**9th August 1974** Facing impeachment over his role in the Watergate burglary and subsequent cover-up, President Richard Nixon announces his resignation. The final straw was the US Supreme Court decision the day before to order the release of tapes of Oval Office conversations. He is succeeded by his Vice President Gerald Ford, who pardons Nixon for any federal offences he might have committed. Nixon is the first US President to resign from office.

### Haile Selassie deposed
**12th September 1974** After more than 700 years, the Ethiopian Empire comes to an end. Plagued by famine and economic malaise, citizens strike in protest against Emperor Haile Selassie. The army and police seize their opportunity, place Haile Selassie under house arrest and take power.

### Perón dead
**1st July 1974** General Perón, stripped of power by a coup in 1955, returns to Argentina from exile with his wife Isabel and is elected President for the third time. Two days later, he suffers a fatal heart attack and Isabel assumes the presidency.

# 1974

**PLO recognized**
*1st October 1974* The Palestine Liberation Organisation is recognised by the UN and the Arab League as the representative of the Palestinian people. PLO leader Yasser Arafat addresses the UN: 'Today I came with an olive branch and the weapon of the freedom fighter. Don't let the olive branch fall from my hands.'

**Lucy in the ground**
*24th November 1974* Bones of a 3.2 million year old hominid are found in Ethiopia. The fossil is named Lucy, after the Beatles song *Lucy in the Sky with Diamonds*. Lucy, probably 1.10 metres tall and weighing 29 kilos when alive, is the oldest two-legged animal ever recovered and one of the most important excavations in history.

## ENTERTAINMENT

**Paint the whole world with a rainbow**
Geoffrey Hughes, who has been a jobbing actor in dramas like *Z Cars* and *Dixon of Dock Green*, joins the Thames Television children's programme *Rainbow* this year and now spends his days with a large, absent-minded bear called Bungle, a sheepish pink hippo called George, and Zippy, a talkative orange creature of indistinct species. Over the next eighteen years, Geff-wee (as George pronounces it) takes on the role of teacher, parent, and peacekeeper to his furry, fuzzy colleagues.

**The Flake girl**
Since the 1960s, the TV commercials for Cadbury's Flake have focused on the sensual, languorous pleasure of solo chocolate consumption, with a succession of Flake girls showing us how it's done.

**'Just an old, saggy cloth cat'**
*Bagpuss*, is first shown on BBC1 on 12th February. Full of gentle, old-world charm, the inhabitants of a Victorian shop run by a little girl called Emily, come to life whenever she brings a new thing to be repaired. It's Bagpuss, a plump, quizzical-looking pink and white striped cat who is the catalyst for the others to wake; a woodpecker bookend called Professor Yaffle, Madeleine the doll, Gabriel the toad and his banjo, and an army of industrious little mice. A 1999 poll votes *Bagpuss* the UK's favourite children's programme.

**Tiswas – Saturday morning mayhem**
Saturday mornings are never the same again after *Tiswas* begins on 5th January on ITV. *Tiswas*, which comes from ATV's Birmingham studios, is chaotic, subversive and a bit rebellious with a gaggle of hyperactive presenters including Chris Tarrant and Sally James, who embrace the custard pies and slapstick, the buckets of water, mischief and mayhem. Bad jokes and impressions are provided by Bob Carolgees and Spit the dog and local comedian Lenny Henry, while Spike Milligan and Jasper Carrot are two more names who often pop up to join in the anarchic fun.

# 1974

### Goodnight, John Boy

Already a huge hit in America, *The Waltons* comes to the UK this year, airing on BBC2 on 18th February. The Waltons - seven siblings, Ma and Pa, Grandma and Grandpa - live in Depression-era Virginia, run a sawmill, wear mainly denim dungarees and every night insist on calling goodnight to each other as they turn out their lights. It's an unapologetic slice of very sweet American apple pie and Britain adores it.

### Kubrick withdraws *Clockwork Orange*

When Stanley Kubrick's *A Clockwork Orange* was released in cinemas in 1971, the film's controversial themes and 'ultraviolence' divided opinion. But following a spate of real-life crimes which some argue are strongly influenced by the rapes and murders depicted in the film, Kubrick and his family begin to receive death threats. In an unprecedented example of self-censorship, he insists Warner Brothers withdraw the film from circulation in the UK. *A Clockwork Orange* remains an underground cult movie until it is once again permitted general release in 2000, a year after Kubrick's death.

### Roobarb (and Custard)

*Roobarb* bounces onto television screens for the first time on 21st October on BBC1 in a cartoon perfectly capturing the universally recognised differences between cats and dogs. Roobarb is an exuberant green dog, and his rival, the laid-back Custard, is a puce-coloured cat who spends most his days calculating how to get the better of Roobarb.

### Opportunity Knocks for Lena

Diminutive Italian-Scottish singing sensation Lena Zavaroni, aged ten, appears on Hughie Green's talent show, *Opportunity Knocks* and becomes the only contestant to win five weeks in a row. Her version of 'Ma - He's Making Eyes at Me' becomes a chart hit for her at the age of thirteen.

### Baker Who?

*Doctor Who* number four is introduced to audiences for the first time on 28th December in an episode called 'Robot'. Tom Baker's Doctor wears a floppy hat, an unfeasibly long stripey scarf, has a penetrating gaze and seems quite excitable. It doesn't take long to win viewers round and for many, Baker remains the definitive Doctor Who, delighting many middle-aged fans when he appears in the show's 50th anniversary special, 'Day of the Doctor' in 2014.

### Miss Pears turns 21

Pears Soap celebrates the 21st birthday of its famous Miss Pears competition by inviting all the past winners to a special party. Since 1958, hopeful parents around the country submit photographs of their offspring each year for this highly-publicised contest in which one little girl is chosen to be the face and brand ambassador for the classic glycerine soap.

# 1974

### Hysteria and tragedy at Cassidy concert
*26th May 1974* Fourteen-year old Bernadette Whelan dies in a hysterical stampede at a David Cassidy concert at White City Stadium in London. The incident has a profound effect on the singer, who quits live performing and his *Partridge Family* TV show.

### Smash hit
Instant mash brand Smash score a smash hit with a TV advertising campaign created by ad agency BMP DDB, featuring metallic aliens chortling over the primitive and labour-intensive way in which earthlings peel and boil their potatoes. 'Get Mash, Get Smash' is the advertising jingle on everyone's lips and the Smash Aliens go on to be voted among the top UK advertisements of all time by the public and advertising industry alike.

### Bedsits and Beckinsale
September treats TV viewers to the launch of not one but two winning sitcoms. ITV's *Rising Damp* starts on 2nd September, with Leonard Rossiter playing Rigsby, the miserly landlord of a creaking Victorian townhouse, whose bedsits are occupied by Richard Beckinsale's medical student, a suave Don Warrington and Frances de la Tour as the romantic spinster Miss Jones, with whom Rigsby is besotted. On BBC1 on 5th September, Beckinsale appears a second time this week as Lennie Godber, the cell mate of Ronnie Barker's Norman Stanley Fletcher ('Fletch') in prison comedy *Porridge*.

### Good clean fun?
Robin Askwith puts on his best cheeky chappie persona as he takes on the role of disaster-prone window cleaner, Timothy Lea, who spends more time in bed with his customers than he does actually cleaning their windows. *Confessions of a Window Cleaner*, releaed 16th August, treads a fine line between sauce and soft porn but the promise of lewd slapstick, full frontal female nudity, and constant views of Askwith's derrière somehow compels people to see it.

### Head-swivelling horror
When William Friedkin's film *The Exorcist* is released in UK cinemas on 14th March, its reputation precedes it, with reports of American audiences suffering shock, fainting and vomiting after witnessing the terrifying demonic possession of twelve-year-old Regan MacNeil, played by Linda Blair. There has never been a horror like *The Exorcist*; seeing it becomes a test of bravery and endurance.

# MUSIC

### Streets of London
*30th January 1974* Singer-songwriter Ralph McTell packs London's Royal Albert Hall on his first headlining appearance. Croydon-born Ralph is best known for the contemporary folk standard *Streets of London*, which he wrote in 1968. He has a surprise hit with the song over Christmas 1974 when its no-room-at-the-inn sentiments strike a chord with a broader audience.

# 1974

**Queen on tour**
1st March 1974 Queen headline their first UK tour. Initially regarded as yet another glam-rock outfit, they are starting to make a big impact as an album band thanks to Freddie Mercury's charismatic vocals and the uniquely sonorous, melody-driven guitar style of former astronomy student Brian May.

**Dolly's debut year**
21st April 1974 Country singer-songwriter Dolly Parton says goodbye to her long-time singing partner Porter Wagoner with the heartfelt I Will Always Love You. In her first solo year, Dolly tops the US country chart with this, Jolene and Love is Like a Butterfly.

**Abba win Eurovision**
6th April 1974 A landmark day in pop music as the Eurovision Song Contest - hosted by the UK at the Brighton Dome - introduces the world to Abba. Comprising two wonderfully costumed Swedish couples who sing in English, they win with Waterloo, written by members Bjorn Ulvaeus and Benny Andersson with producer Stig Anderson. It's the start of an incredible six years for the group who will be the world's leading singles act by 1980.

**Northern soul**
In industrial Lancashire, 'northern soul' rules. Fans and disc jockeys hunt out the best 1960s soul records from the US - the more obscure the better - and dance to them at 'all nighters' at venues such as Wigan Casino. It's now common for the tracks to be turned into national hits by radio play, as happens with R. Dean Taylor's There's a Ghost in My House and Robert Knight's Love on a Mountaintop.

**Lennon's lost weekend**
March 1974 Having parted from Yoko Ono and with the threat of deportation from the US hanging over him, a drunken John Lennon is thrown out of the Troubadour in Los Angeles. He is in the middle of what he will later call his 'lost weekend'; reconciliation with Yoko follows a Thanksgiving Night concert in New York in at which Lennon joins Elton John on stage.

**Cass Elliot dies**
29th July 1974 Aged just 32, the ebullient, wise-cracking Cass Elliot of the Mamas and the Papas dies in her sleep at Harry Nilsson's London flat, where she has been staying during an exhausting two-week spot at the London Palladium.

**Reggae for it now**
26th October 1974 Thanks to names like Desmond Dekker and Jimmy Cliff, Jamaican reggae is no stranger to the UK charts. A No. 1 is a rarity, however. Everything I Own by Kingston's Ken Boothe is a reggae version of a song by David Gates of Bread who wrote it as a tribute to his late father.

# 1974

### A song for Annie
*12th October 1974* Best known for writing *Take Me Home Country Roads* and *Leavin' on a Jet Plane*, country-folk singer John Denver has his only UK chart hit - a No. 1 - with *Annie's Song*, dedicated to his wife of seven years.

### Wailers 'too good'
Having been famously fired from supporting Sly and the Family Stone on tour for being too good, Bob Marley and the Wailers continue to nurture the US and UK markets with their reggae-rock fusion. Eric Clapton's chart-topping US cover of Marley's *I Shot the Sheriff* raises the band's profile despite the departures of key men Peter Tosh and Bunny Wailer.

## MY FIRST 18 YEARS
### TOP 10 — 1974

1. **Tiger Feet** Mud
2. **Jolene** Dolly Parton
3. **Rock Your Baby** George McCrae
4. **The Air That I Breathe** The Hollies
5. **Band on the Run** Wings
6. **Raised on Robbery** Joni Mitchell
7. **I Know What I Like (In Your Wardrobe)** Genesis
8. **Midnight at the Oasis** Maria Muldaur
9. **When Will I See You Again?** The Three Degrees
10. **Spiders and Snakes** Jim Stafford

Open | Search | Scan

### King of clubs
*21st September 1974* Reaching the UK Top Ten is the runaway dance hit of the year, *Queen Of Clubs* by Miami-based showband KC and the Sunshine Band. KC (Howie Casey) is the man behind the airy production sound of the TK label, which has just sold a million with the slinky, sensuous *Rock Your Baby* by George McCrae (photo).

### Wombled out
Bizarrely, the UK's leading chart act of 1974 is not a real group at all but the Wombles, who are songwriter Mike Batt and chums dressed in furry clothing. They follow up *The Wombling Song* with further variations on the wombling theme like *Remember You're A Womble*, *Wombling White Tie And Tails* and *Wombling Merry Christmas*.

PHOTO CREDITS Copyright 2024, TDM Rights BV.
Photos: **A** Harry Dempster - Hulton Archive - Getty Images / **B** David Cannon - Getty Images / **C** Bettmann - Getty Images / **D** Mirrorpix - Getty Images / **E** Independent News and Media - Hulton Archive - Getty Images / **F** Hulton Archive - Hulton Royals Collection - Getty Images / **G** Ulstein Bild - Getty Images / **H** Wally McNamee - Getty Images / **I** Bettmann - Getty Images / **J** Thames Television - Ronald Grant Archive - Mary Evans / **K** Gareth Cattermole - Getty Images / **L** TV Times - Getty Images / **M** Silver Screen Collection - Moviepix - Getty Images / **N** Anwar Hussein - Getty Images / **O** Ronald Grant Archive - Mary Evans / **P** Sunset Boulevard - Corbis Historical - Getty Images / **Q** Michael Putland - Hulton Archive - Getty Images / **R** Hulton Deutsch - Corbis Historical - Getty Images / **S** Steve Morley - Redferns - Getty Images / **T** Robert Riger - Getty Images / **U** David Redfern - Redferns - Getty Images / **V** David Warner Ellis - Redferns - Getty Images.

# 1975

## MY FIRST 18 YEARS

## SPORT

**Fitness guru gets royal recognition**
Fitness pioneer Eileen Fowler, who has inspired the nation to keep fit since the 1950s with her exercise programmes on radio, records, and TV, is awarded an MBE. Fowler continues to evangelise about the benefits of exercise and even after moving into a retirement home in her nineties, encourages other residents to join her in a daily fitness routine.

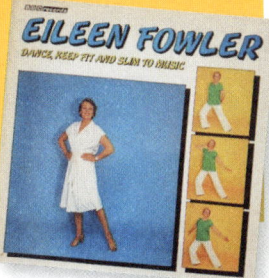

**The Thrilla in Manila**
In a decade defined by epic boxing confrontations, the Thrilla in Manila, between Muhammad Ali and Joe Frazier on 1st October, is perhaps the biggest and the most brutal. It's a gruelling, forty-two-minute marathon with temperatures reaching a muggy 49 degrees, as the two heavyweights slug it out in what is their third meeting. Ali prevails when Frazier's team stop the fight in the fourteenth round, the victory cementing his status as 'The Greatest'.

**Terror on the terraces**
Football hooliganism is rampant by the mid-1970s and has serious consequences for Leeds United who are defeated by Bayern Munich in the European Cup Final. Riots by Leeds fans break out during the match, triggered by a disallowed Peter Lorimer goal. The club is handed a four-year ban from European football which is reduced to two years after an appeal. Two years later, Liverpool is also banned from Europe after riots at a Cup Winners' Cup game against St. Etienne. The so-called 'English disease' will overshadow football for the next decade.

**Arthur Ashe conquers Wimbledon**
It's an all-American affair for the men's singles final at Wimbledon on 5th July as defending champion and favourite Jimmy Connors meets Arthur Ashe in the final. Ashe plays a perfect, tactical match, and when he beats Connors in four sets, he becomes (and remains) the only black man to win the Wimbledon as well as the US and Australian Open titles.

**World Cup cricket**
The cricket World Cup takes place in England from 7th to 21st June, the first major tournament in the history of one-day international cricket. The West Indies under Clive Lloyd emerge the victors.

### 2 JAN 1975
It is announced Charlie Chaplin will receive a knighthood in the New Year Honours.

### 26 FEB 1975
Off-duty Metropolitan Police officer Stephen Tibble, aged 22, is shot and killed at point blank range while pursuing a member of the Provisional IRA.

### 15 MAR 1975
The Army is drafted in to clear 70,000 tonnes of rubbish accumulated during a nine-week binmen's strike in Glasgow.

# 1975

**New start for Martina in the States**
Czech player and rising tennis star Martina Navratilova announces her defection from Czechoslovakia to the US.

**Sobers becomes Sir**
On 19th February, during her Commonwealth tour of the West Indies, the Queen knights cricket hero Gary Sobers at Bridgetown racecourse, in front of a crowd of 10,000 cheering Barbadians.

**Moorgate tube crash**
28th February 1975 London is left reeling when a train entering its final stop at Moorgate underground station fails to slow down and collides with the end of the tunnel. 43 people are killed and 74 injured, prompting the introduction of an automatic system to slow speeding trains on the network, known as the 'Moorgate' protection.

**Local government in Scotland**
16th May 1975 Following major changes to the administrative map in England the previous year, Scotland's local government areas are redrawn leading to the creation of nine new regions and a two-tier system of regions and districts.

## DOMESTIC NEWS

**Black Panther**
14th January 1975 Headlines are dominated by the kidnapping of 17-year-old Leslie Whittle, an heiress taken from her home in Bridgnorth, Shropshire. The kidnapper demands a £50,000 ransom, but confusion regarding the kidnapper's instructions means it is never delivered. On 7th March her body is discovered, and the killer identified as the 'Black Panther', a serial burglar and murderer. Newspapers cover the investigation until Donald Nielson is arrested in December. He spends the rest of his life in prison.

Cassette carousel

**Dibbles Bridge coach crash**
27th May 1975 Tragedy strikes as the brakes fail on a coach carrying 45 female pensioners on a day trip to Grassington. The bus plunges off a bridge near Hebden, North Yorkshire, killing 33 and injuring everyone else on board.

**International Women's Year**
15th January 1975 The United Nations declares 1975 'International Women's Year' in the hope of prompting nations to examine inequality. In November, the UK introduces the Employment Protection Act, which establishes the provision of paid maternity leave, and in December the Sex Discrimination Act 1975 and Equal Pay Act 1970 come into force.

## 23 APR 1975
As South Vietnam falls to the Communists, the British Embassy in Saigon is closed and staff evacuated.

## 22 MAY 1975
One of Britain's leading sculptors, Barbara Hepworth, is killed in a fire at her St. Ives studio.

## 19 JUN 1975
Striking stable-boys march around the course at Royal Ascot on Gold Cup Day. They accept a 19% pay rise in July.

# 1975

### European Space Agency
*31st May 1975* The UK becomes one of the ten founding members of the European Space Agency, which launches its first mission later in the year. The Cos-B space probe is launched to study sources of gamma radiation in the cosmos.

### Snow in June
*2nd June 1975* England is stunned when June brings unexpected snow showers. The brief flurries fall as far south as London, the first time the capital has seen snow in June in almost 200 years.

### EEC referendum
*5th June 1975* The country goes to the polls for a referendum on membership of the European Economic Community, which would later become the European Union. The 'Yes' vote is successful with 67% choosing to remain within the community.

### The Spaghetti House siege
*28th September 1975* The Spaghetti House restaurant in Knightsbridge, London, is robbed by three gunmen who take the staff hostage when the police are called. On the advice of psychologists, police allow the siege to continue for six days in the hope that the gunmen will feel sympathy for their hostages. Eventually, the gunmen release the staff and surrender.

### Balcombe Street siege
*6th December 1975* A year of continuing violence regarding Northern Ireland culminates with the Balcombe Street siege. After months of bombings in London, police give chase to four Provisional IRA operatives who had fired shots into a Mayfair restaurant. The chase ends with the operatives breaking into a flat and taking the two occupants hostage for six days, before eventually surrendering. Events are broadcast live on television across the country. Two of the operatives, Harry Duggan and Hugh Doherty, had been responsible for the assassination of Guinness Book of Records founder Ross McWhirter in November, after he had offered a reward for information about their activities.

### First Ripper victim
*30th October 1975* The murder of 28-year-old Wilma McCann in Leeds is the first in a string of killings committed by the so-called 'Yorkshire Ripper' Peter Sutcliffe. The search for the Yorkshire Ripper becomes one of the decades' biggest news stories.

## 18 JUL 1975
British racing driver Graham Hill announces his retirement from the sport. He is killed in an air crash on 29th November.

## 7 AUG 1975
Temperatures soar to 32 degrees centigrade in London, the highest recorded in 35 years.

## 19 SEP 1975
British Forces Broadcasting Services broadcasts television programmes for the first time from the Trenchard Barracks, Celle, near Hanover.

# 1975

## ROYALTY & POLITICS

**Thatcher becomes Tory leader**
On 11th February, Margaret Thatcher, becomes the first woman leader of a British political party when she defeats four other (male) candidates with 146 out of 215 votes. 'I beat four chaps. Now let's get down to work,' says the 49-year-old mother of twins.

**Politics on the radio**
The idea of broadcasting Parliamentary proceedings has been resisted for some time but on 24th February, a Commons vote approves the presence of microphones in the chamber and in June, during a month-long experiment, Radio 4 listeners can hear for the first time what is debated in Westminster; Labour minister Tony Benn is the first MP to be heard. Permanent radio coverage of Parliament is introduced in 1978, but television must wait until November 1989.

**Queen visits Japan**
Thirty years after the end of the Second World War, the Queen makes the first state visit to Japan as the guest of Emperor Hirohito. She and the Duke of Edinburgh attend a welcome banquet on 7th May and they experience plenty of Japanese culture and tradition during the visit.

**Order of the Bath anniversary**
Prince Charles, sporting a moustache, is installed as Great Master of the Most Honourable Order of the Bath at Westminster Abbey on 25th May, in a service marking the 250th anniversary of the founding of the order by George I.

## FOREIGN NEWS

**Digital watches**
Too expensive and out of reach for the average consumer, digital LED watches start to take off when Texas Instruments starts mass production in a plastic housing. These watches sell for $20 and cost half the price a year later.

**Microsoft launch**
*4th April 1975* After developing an operating system called an interpreter for the Altair 8800, which makes the microcomputer interesting for hobby programmers, childhood friends Bill Gates and Paul Allen launch their own company. Allen coins the name 'Micro-Soft', short for 'microcomputer software'.

---

**30 OCT** 1975
A report is published stating that 6.5 million elm trees have been destroyed due to Dutch elm disease.

**27 NOV** 1975
Ross McWhirter, co-founder of the Guinness Book of World Records with his twin Norris, is shot and killed by the Provisional IRA.

**25 DEC** 1975
Heavy metal band Iron Maiden are formed in east London by bassist Steve Harris.

# 1975

## Fall of Saigon
*30th April 1975* After nearly twenty years of fighting, North Vietnamese forces penetrate Saigon and 'liberate' the capital of South Vietnam. Without the support of the US, South Vietnam is lost. News cameras capture the mass panic of the final moments in the fall of Saigon, as desperate civilians mass around US helicopters sent to rescue the remaining American Embassy staff.

## Khmer Rouge
*17th April 1975* Despite three years of bombing by the US, the Khmer Rouge emerge victorious in the Cambodian civil war. On 17th April, their forces enter the capital Phnom Penh, where they expel the rulers and install dictator Pol Pot as leader. The stage set is set for one of the most brutal regimes in human history.

## Carlos the Jackal
*21st December 1975* With five accomplices, Venezuelan terrorist Ilich Ramírez Sánchez, nicknamed Carlos and called 'the Jackal' by the press, kidnaps delegates to the ministerial conference of the Organization of the Petroleum Exporting Countries (OPEC) in Vienna. They capture 60 and kill three. A day later, the hostage takers are given a free exit by plane to Algiers and Tripoli, where the hostages are freed in return for a ransom of more than $20 million.

## Franco is dead
*20th November 1975* After a three-week-long coma, Spain's fascist dictator General Francisco Franco dies. Two days after his death, the monarchy returns, as he had wished. But against expectations, King Juan Carlos pushes for reconciliation with the socialists, a return to democracy and more freedom for regions such as Catalonia and the Basque Country.

# ENTERTAINMENT

## High-rise horrors
'A night of blazing suspense' is perhaps an understatement for *The Towering Inferno*, a collaboration between Warner Bros. and Twentieth Century Fox based on two separate books about a skyscraper uncontrollably ablaze. This is the disaster movie to end all disaster movies and when it's released in the UK on 29th January, audiences flock to see not only the scorching special effects but an A-list cast who must find a way to escape as the flames lick at their heels. Who will survive, and who will get roasted? *The Towering Inferno* is 165 minutes of catastrophic, nail-biting conflagration and becomes the year's biggest box-office hit.

# 1975

## Six Million Dollar toys

The Six Million Dollar Man action figure is launched in the UK, based on the hit US TV series starring Lee Majors as NASA astronaut Steve Austin who is rebuilt with bionic body parts following a deadly crash. Now kids can have their own thirteen-inch-high Steve Austin, who comes wearing a natty red NASA tracksuit and sneakers. Steve can show off his power by lifting a car engine, you can look through his bionic eye via a hole in his head, and his rubber skin peels back to reveal those $6,000,000 bionics.

## Little House on the Prairie

Following on from the success of *The Waltons*, the next historical family drama from America to hit these shores (on 25th February) is *Little House on the Prairie*. Loosely based on the books by Laura Ingalls Wilder about growing up in the nineteenth-century Mid-West as a child of pioneer settlers, *Little House on the Prairie* isn't afraid to tackle some thorny subjects from racism to disability and has no qualms about tugging at viewers' heartstrings - many were moved to tears when Mary Ingalls wakes up to discover she has gone blind. It also fuels a growing taste for prairie style as frilled floral maxi dresses, patchwork bed covers and characters such as Hollie Hobbie gain in popularity.

## Shark attack

*Jaws* may be one of Stephen Spielberg's earliest films but his ability to keep the tension taut, and to play on audiences' fear of the unseen, turns it into a major movie event in the US this summer before it has its UK film premiere on Christmas Day. Roy Scheider, Richard Dreyfus and Robert Shaw do battle with an underwater menace terrorising the East Coast resort of Amity Island before it picks off any more of its swimmers for a mid-morning snack. The suspense is intensified by John Williams's menacing music, and brilliant lines like, 'We're gonna need a bigger boat.' *Jaws* becomes an instant classic.

## Tune in to Doonican

Irish crooner Val Doonican, known for his easy manner, cosy cardigans, and relaxing rocking chair performances, returns to BBC1 on 24th May with *The Val Doonican Show* after several years at ATV (ITV). A regular on British TV screens since 1963, Doonican is comfortable with his uncool status, having sold millions of records including the completely unthreatening *Val Doonican Rocks, But Gently* in 1967.

## Toffee transformation

Chewy sweets Toff-o-Lux are rebranded as Toffos this year, and if that wasn't enough to rattle toffee fans, they are also launched in a fruit-flavoured version featuring strawberry and banana toffees.

# 1975

### Music hall for the masses
*The Good Old Days*, a recreation for television of the late Victorian and Edwardian music hall, presented with great flourish by Leonard Sachs, and with songs and sketches performed in the style of greats like Marie Lloyd or Harry Lauder, began way back in 1953 and continues to enjoy a loyal following throughout its long, thirty-year run. The live audience is encouraged to dress up in costume and sing along at the end to 'The Old Bull and Bush'. During the 1970s, the waiting list to be part of that audience is 24,000.

### The Good Life
*The Good Life* appears on our screens for the first time on 4th April, with Richard Briers and Felicity Kendal as Surbiton's ever-optimistic pioneers of suburban self-sufficiency, Tom and Barbara Good. *The Good Life* taps into - and encourages - a resurgence in growing your own vegetables, jam making and experimenting with homemade wine, but we tune in just as much to laugh at the barely suppressed snobbery and bemusement of socially mobile, kaftan-wearing neighbour Margo Leadbetter (a magnificent Penelope Keith) and her long-suffering husband Jerry (Paul Eddington).

### Chop Phooey
'Who IS the superhero? Sarge? No. Rosemary? The telephone operator? No. Penry? The mild-mannered janitor? Could be!' *Hong Kong Phooey* karate chops his way onto British TV screens on 17th March, a canine crime-fighter full of enthusiasm but with ambitions far beyond his capabilities. He regularly has to stop to consult the 'Hong Kong Book of Kung Fu', and even his transformation into superhero is marred by getting stuck in a filing cabinet drawer. Thank goodness for Spot the cat (who is actually striped) who covers for his friend's incompetence with casual efficiency.

### TV cops get tough
*The Sweeney* airs on ITV on 2nd January and introduces a whole new side of policing to the British public. This is no cosy drama along the lines of *Dixon of Dock Green*. Taking its title from Sweeney Todd, the Cockney rhyming slang for the Flying Squad, Detective Inspector Jack Regan (John Thaw) and Detective Sergeant George Carter (Dennis Waterman) tackle violent crime head on, frequently throwing out the rule book to bring hardened criminals to heel. Police slang terms are revealed (a 'snout' is an informer, a 'stoppo' is a getaway car), and with so much filming done on location around London, this is drama with a heavy dose of reality.

### Trainspotting
Trainspotters and rail enthusiasts assemble as the National Railway Museum is opened in York this year. The first national museum outside of the capital, the National Railway Museum welcomes 2 million visitors in the first twelve months.

# 1975

**Faultlessly Fawlty**
In 1967, the Monty Python team stay at the Gleneagles Hotel in Torquay and are amused and fascinated by the hotel owner who John Cleese describes as 'the rudest man I have ever come across in my life'. That hotelier becomes the inspiration for Basil Fawlty, the misanthropic owner of *Fawlty Towers*, which begins on BBC2. Written by Cleese and his then-wife Connie Booth (who plays maid Polly), the pair spend weeks writing and fine tuning the script for each episode, and then more weeks editing, during which time Cleese appears in several TV commercials to earn income. The show first airs on 19th September, with Cleese as Basil, Prunella Scales as his domineering wife Sybil and Andrew Sachs as Manuel, the hapless Spanish waiter whose mix-ups and accidents are always because, 'He's from Barcelona'. Just twelve episodes of Fawlty Towers are made, divided into two series. But it's quality not quantity and Cleese and Booth's pursuit of perfection pays off. In 2000, *Fawlty Towers* is voted first out of the 100 best British television programmes of all time by the British Film Institute.

**How we used to live**
Queen Elizabeth, the Queen Mother, visits Beamish Museum near Stanley, Co. Durham on 17th July. Beamish is an open-air museum and pioneer of living history, preserving north-east heritage by authentically recreating typical communities and industries of the area in the late nineteenth and early twentieth centuries.

**Runaround**
Cockney geezer Mike Reid is the MC of ITV's kids' quiz show *Runaround*, which airs for the first time on 2nd September. It's high energy fun with teams zooming around the studio when Reid asks a question and shouts, 'G-g-g-g-g-GO!' jumping in front of what they think is the correct answer. The elusive yellow ball - and two extra points - goes to any brainbox who selects the right answer when nobody else does.

**Bod**
Bod first appears on the BBC in 1974 in a story read on *Playschool*. The BBC decide to bring Bod to life on screen and the resulting animation airs on 23rd December, narrated by John Le Mesurier with a jazzy theme tune by *Playschool* and *Playaway* regular Derek Griffiths. *Bod* is quite odd; a bald little figure of indeterminate gender in a yellow smock and with a circle of acquaintances limited to a policeman, a farmer, a postman and his aunt Flo.

**Comedy's Holy Grail**
'Sets the film industry back 900 years!' and 'Makes Ben Hur look like an epic' are just some of tongue-in-cheek slogans across the film poster for *Monty Python and the Holy Grail*, which opens in the UK on 3rd April. A farcical retelling of the Arthurian legend with non-stop jokes and silliness, it's a film crammed with memorable (and quotable) moments from the ridiculous Knights of 'Ni' to the gory duel where the Dark Knight insists 'Tis only a scratch' as Graham Chapman's King Arthur systematically dismembers him.

# 1975

### Big potato
Mr Potato Head, first launched in 1952, expands in size this year making him safe for small children to play with too.

### A right royal drama
ITV's historical royal drama *Edward the Seventh* begins on 1st April, and traces the life and eventual reign of Edward VII, whose older self is played by Timothy West, with Annette Crosbie as his mother, Queen Victoria. Through the years we witness the appearance of figures both central and peripheral to European history, played by an eclectic cast.

### One Flew Over the Cuckoo's Nest
When Randle P. McMurphy (Jack Nicholson) claims insanity so he can get himself transferred to a state psychiatric hospital in order to avoid hard labour, he doesn't factor in a formidable foe in the form of sadistic Nurse Ratched (Louise Fletcher). Produced by Michael Douglas, whose father Kirk owned the film rights to Ken Kesey's best-selling novel about his experiences working in a Californian Veterans Hospital, *One Flew Over the Cuckoo's Nest* wins five Oscars including Best Actor for Nicholson and Best Actress for Fletcher.

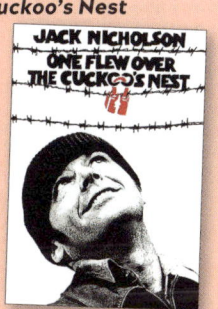

### Galileo, Galileo
*31st October 1975* Queen close out the year with one of the records of the decade. *Bohemian Rhapsody* is a six minute-long multi-layered five-part mini-opera that takes three weeks to record. The band also make their own film for television stations to play when they can't appear live - effectively the first promotional video of the kind that will become commonplace in the 1980s. *Bohemian Rhapsody* stays at No. 1 in the UK for nine weeks.

### Ch-Changes
*March 1975* David Bowie changes style again. As he prepares for filming *The Man Who Fell to Earth*, his *Young Americans* album reveals a new soul-based direction. *Fame*, a collaboration with John Lennon and Carlos Alomar, gives him his first US No. 1.

### Rollermania!
*22nd March 1975* 'Rollermania' explodes as the Bay City Rollers spend five weeks at No. 1 with an old Four Seasons tune, *Bye Bye Baby*. From the Glasgow area, they appeal most to teenage and pre-teenage girls with a tinny and clanky sound that's deliberately under-produced to underline their ingenuousness. In the charts and on teen magazine covers, it is difficult to escape the tartan-covered quintet during 1975. The Rollers offer a final blast of pop hysteria before punk rock and disco take hold.

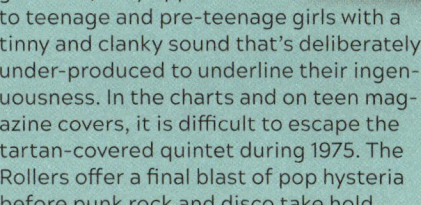

# MUSIC

### Mac additions
*1st January 1975* US rock duo Lindsey Buckingham and Stevie Nicks join Fleetwood Mac, setting the once all-British blues band on a whole new course.

# 1975

**Voulez-vous coucher?**
*23rd March 1975* One of the cheekiest lines in songwriting history - '*Voulez vous couchez avec moi, ce soir?*' - is heard in *Lady Marmalade* by Labelle, now No. 1 in the US. Fronted by Patti Labelle, Labelle is an all-female trio whose space-age stage suits and in-your-face attitude put them light years ahead of previous all-female outfits like the Supremes.

**Gabriel leaves**
*28th May 1975* Peter Gabriel leaves Genesis (photo), the art rock band he formed with fellow Charterhouse public schoolboys Mike Rutherford and Tony Banks in 1967. Stepping up as vocalist is Phil Collins, drummer with the band since 1970, who once played the Artful Dodger in *Oliver!* in the West End. Far from jeopardising the band's future, as some suggest, the switch gives the band a more mainstream direction and a new lease of life.

**Rod goes west**
As Rod Stewart admits he is considering US citizenship, his debut album for Warner Brothers has the appropriate title of *Atlantic Crossing*. Meanwhile Rod's private life goes public as he begins an affair with actress Britt Ekland.

## MY FIRST 18 YEARS
### TOP 10 — 1975

1. **I'm Not in Love** 10cc
2. **Lovin' You** Minnie Riperton
3. **This Old Heart of Mine** Rod Stewart
4. **Jive Talkin'** The Bee Gees
5. **At Seventeen** Janis Ian
6. **Cat's in the Cradle** - Harry Chapin
7. **You Ain't Seen Nothing Yet** Bachman-Turner...
8. **December '63** The Four Seasons
9. **No Woman No Cry** Bob Marley
10. **Mamma Mia** Abba

**Zeppelin in exile**
*May - June 1975* Now the biggest band in the world in terms of earnings, Led Zeppelin enter tax exile in Switzerland after playing a series of four hour shows at Earl's Court. Their first release on their own SwanSong label, *Physical Graffiti*, is an instant chart-topping album in the US and UK.

**Lennon can stay**
*7th October 1975* With John Lennon and Yoko Ono now reconciled, son Sean is born two days after Lennon's deportation order is rescinded. He receives his Green Card allowing him permanent residence in the US nine months later.

---

PHOTO CREDITS Copyright 2024, TDM Rights BV.

Photos: **A** Bettmann - Getty Images / **B** Bettmann - Getty Images / **C** PA Images - Getty Images / **D** Philippe Achache - Gamma Rapho - Getty Images / **E** Keystone - Hulton Royals Collection - Getty Images / **F** Doug Wilson - Corbis Historical - Getty Images / **G** Roland Neveu - LightRocket - Getty Images / **H** Keystone France - Gamma-Keystone - Getty Images / **I** Keystone - Hulton Archives - Getty Images / **J** Fotos International - Archive Photos - Getty Images / **K** Tony Russell - Redferns - Getty Images / **L** Ian Tyas - Hulton Archive - Getty Images / **M** Yorkshire Television - AF Archive - Mary Evans / **N** Ronald Grant Archive - Mary Evans / **O** Ronald Grant Archive - Mary Evans / **P** Ronald Grant Archive - Mary Evans / **Q** LMPC - Getty Images / **R** Michael Putland - Hulton Archive - Getty Images / **S** The Land of Lost Content Collection - Mary Evans Picture Library / **T** Michael Ochs Archives - Getty Images / **U** RB - Redferns - Getty Images / **V** Jorgen Angel - Redferns - Getty Images.

# 1976

## SPORT

### Ice gold perfection
On 11th February, at the Winter Olympics in Stockholm, Birmingham's John Curry wins the gold medal in the men's figure skating. Curry's early ambitions to be a ballet dancer were quashed by his father but there is a balletic quality to his performance, which combines grace with athleticism.

### Life in the fast lane
Marlboro Maclaren's chances of victory in this year's Formula One Championship rest on the final race at the Fuji Speedway track in Japan, and the ability of their British driver, James Hunt, to secure a place in the top four. Hunt has been chasing his Austrian rival, Niki Lauda, all season and when they line up on the grid on 24th October, he needs just three points to take the championship. In treacherous, monsoon conditions James Hunt has the drive of his life, continuing through the spray despite a puncture, and a delayed pit stop, while Lauda is forced to withdraw from the race. Hunt comes third, enough to win the championship by a single point. Charismatic with dashing good looks and a playboy reputation, the win seals Hunt's position as one of the country's modern-day heroes.

### Borg begins
On 3rd July, cool, calm and collected Swede Bjorn Borg defeats Ile Nastase in the men's singles final at Wimbledon in three sets and secures the first of five consecutive titles at the All England club.

### Seven times Derby winner
Lester Piggott becomes the most successful jockey ever in the Derby when he wins the race for the seventh time on Empery on 2nd June. Piggott's seven titles put him ahead of the six wins of both Jim Robinson in the 1830s, and the legendary Steve Donoghue. He will go on to consolidate his achievement, winning the race twice more, in 1977 and 1983.

### 13 JAN 1976
Queen of crime writing Agatha Christie dies at the age of 85.

### 2 FEB 1976
The Queen opens the huge National Exhibition Centre (NEC) in Birmingham.

### 20 MAR 1976
The speedy Oxford crew win the Boat Race in 16 minutes, 58 seconds; a record for the event.

# 1976

### Montreal Olympics
One of Britain's three gold medals is thanks to swimmer David Wilkie who sets a new world record of 2:15:11 in the men's 200 metre breaststroke. It is the first Olympic gold swimming medal for Great Britain in 68 years. Elsewhere, sporting history is made by Romanian gymnast Nadia Comaneci who is awarded the first ever 10.0 score on the asymmetric bars in the team competition, followed by six more perfect scores in individual events on her way to winning three gold medals

Montréal 1976

### Concorde arrives!
*21st January 1976* Supersonic jet Concorde makes its first commercial flight between London and Bahrain, launching the era of supersonic passenger flights. Concorde becomes an icon of luxury and modernity but suffers with sales thanks to its high cost and the difficulties flying it over land thanks to its sonic boom.

## DOMESTIC NEWS

### Northern Ireland
*5th January 1976* A year of continuing violence in Northern Ireland begins with the Kingsmill Massacre in South Armagh, in which ten protestant men are killed by members of the Provisional IRA. Twelve bombs strike the West End of London later in the month, and in July Christopher Ewart-Biggs, the UK's ambassador to Ireland, is assassinated by landmine. The year also brings large peace demonstrations, with 10,000 Protestant and Catholic women marching in August, and a Derry Peace March attracting 25,000 people in September. The same year the Guildford Four and the Maguire Seven are wrongly convicted for the Guildford pub bombings, their convictions overturned in 1989 and 1991.

### Britain's Buddhist temple
Britain gets its very first purpose-built Buddhist temple. Following the Thai style of Buddhism, the Wat Buddhapadipa opens in Wimbledon following a move from its original location on a residential street in East Sheen.

**DO YOU REMEMBER THIS?**

Marbles

### Third Cod War
*1st June 1976* Iceland and the UK finally agree an end to the Third Cod War, with the UK accepting Iceland's definition of its territorial waters. The eleven-month conflict has resulted in 55 separate incidents, mostly involving the aggressive ramming of ships on both sides.

## 26 APR 1976
Comedy actor and *Carry On* star Sid James dies after suffering a heart attack on stage at the Sunderland Empire.

## 10 MAY 1976
Embroiled in scandal, Jeremy Thorpe resigns as leader of the Liberal Party.

## 22 JUN 1976
The sizzling 'summer of '76' begins with a heatwave that will be remembered for decades to come.

# 1976

## Ford Fiesta launches
*14th July 1976* Nation's favourite the Fiesta is launched by Ford, due to be manufactured at the company's Dagenham plant in Essex. The three-door hatchback is the smallest car Ford has produced so far and becomes popular as a 'run-around' vehicle and especially with learner drivers, making it one of the best-selling cars of the next 40 years.

## Art fraud exposed
*16th July 1976* A series of articles published in *The Times* begin to unravel the story of prolific forger Tom Keating. Convinced dealers are interested only in big names and not the artistic value of a work, Keating has been saturating the market with hundreds of fakes since the 1950s. He is convicted in 1979 and goes on to lead a successful Channel 4 documentary about painting in the 1980s.

## Big Ben clock stops
*5th August 1976* After more than 100 years of use, the chiming mechanism in the Great Clock of Westminster breaks. The mechanism is badly damaged and is shut down for 26 days while repair is made, the longest break in service since its construction. Westminster feels eerily quiet without its familiar tolls.

## Riots at Notting Hill
*30th August 1976* The Notting Hill Carnival descends into chaos as mounted police officers attempt to break up the 150,000-strong crowd. Whilst arresting pickpockets at the event, tension had risen between the police and young black attendees who felt unfairly targeted. Violence breaks out and 100 police officers and 60 carnival attendees are injured.

## Hull Prison riot
*1st September 1976* A three-day long riot breaks out at HM Prison Hull. Protesting against alleged prison guard brutality, 100 prisoners take over the prison, destroying two-thirds of the compound. The riot ends peacefully, but the prison closes for a year to allow for the £3 million worth of repairs.

## Renee MacRae disappearance
*12th November 1976* 36-year-old mother Renee MacRae disappears with her three-year-old son Andrew in what becomes the country's longest-running missing persons case. In 2022, MacRae's lover, and Andrew's father, William MacDowell is found guilty of their murders, although their bodies are never found.

## 14 JUL 1976
Drought Bill introduced to tackle the country's worst drought in 250 years.

## 1 AUG 1976
Grand Prix champion Niki Lauda suffers severe burns in an accident during the German Grand Prix.

## 29 SEP 1976
With the pound falling to $1.64, Britain applies to borrow £2.3 billion from the IMF.

# 1976

### Bank of America robbery
*16th November 1976* The perpetrators of what is believed to be the world's largest bank heist are sentenced to a total of 100 years in prison. The seven men are responsible for a robbery at the Mayfair branch of the Bank of America last year, in which safety deposit boxes worth £8 million were stolen, and only £500,000 of the loot is ever recovered.

### International Monetary Fund loan
*15th December 1976* Chancellor of the Exchequer, Denis Healey, announces an agreed £2,300,000,000 loan from the International Monetary Fund to ease the country's financial woes. The loan comes on the condition that public spending be cut and is received against a backdrop of pay freezes and inflation at 16.5%, one of the highest levels since records began.

### Extreme weather
1976 brings extreme weather to the United Kingdom. In January, the Gale of 1976 sees hurricane-force winds of 105 miles per hour. In June and July, an extreme heat wave sees fifteen consecutive days of temperatures over 26.7°C. The temperature reaches a peak of 35.9°C before August and September bring drought.

### Callaghan takes over at No. 10
On 16th March, Prime Minister Harold Wilson announces his resignation and recommends Foreign Secretary and former Home Secretary James Callaghan (photo) as his successor. Callaghan, aged 64, becomes Prime Minister on 5th April. Wilson's departure triggers controversy when he includes some questionable individuals in his resignation honours list.

### Divorce in the Firm
A statement from Kensington Palace on 19th March announces that Princess Margaret and Lord Snowdon have mutually agreed to live apart. Although the statement goes on to say 'There are no plans for divorce proceedings' the couple do indeed divorce two years later.

## FOREIGN NEWS

### Dirty War
*24th March 1976* In Argentina, President Isabel Perón is kidnapped and deposed by the military, and replaced by Lieutenant General Jorge Videla. Under the name 'Dirty War', the Videla junta is responsible for the disappearance of tens of thousands of trade union workers, students and other left-wing activists.

## ROYALTY & POLITICS

### Hot property
The Queen buys the 730-acre Gatcombe Park estate in Gloucestershire for Princess Anne and Captain Phillips at a reported cost of £300,000, leading to criticism by several Labour MPs.

### 4 OCT 1976
British Rail launch the new Intercity 125 train which initially runs out of Paddington to Bristol and South Wales.

### 27 NOV 1976
The Mini continues to be a popular choice of motor. The four millionth rolls off the assembly line this month.

### 10 DEC 1976
Mairead Corrigan and Betty Williams, founders of the Ulster Peace Movement, are awarded the Nobel Peace Prize.

# 1976

### First Apple
*1st April 1976* Having built a prototype of an assembled personal computer with Steve Jobs in 1975, Steve Wozniak offers the design to his employer HP and to game console manufacturer Atari, but neither party is interested. Wozniak and Jobs then decide to market their computer themselves. Jobs, who follows a fruit diet, comes up with the name: Apple Computer Company. From 11th April, the Apple I is on sale for $666.66.

### Judgement of Paris
*1st May 1976* In a blind wine tasting soon to be known as 'the judgement of Paris', an eleven-member jury of nine connoisseurs from France, the UK and US chooses both the white chardonnay and the red cabernet sauvignon from California over the French chardonnay and Bordeaux - a serious blow to the French ego. The so-called 'new wines' are conquering the world.

### CN Tower opened
*26th June 1976* The Canadian National (CN) Tower is opened in Toronto, Canada, at this point the highest free-standing structure on the planet at 553 metres.

### Operation Entebbe
*27th June 1976* Palestinian militants hijack an Air France plane in Greece and fly it to Entebbe in Uganda, where they are welcomed by dictator Idi Amin. They demand the release of militants imprisoned in Israel and other countries in return for the hostages. 148 non-Jewish hostages are released over the next two days but an Israeli force of 100 commandos mounts a rescue of the remaining hostages on 4th July. Three hostages are killed but 102 are brought to safety, while all the hijackers and 45 Ugandan soldiers are killed. The rescuers' sole fatality is Yonatan Netanyahu, brother of future Israeli Prime Minister Benjamim Netanyahu.

### Soweto uprising
*16th June 1976* In South Africa, the apartheid regime comes under further pressure when police in Soweto open fire on students demonstrating against the introduction of Afrikaans as the dominant language of education. Several hundred demonstrators are killed. A photo of the shot twelve-year-old student Hector Pieterson being carried away shocks the world.

### Red planet
*20th July 1976* In the search for life on other planets, NASA sent an unmanned space mission to Mars on 20th August 1975. Now Viking 1 becomes the first spacecraft in history to successfully soft land on the red planet. The probe soon transmits the first images of Mars to Mother Earth.

# 1976

### Robbery of the century
*16th - 17th July 1976* Six robbers spend four months drilling their way through the sewer system to the vaults of the Société Générale bank in Nice. During the weekend after the 14th July national holiday, the robbers strike: 337 safes are emptied containing almost 50 million French francs. Before they leave, the thieves leave a message: 'Without weapons, without hatred and without violence.' Not a single franc from the loot is ever recovered.

### Mao is dead
*9th September 1976* The architect of Chinese communism and one of the dominant political figures of the 20th century, Chairman Mao Zedong of the People's Republic of China dies in Beijing aged 82.

### Carter is President
*2nd November 1976* Jimmy Carter (photo right) wins the US presidential election, defeating incumbent Gerald Ford in a close race. He is the first candidate from the southern states to become President since the American Civil War.

# ENTERTAINMENT

### Emu attacks Parky
On 27th November, Rod Hull and Emu are invited onto chat show *Parkinson* but Emu takes a marked dislike to host Michael Parkinson, rips up his notes and eventually attacks and unseats him. Rod, meanwhile, is powerless to stop him.

### *Roy of the Rovers* scores
Roy Race of Melchester Rovers, aka Roy of the Rovers, first made an appearance in *Tiger* comic back in 1954, but 22 years later, his continuing popularity means he's promoted to the first division and gets to headline his own comic with the first issue on 25th September. With guest appearances by real-life players and even the former England manager Alf Ramsey popping up, plus dramatic storylines including a worrying number of kidnappings, at its peak *Roy of the Rovers* sells an extremely respectable 450,000 copies.

### Carry On Budgie
Budgerigars have been popular pets since the Victorian era but in the 1970s, it seems as if every home has a cage hanging in the corner with a gaudy plastic cover. Riding on the crest of the budgerigar wave is *World of Budgerigars*, a short film on how to care for your feathered friends, starring, unexpectedly, Sid James, who listens attentively to the advice delivered with deadpan solemnity by budgie expert Philip Marsden.

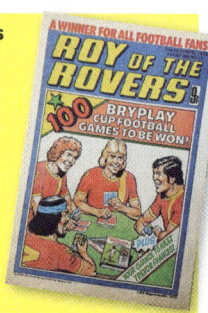

# 1976

### Green Cross Code for roads

Since the 1950s, children have been schooled in crossing the road safely by Tufty the Squirrel. Tufty appears as a puppet in public information films and is the face of the Tufty Club which by the early 1970s has two million members. But there is a new road safety kid on the block by this year, with special superpowers. The Green Cross man extols the importance of the Green Cross Code's essential rules of Stop, Look, Listen, Think and, if he spots anyone ignoring this advice, can teleport in an instant to intervene and save kids getting squashed by an Austin Allegro. The Central Office of Information engages 6 ft 6 in bodybuilder, weightlifter and actor David Prowse, who dons the special green and white suit in his quest to rid the world of road accidents.

### Open All Hours

Ronnie Barker creates another sitcom anti-hero in the form of Albert Arkwright, the penny-pinching, stuttering shopkeeper of a Doncaster corner shop, assisted by his luckless nephew Granville (David Jason) as he tries to charm Lynda Baron's Nurse Gladys and avoid injury by a temperamental cash register. Barker's comic timing and knack for verbal acrobatics, not to mention the on-screen chemistry with Jason, guarantees *Open All Hours* - which opens on BBC1 on 20th February - is a comedy classic.

### Starsky and Hutch

Some of TV's most successful crime-busting duos are based on a personality balance of yin and yang. That's the case with Starsky & Hutch, who first appear on British TV screens on 23rd April. Starsky is a streetwise, ex-US Army veteran from Brooklyn, prone to moodiness and fond of shawl-collars. His partner Hutch is a more reserved, cerebral type with Nordic good looks. Together they tear around the streets of Bay City, California in a red and white striped Ford Gran Torina, on the hunt for drug dealers, pimps and other lowlifes, often tipped off by their friend, fly guy and bar owner Huggy Bear.

### High spirits

They've got spooks and ghouls and freaks and fools at *Rentaghost*, an agency run by ghosts for all your haunting needs. Unfortunately, the three ghosts available - Mr Timothy Claypole, a Tudor jester, a fey Victorian gent called Hubert Davenport, and the more recently deceased Fred Mumford - were all failures in life and are equally hopeless in death. The first series of *Rentaghost* begins on BBC1 on 6th January.

69

# 1976

**Saturday Swap Shop**
Swapping things is the basic premise for the BBC's new Saturday morning show, the *Multi-Coloured Swap Shop* which opens for business on BBC1 at 9:30am on 2nd October, hosted by Noel Edmonds. Kids can phone in to swap their action man for a Stylograph; their stamp albums for a Viewmaster, while out in the field, perpetually excited Keith Chegwin supervises outdoor 'swaporamas' at various venues around the country. Interspersed with the swapping are interviews with celebrity guests, news segments courtesy of John Craven, interactions with Posh Paws (Edmonds' prehistoric, purple sidekick), music performances and videos.

**I, Claudius**
Showered with BAFTA awards and still considered a taboo-breaking landmark in historical television drama, *I, Claudius* begins on BBC1 on 20th September. Based on the novels of Robert Graves, the adaptation by Jack Pulman does a fine job at leading the viewer through the complicated web of corruption, debauchery, power struggles, treachery and murder marking the early days of Imperial Rome, with Derek Jacobi, as the Emperor Claudius, unravelling the story as narrator. The huge cast includes Sian Phillips as the scheming Livia (never far from a vial of poison), John Hurt as Caligula and Brian Blessed, in booming form, as Augustus.

**Muppetry**
*The Muppet Show* is Jim Henson's move away from *Sesame Street* to a puppet show with a broader appeal. *The Muppet Show* is made at Elstree Studios and airs on ITV on 5th September with a vivid cast of hundreds including a skinny green frog called Kermit who acts as MC; temperamental diva, Miss Piggy; a struggling stand-up called Fozzie Bear, a groovy house band - Dr. Teeth and the Electric Mayhem (with a lunatic, Keith Moon-style drummer called Animal); Gonzo, Rowlf, and many more.

**Happy Days**
*16th October 1976* The show's central character, Arthur 'Fonzie' Fonzarelli, played by Henry Winkler, is a global phenomenon. Kids everywhere try to channel The Fonz's cool, impersonating the click of his fingers, the thumbs up and the drawled, 'He-ey'. Fonzie appears on magazine covers, annuals, posters, bubblegum packets and there is, of course, a play figure. Goofy teen Richie Cunningham is played by Ron Howard, who goes on to become a successful Hollywood film director.

# MUSIC

**1976**

**Patti's in town**
*16th March 1976* Punk rock may come to be seen as a very British phenomenon but its roots are on the US east coast with Iggy and the Stooges, the New York Dolls and Television. Another big influence is the Ramones, whose buzzsaw sound is what every punk band wants to emulate. Now rock journalist and poet Patti Smith adds another dimension with the stunningly unadorned and daring debut album *Horses*, produced by Velvet Underground's John Cale.

**Eurovision win**
*3rd April 1976* This year's Eurovision Song Contest, held in the Hague, sees Brotherhood of Man represent the UK with *Save Your Kisses For Me*. And what do you know, the UK has a winner for only the third time in Eurovision history. A cutesy love song from a father to his three-year-old, it gives the group a whole new lease of life after a couple of hits in the early 70s.

**On a dark desert highway**
As ego clashes and general excess start to pull the Eagles apart, they peak with an album that articulates all that's enervating and vacuous about the cocaine-fuelled Californian rock lifestyle. *Hotel California* has elements of the country rock they once championed on *Desperado* and *Take It Easy* but it's a self-loathing set that nevertheless becomes the sixth best selling album of the whole decade.

**Frampton live**
*8th April 1976* Peter Frampton achieves platinum status for sales of his double album *Frampton Comes Alive!*, which includes the hit *Show Me The Way*. Recorded at San Francisco's Winterland Ballroom, it's a stunning comeback for a guitarist whose career stalled after leaving Humble Pie.

**Forever Demis**
*17th July 1976* Sitting atop the singles chart is the long-haired, kaftan-clad Demis Roussos, whose distinctive high trill once adorned the progressive rock band Aphrodite's Child. He has a huge fanbase among British holidaymakers who first heard his music in the tavernas and discotheques of the Greek islands. The single is made up of four tracks and titled *Roussos Phenomenon*, with most radio airplay going to the dreamy *Forever And Ever*.

**Elton and Kiki**
*24th July 1976* The big hit of the long, hot drought-ridden summer of 1976 is Elton John's duet with Kiki Dee, *Don't Go Breaking My Heart*. Oddly, they don't actually record the track together: Elton makes his vocal in Canada and ex-Motown artist Kiki adds hers in London. It is Elton's first UK No. 1.

# 1976

**Here comes Summer**
Clubs and discotheques playing black-originated dance music have been part of the New York scene since the late 60s. Now disco music becomes a truly global phenomenon as producers Giorgio Moroder and Pete Bellotte and former *Hair* performer Donna Summer begin collaborating at the Musicland studios in Munich. On *Love to Love You Baby*, over a looping part-synthesised backing track, Summer adds moans of ecstasy as if approaching climax. Released as a seventeen-minute twelve-inch single, it causes a sensation in the discos and clubs of Europe. By the time Summer makes the even more orgasmic *I Feel Love* in 1977, they have established the blueprint for what becomes known as 'Eurodisco'.

### MY FIRST 18 YEARS TOP 10 — 1976

1. **The Boys are Back in Town** *Thin Lizzy*
2. **This Masquerade** *George Benson*
3. **If You Leave Me Now** *Chicago*
4. **You to Me are Everything** *The Real Thing*
5. **Let's Stick Together** *Bryan Ferry*
6. **Beautiful Noise** *Neil Diamond*
7. **All By Myself** *Eric Carmen*
8. **Blitzkrieg Bop** *The Ramones*
9. **Free** *Deniece Williams*
10. **Golden Years** *David Bowie*

Open Spotify | Search | Scan

**Abba go regal**
*4th September 1976* A triumphant year for Abba brings no fewer than three No. 1s including their majestic contribution to the growing disco boom, *Dancing Queen*. It is quintessential Abba: soaring, heart touching and an instant dancefloor filler.

**Punk grabs the headlines**
*1st December 1976* Punk rock has been making waves in the press all year. Now comes the moment when its notoriety goes national. On the TV programme *Today*, the Sex Pistols scoff and swear their way through a live interview with unamused host Bill Grundy. Even though they haven't played a note, suddenly they are every stroppy and disaffected kid's dream. With their *Anarchy in the UK* tour about to start, sixteen of the nineteen planned gigs are cancelled on local authority orders.

**10cc split**
*27th November 1976* Founder members Lol Creme and Kevin Godley leave 10cc to pursue other projects, including a new guitar-attachable gadget called a 'Gizmo'. Graham Gouldman and Eric Stewart - the creators of No. 1s *I'm Not in Love* and *Dreadlock Holiday* - will carry on as a duo under the 10cc banner.

PHOTO CREDITS Copyright 2024, TDM Rights BV.
Photos: **A** Bettmann - Getty Images / **B** Tony Evans Timelapse Library Ltd - Hulton Archive - Getty Images / **C** PA Images Archive - PA Images - Getty Images / **D** BWP Media - Getty Images / **E** Classicsworld - New retro-ads - Getty Images / **F** PA Images - Getty Images / **G** European Communities - Christian Lambiotte / **H** SSPL - Getty Images / **I** Keystone - Hulton Archive - Getty Images / **J** Wally McNamee - Corbis Historical - Getty Images / **K** Central Press - Hulton Archive - Getty Images / **L** Denis Tabler - Shutterstock / **M** BBC TV - AF Archive - Mary Evans / **O** Evening Standard - Hulton Archive - Getty Images / **P** ABC - AF Archive - Mary Evans / **Q** PA Images - Getty Images / **R** BBC - Ronald Grant Archive - Mary Evans / **S** The Jim Henson Company - AF Archive - Mary Evans / **T** Ronald Grant Archive - Mary Evans / **U** Andrew Putler - Redferns - Getty Images / **V** David Redfern - Redferns - Getty Images / **W** GAB Archive - Redferns - Getty Images / **X** Michael Ochs Archives - Getty Images / **Y** Mirrorpix - Getty Images.

# 1977

## MY FIRST 18 YEARS

## SPORT

**Red Rum hat trick**
Despite doubters claiming that at twelve years old he is too old, Red Rum, ridden by Tommy Stack, wins the Grand National at Aintree on 2nd April, his third victory in the event, making him the only horse to win the race three times.

**Liverpool conquer Europe**
Liverpool FC win their first European Cup title, beating Borussia Monchengladbach in the final. It begins a golden age of European Cup football for the club as they reach five finals in nine years, winning the title four times in total.

**Boycott's Ashes century**
On 11th August, England's opening batsman, Geoffrey Boycott, scores 191 against Australia in the 4th Test match of the summer Ashes series in front of a full house at his home ground of Headingley; the first cricketer to score his one hundredth first-class century in a Test match. Never afraid to court controversy, when his cricket career ends, Boycott goes on to commentate on radio and television and is notorious for his outspoken views on modern players' techniques.

**Wade wins Wimbledon**
British player Virginia Wade is a veteran of Wimbledon, having played there for sixteen years yet never having reached the final; until now. She beats Chris Evert in the semi-final to face the Netherlands' Betty Stove in the final and wins in three sets. The timing is perfect. Not only does 1977 mark the centenary of the founding of the Wimbledon Championships but it is the Queen's Silver Jubilee year and Wade's victory is played in front of Her Majesty, attending the tournament for the first time since 1962.

**Bras ban bounce**
The first sports bra, the 'Jockbra', later renamed the 'JogBra', is invented this year by Lisa Lindahl, a student at the University of Vermont, in collaboration with theatre costume designer Polly Smith and her assistant, Hinda Schreiber.

DO YOU REMEMBER THIS?

Flash cubes

**29 JAN 1977**
Seven IRA bombs explode in Oxford Street and surrounding area, damaging buildings, and causing fire at Selfridge's department store.

**18 FEB 1977**
Rock band KISS play their first concert in New York.

**28 MAR 1977**
Yorkshire and Tyne Tees television conduct a nine-week experiment in breakfast television.

# 1977

## DOMESTIC NEWS

### Two-inch TV launched
10th January 1977 A new two-inch screen television is launched by Sinclair Radionics as an update to their 1966 world-leading design. Able to fit in your pocket, with a pull-out aerial, the television is more portable than ever.

### Dounreay explosion
10th May 1977 At the Dounreay nuclear facility in Caithness, a shaft containing radioactive waste, sodium and potassium is flooded with seawater, leading to an explosion. The lids of the shaft are dislodged, and radioactive particles enter the surrounding area.

### British cars in trouble
15th March 1977 Under threat of government withdrawal, part-nationalised car manufacturer British Leyland announce the termination of 40,000 workers who have gone on strike, after industrial action costs the company £10 million a week. Car industry figures released in September show that foreign-made cars are outselling British cars for the first time, although companies like Vauxhall are still the market leaders. Vauxhall launches the Luton-made Cavalier in August.

### Queen visits Northern Ireland
10th August 1977 Under tight security, the Queen visits Northern Ireland, as part of a tour celebrating her Silver Jubilee. For the first time in her reign, she travels by helicopter in order to avoid ambush, and no one without a pass is allowed within a mile of her.

### Economic trouble continues
29th March 1977 The government announces that they are cutting income tax from 35 pence in the pound to 33 pence on the condition that trade unions agree to a third year of wage restraints. Government figures launched earlier in the month reveal that rampant inflation has led to prices rising 70% since 1973.

### 11 APR 1977
London Transport launch a special series of AEC Routemaster buses to mark the Queen's Silver Jubilee.

### 29 MAY 1977
11-year-old Nigel Short becomes the youngest player to qualify for the national chess championship.

### 6 JUN 1977
Beacons are lit across the country to mark the Silver Jubilee, sparking a week of festivities.

# 1977

### Battle of Lewisham
*13th August 1977* A march by 500 members of the far-right National Front is confronted en route from New Cross to Lewisham by around 4,000 counter-protesters. Protestors block streets and throw bottles and bricks at the marchers. Mounted police deploy smoke bombs and enter the crowd, and the march is diverted after protesters occupy Lewisham town centre. 111 people are injured in the violence and over 200 arrested. Days later riots break out in Birmingham during further National Front demonstrations.

### Laker launches Skytrain
*26th September 1977* Laker Airlines launches its 'Skytrain' flights from London Gatwick to New York's JFK, ushering in the era of budget travel. It is the first airline in the UK to offer international travel at such affordable rates.

### Jeremy Thorpe allegations
*27th October 1977* Former leader of the Liberal Party, Jeremy Thorpe, denies allegations made by airline pilot Andrew Newton that he had paid him to kill his former lover, Norman Scott. The allegations are printed in London's *Evening News* and cause a sensation, with the case going to trial in 1979. Thorpe is found innocent, but the scandal contributes to the decline of the Liberal Party.

### Yorkshire Ripper hunt continues
*28th October 1977* The police appeal to the public for help in finding and identifying the so-called Yorkshire Ripper, who they believe has attacked five women already this year, killing four of them. Another woman would be injured before the year is out.

### Firefighters strike
*14th November 1977* The first ever national strike of firefighters is called as they negotiate for a 30% wage increase. The strike lasts nine weeks, into January of 1978, and sees so-called 'Green Goddess' fire engines take to the streets, operated by the British Army. Despite attempts by the army to fill the firefighters' shoes, 119 people die in fires across the country before the year is out. In January the strike is settled with a 10% pay rise.

## ROYALTY & POLITICS

### One is a grandmother
Princess Anne gives birth to a baby boy, Peter Phillips, on 15th November. The Queen receives a message about the safe arrival of her first grandchild just before an investiture ceremony at Buckingham Palace. Arriving ten minutes late, she tells those waiting the good news, adding proudly, 'I am now a grandmother.'

---

**JUL 1977** The average house price in London and the south-east is now £16,731.

**23 AUG 1977** New, smaller pound notes are introduced.

**8 SEP 1977** Jimmy McCulloch leaves Wings, leading to another reshuffle for Paul McCartney's band.

# 1977

### Shops go Jubilee crazy
The Silver Jubilee, the first major royal event since the 1953 Coronation, sees shops flooded with Jubilee memorabilia. There are the expected t-shirts, mugs, hats and flags, but even food manufacturers jump on the Jubilee bandwagon. Shoppers can buy Silver Jubilee ice cream, ice lollies and frozen mousse, Silver Jubilee margarine and cans of strawberry flavoured 'Jubilade' from the Co-op!

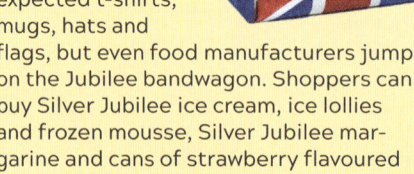

### Roy Jenkins becomes head of EEC
Home Secretary Roy Jenkins resigns from both the Cabinet and his parliamentary seat on 3rd January to become president of the EEC commission in Brussels. Disillusioned about the Labour Party's views on Common Market membership, the position suits the Europhile Jenkins. It is speculated that he will return to form an alternative party in the near future.

### Death of Anthony Eden
Former Prime Minister Sir Anthony Eden dies at his home, Alvediston Manor, Wiltshire, on 14th January at the age of 79.

## FOREIGN NEWS

### Chinese New Year disaster
*18th February 1977* A huge fire in Khorgas, China, claims 694 lives at a military-run agricultural colony. The fire starts when a firecracker ignites wreaths to the late Mao Zedong during a Chinese New Year celebration.

### Tenerife plane crash
*27th March 1977* Dense fog, miscommunication and inadequate equipment combine to cause the worst air disaster in history, though neither of the planes involved are airborne at the time. A KLM jumbo jet collides with a Pan Am Boeing at Tenerife Airport, resulting in 583 fatalities.

### Blackout!
*13th July 1977* Much of New York City suffers an electricity blackout lasting 24 hours following a lightning strike on a Hudson River substation. There is widespread looting and arson, LaGuardia and Kennedy airports are closed down for eight hours and most television stations are forced off air during the hottest week of the year.

## 2 OCT 1977
Niki Lauda wins his second Formula 1 World Drivers' Championship.

## 4 NOV 1977
The tv series *The Incredible Hulk* with body builder Lou Ferrigo premieres.

## 25 DEC 1977
British-born comic screen legend Charlie Chaplin dies aged 88.

# 1977

## To the North Pole
**17th August 1977** Ships have been trying to reach the North Pole for decades. Now the Soviet vessel *Arktika* succeeds for the first time. The nuclear icebreaker is powered by two nuclear reactors that provide power via four steam turbines. The ship makes its way between ice floes up to three metres thick.

## Biko killed
**12th September 1977** Prominent anti-apartheid activist Steve Biko is tortured, beaten and left for dead by South African police. He is taken to hospital but dies of a brain haemorrhage, causing international outrage.

## Milk elected
**8th November 1977** Harvey Milk becomes the first openly gay man to be elected to any government post in the US when he is voted San Francsico's City Supervisor. He becomes an icon to the US gay community during his tenure, which is cut short by his assassination just over a year later.

## First steps to peace
**19th November 1977** Egyptian President Anwar Sadat lands at Ben-Gurion Airport in Tel-Aviv and becomes the first Arab leader to make an official visit to Israel. His historic speech in the Israeli Knesset marks a turning point in Middle East geopolitics and paves the way to peace between Egypt and Israel after 30 years of tension and war.

# ENTERTAINMENT

### Abigail's Party
Mike Leigh's *Abigail's Party* opens at Hampstead Theatre on 18th April, and is such a hit it has a second run before becoming a BBC *Play for Today*. On 1st November, the nation is introduced to Beverly as she and her husband Laurence entertain their new neighbours in an evening that slowly reveals, by way of chilled Beaujolais and Demis Roussos, the petty prejudices, middle-class aspirations and compelling need to keep up appearances in 1970s suburban Britain.

### All Aboard the SkylArk
Grange Calveley, the creator of *Roobarb and Custard*, is behind a new BBC children's animation, *Noah and Nelly in...SkylArk*. Captain Nutty Noah, and champion knitter Nelly, equipped for wet weather in their yellow sou'westers, travel to fantastical places with an ark full of strange animals, each with two heads - a happy one at one end, a grumpier one at the other.

# 1977

### Putty in Hart's hands
Morph, a little man made from plasticine, joins Tony Hart's popular art programme, *Take Hart* on BBC1, making his first appearance on 15th February. Created by stop-animation specialists Aardman Animations, Morph shape-shifts, speaks in (very expressive) gibberish, sleeps in a wooden box, and provides a comic foil to Hart's calm, industrious presence. Later, Morph is joined by Chas, who is naughtier with a dirty laugh, and sometimes tests the patience of the serene Mr. Hart.

### Charlie's Angels
The Glamo-meter is dialled up to the max when the much-anticipated *Charlie's Angels* airs for the first time on UK television on 3rd January. Flicked hair, boob tubes and lip gloss share just as much screen time as the handguns as Kelly, Jill and Sabrina chase down criminals at the behest of the unseen Charlie.

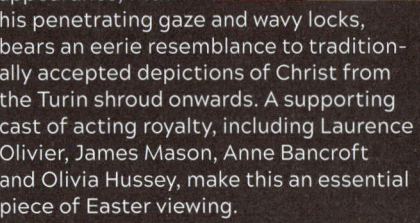

### Christ alive
Beginning 3rd April, Robert Powell stars as the main man in the Biblical mini-series, *Jesus of Nazareth* directed by Franco Zefferelli. Powell's appearance, with his penetrating gaze and wavy locks, bears an eerie resemblance to traditionally accepted depictions of Christ from the Turin shroud onwards. A supporting cast of acting royalty, including Laurence Olivier, James Mason, Anne Bancroft and Olivia Hussey, make this an essential piece of Easter viewing.

### Poldark - Ross Rides Again
The 1975 series of *Poldark*, the eighteenth-century Cornish saga based on Winston Graham's novels, has been a smash hit success, with average UK audiences of 15 million gripped by the sex, scandal and smuggling among the tin mines. On 20th November, Ross Poldark returns to screens for a new season, using three more of Graham's novels for the storylines. Poldark's producers would like to make a third series, but Graham cannot write fast enough to keep up with demand. His later books are instead incorporated into a 2015 adaptation when the Poldarks captivate a whole new generation. Fans of the 1970s original are delighted to spot the first Ross, Robin Ellis, taking on a cameo role as Judge Hayter.

### Tapping in
*1st December 1977* As part of the TV special, *All Star Record Breakers*, multi-talented Roy Castle, host of *Record Breakers*, joins a mass tap-dancing world record at BBC Television Centre as 500 dancers tap their way around the centre's famous central, circular 'doughnut'. Castle was already a tap-dancing world record holder having recorded the fastest tap dance in 1973, achieving an astonishing 1,440 taps per minute.

# 1977

### Generation gap
Bruce Forsyth has been the host of *The Generation Game*, television's most successful Saturday night show, since 1971. He's on hand with quips and guidance as pairs of contestants (who are always related) attempt various skilful tasks like potter's wheels, Highland dancing or icing a cake in order to score enough points and win a chance to recall all the prizes that pass before them on a conveyor, including the ubiquitous 'cuddly toy'. But Forsyth decides to leave this year, lured over to ITV to front *The Big Night*, and presents his last *Generation Game* on 31st December. He's replaced by Larry Grayson in 1978 who, assisted by 'the lovely Isla St. Clair' brings his own brand of high camp to a show that continues to enjoy huge popularity on his watch.

### Roots
Based on Alex Haley's 1976 novel, *Roots - The Saga of an American Family*, the American miniseries *Roots* begins on BBC1 on 8th April after winning critical acclaim in America. A sprawling story that tells of the struggles of successive generations from the capture and enslavement of Kunta Kinte in eighteenth-century Gambia to the eventual liberation of his descendants from the brutal inhumanity of slavery, *Roots* is powerful, thought-provoking, necessary television - a historical drama that has everyone talking, and one that still ranks as one of the most-watched television events of all time.

### The Flumps
*The Flumps*, a family of furry, bobble hat-wearing creatures with Yorkshire accents, who live at the bottom of an abandoned garden, arrive on BBC1 on 14th February.

### Brain AND brawn
The ultimate test in physical and mental prowess, *The Krypton Factor*, named after Superman's home planet, is the TV contest that puts other quiz shows in the shade. Hosted by Gordon Burns, participants must face a series of tough challenges every heat in order to reach the final and the possibility of being crowned British Super Person of the Year. Their mental dexterity and spatial awareness are tested with fiendish puzzles, they scramble through an Army assault course to prove their fitness, take an observation test, and answer general knowledge questions.

### Poems for the populace
After appearing on *Opportunity Knocks* in 1975, Pam Ayres has become a favourite TV personality; audiences adore her comic poems about the trivial and everyday, delivered in her slow Oxfordshire burr, with the occasional smirk suggesting she might corpse on-air. She is given her own ITV show, *The World of Pam Ayres,* which first broadcasts on 2nd September.

# 1977

### Bye bye Bing
On 11th September, Bing Crosby and David Bowie record *Peace on Earth/The Little Drummer Boy* at ATV's Elstree Studios as part of Crosby's *Merrie Olde Christmas Special*. The pair perfect the duet in just three takes and afterwards, Crosby compliments Bowie as 'a clean-cut kid and a real fine asset to the show'. Just over a month later, Crosby dies suddenly on 14th October while in Spain, suffering a massive heart attack. When the Christmas Special is broadcast on Christmas Eve, there is a particular poignancy in seeing these two musical icons, each from a different generation, performing together.

### Star Wars and other mega movies
1977 is a bumper movie year with something for everyone. Aliens really do exist according to Stephen Spielberg's *Close Encounters of the Third Kind*, while boxing epic *Rocky*, with its thumping theme song *Eye of the Tiger* makes its slurring star Sylvester Stallone a household name. *Saturday Night Fever* presents hip-wiggling John Travolta to audiences and disco music to the masses with a multi-million selling soundtrack. And on 25th May, the words, 'A long time ago, in a galaxy far, far away', introduce UK audiences to *Star Wars*. Director George Lucas's intergalactic saga combines pioneering special effects and memorable characters with old-fashioned, compelling storytelling. The force is strong in this film and Lucas's creation goes on to form the foundation of the world's most successful film franchise.

### Atari 2600
The Atari 2600, is launched on 11th September, 1977. Unlike the first generation of game consoles, which only allow for one game on the device (boring!), Atari 2600 comes with a full complement of nine cartridge games including *Outlaw*, *Space War* and *Breakout*. Gamers can simply switch cartridges to their heart's content. It sells a staggering 30 million consoles around the world.

## MUSIC

### Sex Pistols dropped
*6th January 1977* Under pressure from shareholders and the press, EMI drops the Sex Pistols, who replace Glen Matlock with Sid Vicious and they sign with Virgin.

### Rumours
*4th February 1977* Released today, Fleetwood Mac's *Rumours* turns the emotional lives of the band into public property. Written and recorded when band relationships were breaking down, new ones were forming and members were barely talking to one another, the album nevertheless evolves into the quintessential bitter-sweet California rock record. As Stevie Nicks puts it, 'We created the best music in the worst shape.'

### Disco milestone
*26th April 1977* Studio 54, soon to be the most famous and exclusive discotheque in the world, opens in Manhattan. Cementing the perception of disco as flamboyant, escapist and sexually free, it comes at the perfect time, just as the Bee Gees' *Saturday Night Fever* soundtrack is sweeping the globe and making a style that was associated strongly with the gay community into something accessible to gay and straight alike.

# 1977

## Supremes disband
*12th June 1977* As Diana Ross begins filming the Motown-financed movie *The Wiz*, her former group the Supremes call it quits with an emotional concert at London's Theatre Royal Drury Lane.

## Lynyrd Skynyrd
*20th September 1977* Steve Gaines and Ronnie Van Zant of southern rock band Lynyrd Skynyrd are killed with four others when their plane crashes in Mississippi. The band are best known for *Sweet Home Alabama*, a riposte to Neil Young's redneck-baiting *Southern Man*.

## Billy's movin' out
*29th September 1977* After six years as a solo artist, Billy Joel enters the big league of singer-songwriters with breakthrough album *The Stranger* and a trio of hit singles - *Movin' Out, Just the Way You Are* and *She's Always a Woman*.

## Elvis is dead
*16th August 1977* The king of rock dies of heart failure at 42. Elvis Presley is found by his girlfriend Ginger Alden in his bathroom at Graceland. Two days later, 75,000 gather for his funeral. His death renews mass interest in his music and *Way Down*, recorded just days before, becomes the first of many posthumous hits.

## Bat Out of Hell
*21st October 1977* The surprise hit album of the year is *Bat Out of Hell*. Conceived and performed by giant-voiced Meat Loaf and Jim Steinman, it's a piece of Gothic rock theatre in *Rocky Horror Show* vein, with grandiose power ballads and Springsteen-like production values. The seventh biggest selling LP in history, it shifts over 43 million worldwide.

## Bolan killed
*16th September 1977* Glam rock pioneer Marc Bolan is killed when a car driven by his wife Gloria hits a tree on Barnes Common. He was 29 years old and always feared that he would die before reaching 30.

# 1977

**From punk to new wave**
While Sex Pistols-inspired punk rock isn't exactly all over the charts in 1977, it marks a sea change in music. Young bands are forming and making music with just three chords, as punk fanzine *Sniffin' Glue* tells them to do. The Clash debut with *White Riot*, John Peel invites punk bands to play radio sessions, Siouxsie and the Banshees (photo) get record deals and the Damned, Buzzcocks, Angelic Upstarts and Big in Japan are not far behind. Though much older, the Stranglers pass for punk and deliver the right punk attitude on *No More Heroes*. Most significantly, punk opens the door to fringe musicians with more than a touch of anger and insolence, like Elvis Costello and Ian Dury. The industry prefers the term 'new wave', which sticks. Suddenly established bands from Pink Floyd to ELO are sounding like dinosaurs.

## MY FIRST 18 YEARS
### TOP 10 — 1977

1. **Chanson d'amour** *Manhattan Transfer*
2. **Holidays in the Sun** *The Sex Pistols*
3. **Sex and Drugs and Rock'n'roll** *Ian Dury*
4. **Go Your Own Way** *Fleetwood Mac*
5. **Roadrunner** *Jonathan Richman*
6. **No More Heroes** *The Stranglers*
7. **I Feel Love** *Donna Summer*
8. **Knowing Me Knowing You** *Abba*
9. **Show Some Emotion** *Joan Armatrading*
10. **Sir Duke** *Stevie Wonder*

**Mull of Kintyre**
*3rd December 1977* Complete with bagpipes, Paul McCartney's wistful tribute to his Scottish bolt hole, *Mull of Kintyre*, monopolises the No. 1 spot for nine weeks. With domestic sales alone topping two million, it is the biggest selling single in the UK to date.

**Iggy and Bowie**
No longer fronting the Stooges, godfather of punk Iggy Pop is invited on tour by David Bowie, who also produces Iggy's two solo albums, *The Idiot* and *Lust for Life*. Iggy's *The Passenger* from the latter becomes his best-known song and is still being used in television commercials 45 years later.

PHOTO CREDITS Copyright 2024, TDM Rights BV.
Photos: **A** Peter Robinson Empics - PA Images - Getty Images / **B** PA Images Archive - PA Images - Getty Images / **C** FPG - Archive Photos - Getty Images / **D** Serge Lemoine - Hulton Royals Collection - Getty Images / **E** Central Press - Hulton Archive - Getty Images / **F** Evening Standard - Hulton Archive - Getty Images / **G** The Land of Lost Content Collection - Mary Evans Picture Library / **H** Bettmann - Getty Images / **I** Imperial War Museum / **J** Allan Tannenbaum - Archive Photos - Getty Images / **K** Lev Fedoseyev - TASS - Getty Images / **L** San Francisco Chronicle - Hearst Newspapers - Getty Images / **M** BBC TV - Ronald Grant Archive - Mary Evans / **N** David Hume Kennerly - Getty Images / **O** Ronald Grant Archive - Mary Evans / **P** Allstar Picture Library - Mary Evans / **Q** Ronald Grant Archive - Mary Evans / **R** TV Times - Getty Images / **S** Ronald Grant Archive - Mary Evans / **T** Sean Dempsey - PA Images - Getty Images / **U** TV Times - Getty Images / **V** Screen Archives - Moviepix - Getty Images / **W** Sunset Boulevard - Corbis Historical - Getty Images / **X** The Washington Post - Iconic toys - Getty Images / **Y** Wikipedia - Studio 54 - / **Z** Michael Ochs Archives - Getty Images / **A2** Images Press - Archive Photos - Getty Images / **B2** Paul Natkin - Getty Images / **C2** Fin Costello - Redferns - Getty Images / **D2** Richard McCaffrey - Michael Ochs Archives - Getty Images.

# 1978

## MY FIRST 18 YEARS

## SPORT

### Prince of sails
Windsurfing, or sail boarding, introduced at the beginning of the decade, is all the rage. In August, 'Action Man' Prince Charles is photographed windsurfing in Australia and the image is published around the world, fuelling interest further.

### World Cup woes
Argentina win the World Cup, beating the Netherlands 3-1 in extra time in the final on 25th June. It is a controversial tournament. Argentina has recently become a military dictatorship and the World Cup is seen as an opportunity to legitimise the regime and bolster national pride. Argentina's win is overshadowed by allegations of match fixing, intimidation, and scheduling of matches to favour the home side. England fail to qualify for the tournament and the only home side to do so, Scotland, are knocked out in the group stages.

### Tractor Boys lift the Cup
Bobby Robson's Ipswich Town face Arsenal in the FA Cup final on the 6th May. It's the East Anglian club's first time in the FA Cup final against a team who have won four times. Ipswich dominate the match with several chances at the goal before Roger Osborne scores in the 77th minute to secure the cup for his team.

### Martina wins at Wimbledon
Martina Navratilova wins her first Wimbledon ladies' singles title (and her first Grand Slam title), beating no. 1 seed Chris Evert in the final, 2-6, 6-3, 7-5. Elsewhere the Great Britain team enjoy a strong run in the Davis Cup. They eventually lose in the final to a US team inspired by tennis 'superbrat' John McEnroe.

## DOMESTIC NEWS

### North Sea storm surge
*11th January 1978* A huge storm surge in the North Sea sees damage done to coastal areas as floods affect the coastline from the Humber to the Thames. Pleasure piers in Herne Bay, Margate, Hunstanton and Skegness are severely damaged, with some never recovering.

**1 JAN 1978** The otter becomes a protected species in Britain, bringing otter hunting to an end.

**17 FEB 1978** Twelve people are killed when La Mon restaurant in Belfast is bombed.

**25 MAR 1978** Oxford win the Boat Race after Cambridge sink a mile from the finish line.

# 1978

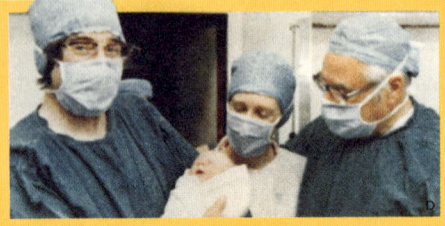

**First 'Test tube' baby**
*25th July 1978* The first success from pioneering new fertility treatment 'in vitro fertilisation' results in the birth of Louise Brown in Oldham. The new treatment gives hope to millions worldwide who struggle to conceive.

**El Al bus shooting**
*20th August 1978* Gunmen from the Popular Front for the Liberation of Palestine open fire on a bus in Grosvenor Square, London, in broad daylight. The bus carries staff from the Israeli airline El Al, and the terrorists use guns and grenades to carry out their attack. Nine people are injured, and one flight attendant is killed.

**Murder by umbrella**
*7th September 1978* Georgi Markov, a Bulgarian dissident, dissenter, and BBC journalist, collapses at work at after being stabbed by a poisoned umbrella as he crosses Waterloo Bridge. He dies in hospital four days later in what was widely considered to be an assassination by the Bulgarian Secret Service and the KGB.

**Flipping amazing**
Constructed in pressurised concrete, the UK's first permanent skateboard park opens in Hornchurch, East London. It's a sign of the growing popularity of a hobby-sport that started in the 1960s in California. Armed with boards customised in street art style and dressed in a uniform of baseball caps, baggy pants and Vans shoes, skateboarders are now showing off a dazzling repertoire of heelflips, kick turns and tail slides.

**West Brom/Nuneaton shootings**
*26th - 28th October 1978* Foundry worker Barry Williams kills five people and wounds four more in a rampage that begins in West Bromwich and ends in Nuneaton. He is arrested by police after a high-speed chase and is convicted of manslaughter on grounds of diminished responsibility.

VHS video cassettes

**Bridgewater murder**
*19th September 1978* The nation is gripped as police investigate the murder of thirteen-year-old newspaper boy Carl Bridgewater, who is shot dead whilst disturbing a burglary at a West Midlands farmhouse. Four men are arrested and tried in December for the murder, but their convictions are quashed in 1997 and the murder remains unsolved.

## 3 APR 1978
Vanessa Redgrave wins an Oscar and makes a speech condemning those who had threatened her for making a documentary about Palestine.

## 1 MAY 1978
The nation enjoys its first early May Bank Holiday.

## 27 JUN 1978
Oil output from the North Sea exceeds one million barrels a day making Britain the world's 16th biggest oil producer.

# 1978

## Bakeries ration bread
*4th November 1978*
After strikes in bakeries across the country, the nation is gripped by a surge of panic-buying, forcing bakeries to ration the sale of bread. The shortages last until 10th November, when bakers go back to work and calm resumes.

## British Embassy burned
*5th November 1978* Students from the University of Tehran take to the streets, attacking Western symbols such as hotels and cinemas. The British Embassy is burned and vandalised as the country moves closer to full-scale revolution.

## Concrete cows
Milton Keynes unveils the iconic 'Concrete Cows' by American artist Liz Leyh, her parting gift to the city. Over the years the sculptures become the subject of a lot of local fun, including amusing graffiti, interesting paint jobs, the addition of a papier-mâché bull, and even a calf kidnapping as part of a university fundraising stunt.

# ROYALTY & POLITICS

## Prince Michael of Kent weds
Prince Michael of Kent, younger brother of the Duke of Kent and cousin of the Queen, marries Baroness Marie-Christine von Reibnitz, Vienna on 30th June. Marie-Christine is a Roman Catholic and therefore Prince Michael loses his place in the order of succession.

## Tories get boost from ad men
A little-known advertising agency, Saatchi & Saatchi, run by brothers Maurice and Charles Saatchi, is appointed by the Conservatives in March and tasked with creating a campaign to hammer home the Tory message in the run-up to a General Election. Their poster 'Labour Isn't Working' showing a dole queue snaking out of an employment office, becomes a landmark piece of political campaigning, and catapults Saatchi & Saatchi into the major league.

### 17 JUL 1978
Protestors, led by the Bangladeshi community, demonstrate in the Brick Lane area of east London against the National Front.

### 3 AUG 1978
The 11th Commonwealth Games opens in Edmonton, Canada.

### 23 SEP 1978
Government announces plans to replace O-level and CSE examinations with a single exam. The GCSE finally comes into effect in 1988.

# 1978

## FOREIGN NEWS

### Aldo Moro kidnapped
*16th March 1978* Terrorists from the Red Brigades kidnap former Italian Prime Minister Aldo Moro and kill his five bodyguards. Mass demonstrations follow throughout Italy and normal life comes to a halt while the government refuses to give into the kidnappers' demands. His body is found in the boot of a red Renault 4 on 9th May.

### Three Popes in one year
*6th August 1978* Pope Paul VI dies after a heart attack. After a short conclave, Albino Luciani is elected the new Pope John Paul I. But the 'laughing Pope' does not have long to live himself. He dies on 28th September. After the second conclave in three months, Poland's Karol Józef Wojtyła is elected as the first non-Italian pope since Adrian VI in 1522. Taking the title of Pope John Paul II, his reign proves one of the most active and far reaching of any Holy Father in history.

### Amoco Cadiz oil spill
*17th March 1978* The mammoth tanker *Amoco Cadiz* is en route to Rotterdam with a cargo of 1.6 million barrels of crude oil when it encounters heavy weather off the Brittany coast and runs aground. The next morning the ship breaks in two. This causes the largest oil spill in history as 220,000 tons of oil leak into the sea. The coast is smeared with oil for hundreds of kilometres, and dead birds and sea creatures are still washing ashore many months later.

### A ballooning first
*12th August 1978* Three Americans - Ben Abruzzo, Maxie Anderson and Larry Newman - are the first to cross the Atlantic by gas balloon on Double Eagle II. The 5,001-kilometre journey takes 136 hours and six minutes.

## 30 OCT 1978
Following a dispute between management and unions, publication of *The Times* and *Sunday Times* is suspended.

## 4 NOV 1978
France performs nuclear test at Mururoa atoll.

## 17 DEC 1978
Police increase security as the IRA embark on a Christmas bombing campaign.

# 1978

### Camp David
*17th September 1978* Egyptian President Sadat and Israeli Prime Minister Begin conclude the Camp David Accords, in which Egypt recognises Israel's right to exist and Israel returns the Sinai desert to Egypt after eleven years. Both receive criticism from their own supporters and the United Nations rejects large parts of the agreement. The historic progress they have made is enough to secure Sadat and Begin a joint award of the Nobel Peace Prize.

### Jonestown massacre
*18th November 1978* People's Temple cult leader Jim Jones orders a mass murder-suicide at the community of Jonestown that he has established in Guyana. Over 900 lose their lives including 270 children. The massacre is triggered by the shooting of Congressman Leo G. Ryan, who was visiting Jonestown to investigate claims that people were being held against their will.

### China after Mao
*1st December 1978* After the death of Mao Zedong, his critics gain the upper hand in the Communist Party of China. In December, the rehabilitated moderate Vice Prime Minister Deng presents his 'open-door policy' as de facto leader of the People's Republic of China and states that revolutionary 'capitalism with socialist features' will be the turning point in China's modern history. Deng breaks definitively with Mao's ideas and makes possible enormous economic reforms, development and growth by opening the nation to foreign trade and diplomacy.

### Golda Meir dies
*8th December 1978* Golda Meir, the Ukraine-born Prime Minister of Israel who led her country during the Yom Kippur War, dies in Jerusalem at the age of 80.

### Spain's new constitution
*29th December 1978* Following the death of Franco in 1975 and elections in 1977, democratic government is restored to Spain by the passing into law of the Spanish Constitution.

## ENTERTAINMENT

### *Grease* is the Word
The release of the original soundtrack album of 1950s high school musical, *Grease*, two months before that of the film itself is a canny move. The singles *You're The One That I Want* and *Summer Nights* are the sound of summer this year, spending nine and seven weeks respectively at No. 1 in the UK music charts, while three more tracks are top ten hits. By the time the film opens on 14th September, cinema audiences know every single word and are up and dancing in the aisles. *Grease* cements the star status of the leads, John Travolta and Olivia Newton John as Danny and Sandy, and rakes in £14.7 million at the UK box office. Britain, it seems, is hopelessly devoted to *Grease*.

### Space Invaders
Arcade game *Space Invaders* is launched this year. The game, where players have to move a shooter across the bottom of the screen to evaporate approaching aliens, becomes an instant classic and the highest-grossing video game of all time.

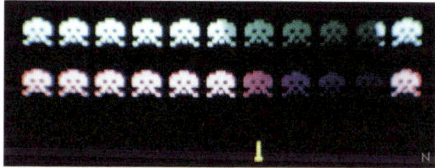

# 1978

### Skool dayz
A new BBC children's drama, *Grange Hill*, begins on 8th February. Set in a typical North London comprehensive, *Grange Hill*'s creator, Phil Redmond, doesn't flinch from showing the grittier side of school life, and storylines on bullying, racism, shoplifting, teenage sex, pregnancy and, by the 1980s, drug abuse, all contribute to the show's controversial reputation. Kids love it; life at Grange Hill is relatable and educational (although not, perhaps in the way, school should be). It continues to be a regular fixture on the BBC for the next 30 years.

### The Water Babies
Starring James Mason, Bernard Cribbins and Billie Whitelaw, *The Water Babies* blends live action with animation (the latter created in Poland) to retell Charles Kingsley's morality story of Tom the Chimney Sweep. The cartoons are crude, but it has a certain charm and the film is redeemed by some toe-tapping tunes including the catchy *High Cockalurum*.

### Simon says
Blinking and beeping electronic game Simon, named after the Simple Simon copying party game, is launched this year by Milton Bradley. It's a circular device requiring players to copy light sequences; simple at first, and then increasingly, panic-inducingly complex, until you make a mistake and Simon makes his displeasure known.

### Cheggers Plays Pop
Permanently upbeat Keith 'Cheggers' Chegwin, having found fame via *Multi-Coloured Swap Shop*, hosts his own quiz show for kids, in which two teams (the Reds and the Yellows) supported by their screaming supporters compete in a variety of challenges, races and quizzes based on their pop music knowledge. Team captains are harvested from the current crop of music celebrities. Throughout, Cheggers' enthusiasm is as sparkling as his wardrobe of glam rock-inspired bomber jackets.

### Don't Cry For Me
The Andrew Lloyd Webber and Tim Rice musical *Evita*, telling the life story of the divisive Argentine leader Eva Perón, opens in London's West End on 21st June. The concept album *Evita* has already been released in 1976, with the single *Don't Cry For Me, Argentina*, reaching no. 1 in the UK music charts. With everyone already humming tunes from the album, and rave reviews in the press for the show, *Evita* is a resounding success and runs in London until 1986.

# 1978

### Superhero saviours

You can't move for superheroes in 1978. DC Comics' *Superman* comes to the big screen, opening in the UK on 14th December. Christopher Reeve is perfectly cast as the hunky, caped Krypton native who masquerades as mild-mannered, short-sighted *Daily Planet* reporter Clark Kent, in between wooing Lois Lane and single-handedly saving the planet. The not-so-jolly green giant, *The Incredible Hulk* (a role admirably grunted by Lou Ferrigno), the alter ego of Dr. David Banner (Bill Bixby), started as a Marvel comic strip and debuts on ITV on 26th May.

### Watership Down

Often remembered as the film that traumatised a generation of children, *Watership Down*, the feature-length animation, is released on 19th. It is given a 'U' classification by the British Board of Film Censors, which claims, 'Animation removes the realistic gory horror in the occasional scene of violence and bloodshed, and we felt that, while the film may move children emotionally during the film's duration, it could not seriously trouble them once the spell of the story is broken.' Parents who have to deal with children having nightmares about a warren of bunnies being murdered disagree and in 2022, the film is finally re-classifed as a PG (Parental Guidance).

### Wedded bliss?

Barbados-born singer Janice Hoyte, becomes the UK's first West Indian game show hostess when she joins Alan Taylor on ITV's *Mr and Mrs*. The show tests married couples on their knowledge of each other with often cringeworthy results.

### Doings of the Ewings

*Dallas*, Aaron Spelling's long-running drama about the family feuds, sibling rivalries, shady deals and bed-hopping antics of the oil barons of Texas airs on BBC1 for the first time on 5th September. There is never a dull moment in this soapiest of soaps as the dysfunctional millionaire Ewings of South Fork ranch provide British viewers with quite a contrast to the cobbles of *Coronation Street*, but also prove that money can't necessarily buy you happiness.

### Five go on television

Enid Blyton's intrepid quintet, the *Famous Five*, are given a 1970s revamp for TV, with mystery-solving cousins Julian, Dick, Ann and George sporting flares and sneakers, rather than shorts and sandals. Toddy, a border collie, plays the fifth member, Timmy the dog. The series begins on ITV on 3rd July and inspires a range of merchandise, re-packaged editions of Blyton's books featuring the actors and even a release of the theme tune. Sadly, two series of half-hour episodes use up all 21 of the Famous Five adventures, and the estate refuses permission for any more to be written.

# 1978

**Paint Along with Nancy**
*Paint Along with Nancy* debuts, a daytime ITV programme that encourages viewers to create their own artistic masterpiece by following the step-by-step advice of Nancy Kominsky, as she dollops paint on to a canvas with what appears to be a kitchen knife.

**All Creatures Great and Small**
The popular stories of life as a Yorkshire vet by Alf Wright, writing under the pen name of James Herriott, have already been made into two feature films. Now James Herriott is adapted for television with Christopher Timothy as James, Robert Hardy as the ebullient Siegfried Farnon and Peter Davidson as his younger brother, Tristan. First broadcast on 8th January, the combination of authentic veterinary scenes, colourful local characters, Tricki Woo the pampered Pekingese, and the glorious North Yorkshire scenery, introduced in the opening credits to the tune of *Piano Parchment* composed by Johnny Pearson, combine to make this nostalgic series one of the BBC's greatest successes.

**The Kenny Everett Video Show**
Mischievous and multi-talented Radio 1 DJ Kenny Everett gets his own Thames Television comedy sketch show beginning 3rd July, featuring characters such as Sid Snot, Captain Kremmen and Marcel Wave. He defects back to the BBC in 1982 and creates a new set of characters including General Cheeseburger, agony aunt Verity Treacle and the fabulous, pneumatic blonde actress Cupid Stunt (Everett in drag) who would end each gossipy monologue by extravagantly crossing her legs, revealing racy red underwear, and declaring, 'It's all done in the best POSSIBLE taste'.

**Win or Dusty Bin?**
ITV game show *3-2-1* begins on 29th July hosted by Ted Rogers, whose blink-and-you'll-miss-it hand gesture showing 3, 2, 1 fingers, has kids around the country trying to replicate it. The show is renowned for its extravagant and often rather unusual prizes with contestants being offered all kinds from a St. Bernard dog to a year's supply of fish. The booby prize is a dustbin, represented by Ted's sidekick, Dusty Bin.

# 1978

# MUSIC

### Sandy Denny is dead
*21st April 1978* Singer-songwriter Sandy Denny, former Fairport Convention member and in many ways the first lady of UK folk music, dies aged 31 of head injuries sustained in a fall at her home in Surrey.

### Pistols down
*18th January 1978* At the close of a chaotic US tour, Johnny Rotten announces the end of the Sex Pistols. In October, Sid Vicious is arrested for the fatal stabbing of his girlfriend Nancy Spungen in a New York hotel room.

### Jamming for Jamaica
*22nd April 1978* Flying high with his *Exodus* album and the singles *Jamming* and *Is This Love*, Bob Marley brings warring factions together in Jamaica at a 'One Love Peace Concert' in Kingston.
At the close, he joins hands with political rivals Michael Manley and Edward Seaga in a show of unity.

### Here's Harry
*18th February 1978* Making their UK chart debut with *Denis* are Blondie, a New York band who play hard-driving, punkish pop with echoes of the 60s girl group sound. Knowing, sexy and fronted by the fabulously photogenic Debbie Harry, Blondie are set to be the biggest band of the post-punk era despite being virtually unknown in their native US.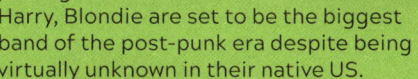

### Wayne's War
*9th June 1978* Producer-composer Jeff Wayne unveils his *War of the Worlds* concept album, based on the H. G. Wells novel. Written in rock opera style, the double LP set features David Essex, Justin Hayward, Phil Lynott of Thin Lizzy and actor Richard Burton as narrator.

### Bush heights
*11th March 1978* At No. 1 in the UK is a major new artist. *Wuthering Heights* features the strange, ethereal voice of its composer, eighteen-year-old Kate Bush, and has all the atmosphere and mystery of the Emily Brontë novel that inspired it. Not only is her singing a revelation, she has a stunningly choreographed stage act to match it. Backing her on *Wuthering Heights* is Pink Floyd guitarist Dave Gilmour, who first brought her to the attention of EMI Records.

# 1978

## Keith Moon dies
*7th September 1978* The Who's drummer Keith Moon dies aged 32 after taking an overdose of prescription drugs. He is found dead at the same London flat in which Cass Elliott died in 1974.

## Ra-ra-Rasputin
*18th October 1978* History teachers despair as *Rasputin* by Boney M begins its chart rise: calling mad monk Rasputin 'lover of the Russian queen' isn't historically accurate. Boney M is the creation of German producer Frank Farian, who matched together Maizie Williams, Bobby Farrell, Liz Mitchell and Marcia Barrett in 1976. With their singalong vocals and Bobby's engagingly gangly dancing, they are now the biggest pop act in Europe.

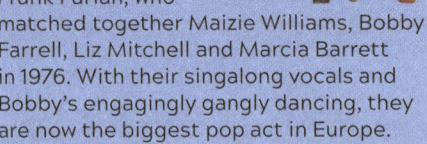

## MY FIRST 18 YEARS TOP 10 — 1978

1. **Three Times a Lady** *The Commodores*
2. **FM (No Static at All)** *Steely Dan*
3. **Baker Street** *Gerry Rafferty*
4. **Because the Night** *The Patti Smith Group*
5. **Up Town Top Ranking** *Althia and Donna*
6. **Blame it on the Boogie** *The Jacksons*
7. **More Than a Woman** *Tavares*
8. **Pump it Up** *Elvis Costello*
9. **Teenage Kicks** *The Undertones*
10. **Mr Blue Sky** *Electric Light Orchestra*

Open | Search | Scan

## Under a groove
*9th December 1978* Scornful of disco's purloining of black music, George Clinton has reinvented funk-soul with his bands Parliament and Funkadelic. Now in London with an elaborate space age stage show starring both bands and ex-James Brown sideman Bootsy Collins, he closes the year with one of the greatest dance anthems ever, *One Nation Under the Groove* for Funkadelic.

## Weller at Wembley
*29th November 1978* The Jam headline the Great British Music Festival at Wembley Arena. Having come through the first wave of punk rock looking and sounding like a throwback to the 1960s mod era, the three-man Jam are now becoming hugely influential. Leader Paul Weller's songs have fiercely political themes and an edgy, biting quality that matches the group's dour demeanour. Their latest single is *Down In The Tube Station At Midnight* from the band's new *All Mod Cons* album.

PHOTO CREDITS Copyright 2024, TDM Rights BV.
Photos: **A** Tim Graham - Tim Graham Photo Library - Getty Images / **B** Tony Duffy - Getty Images Europe - Getty Images / **C** Peter Robinson Empics - PA Images - Getty Images / **D** Keystone - Hulton Archive - Getty Images / **E** Malcolm Clarke - Hulton Archive - Getty Images / **F** Ian Tyas - Hulton Archive - Getty Images / **G** Hulton Archive - Hulton Royals Collection - Getty Images / **H** Chris Ware - Hulton Archive - Getty Images / **I** Bettmann - Getty Images / **J** Yves Gladu - Gamma-Rapho - Getty Images / **K** Vittoriano Rastelli - Corbis Historical - Getty Images / **L** Keystone - Hulton Archive - Getty Images / **M** Foto International - Moviepix - Getty Images / **N** Peter Macdiarmid - Getty Images / **O** Ronald Grant Archive - Mary Evans / **P** Ronald Grant Archive - Mary Evans / **Q** Fin Costello - Redferns - Getty Images / **R** Michael Ochs Archives - Moviepix - Getty Images / **S** Columbia - AF Archive - Mary Evans / **T** Archive Photos - Getty Images / **U** Bettmann - Getty Images / **V** BBC - Ronald Grant Archive - Mary Evans / **W** BBC - Ronald Grant Archive - Mary Evans / **X** Ronald Grant Archive - Mary Evans / **Y** Michael Brennan - Hulton Archive - Getty Images / **Z** Mondadori Portfolio - Mondadori Portfolio Editorial - Getty images / **A2** Chris Walter - WireImage - Getty Images / **B2** Mirrorpix - Getty Images / **C2** GAB Archive - Getty Images / **D2** GAB Archive - Redferns - Getty Images.

# 1979

## MY FIRST 18 YEARS

## SPORT

**Bat out of hell**
Viv Richards hits one of the most memorable innings ever witnessed at Lord's, when he scores an unbeaten 138 runs in a victory for the West Indies over England in the Cricket World Cup final, held in England from 9th to 23rd June.

**Superhero Capes**
The inaugural *Britain's Strongest Man* competition takes place in Woking and is broadcast on ITV in a show hosted by Derek Hobson and bubbly Barbara Windsor in front of a mainly juvenile audience. Field athlete Geoff Capes wins the title and is invited in 1980 to take part in Europe's Strongest Man and then World's Strongest Man in New Jersey where he finishes third.

**Go Coe go**
On 15th August, Sebastian Coe achieves a world record for the 1500 metres at the Weltklasse meeting in Zurich, his time, 3:32:1 shaving a tenth of a second off the record set five years earlier. Coe had already set new world records for the 800 metres and the mile at a meeting in Oslo a month earlier, therefore smashing three world records in the space of just 41 days.

**CHiPs boosts BMX**
ITV shows the US cops programme *CHiPs* this year, which features a storyline involving a kids' bicycle motorcross team, therefore introducing BMX racing to the British public. The following year, the first BMX track is opened at Landseer Park in Ipswich, and sales of BMX bikes soar.

**The one-million-pound man**
First Division champions, Nottingham Forest under Brian Clough, sign Birmingham City forward Trevor Francis for the sum of £1,000,000, the first British football club to pay a seven-figure fee for a player. Francis repays the investment on 30th May when he heads a goal to secure victory for Forest against Malmo in the final of the European Cup.

**16 JAN 1979**
BBC's landmark nature programme, *Life on Earth*, begins, presented by David Attenborough.

**18 FEB 1979**
Snow falls in Sahara Desert.

**3 MAR 1979**
*The Deer Hunter* opens in UK cinemas, the first of a string of Vietnam War films over the next decade.

# 1979

**Seve saves the day**
On 20th July, Seve Ballesteros becomes only the second European to win the British Open at Lytham St. Annes, where despite hitting his tee shot into a car park on the sixteenth hole, he still makes a birdie, and eventually triumphs by three strokes to lift the claret jug.

**Anti-Nazi protester killed**
*23rd April 1979* Blair Peach, an Anti-Nazi League protester is killed during an anti-National Front demonstration in Southall. Peach, a teacher from New Zealand, receives a blow to the head as violence breaks out between police and protesters. Anger regarding Peach's death motivates a number of riots and demonstrations into the 1980s.

## DOMESTIC NEWS

**'The Winter of Discontent'**
The strikes and pay disputes that had characterised the end of 1978 blossom as 1979 begins into the so-called 'Winter of Discontent'. In January lorry drivers go on strike, leading to huge shortages of food and heating oil. Ten days later they are joined by rail workers, and by January 22nd tens of thousands of public sector employees take industrial action too. The strike is accompanied by cold weather, freezing rain, and snow, adding to the country's misery. In February the weather and fuel shortages lead to over a thousand schools closing before an agreement is eventually struck at the end of the month.

**Jubilee Line opens**
*1st May 1979* London's newest tube line, the Jubilee Line is opened by Prince Charles, who poses for photographs at the helm of one of the new trains. Connecting Stanmore to Charing Cross, the line is named in honour of the Queen's silver jubilee two years previously but opens late due to problems installing the escalators.

**Devolution referendum**
*1st March 1979* Scotland and Wales hold major referendums on the devolution of government powers, and the creation of separate Welsh and Scottish assemblies. In Wales, voters reject devolution with 79.7% against the idea, and in Scotland, whilst a majority vote for devolution, they represent less than 40% of the electorate, so the act is repealed.

**Privatisation**
*21st May 1979* The government announces its proposals to begin a wide-sweeping programme of privatisation across the nation, with the selling of various nationalised industries. The programme begins with British Petroleum, which the government starts to disinvest from later in the year.

### 17 APR 1979
A remote-controlled 1,000-pound bomb, detonated by the Provisional IRA, kills four police officers at Bessbrook, Co. Armagh.

### 27 MAY 1979
With a drop in oil production in the wake of the Iranian Revolution, queues form at petrol stations as motorists panic buy.

### 26 JUN 1979
Muhammad Ali announces his retirement from boxing.

# 1979

### Thorpe Park
*24th May 1979* Thorpe Park in Surrey opens for the first time as a leisure and water sports facility. Attractions include a replica Stone Age cave and Norman castle, which delight visitors. In the 1980s it is redeveloped as a theme park with rides, becoming one of the most popular in the country.

### Isle of Man millennium
*5th July 1979* The Isle of Man celebrates 1,000 years of its parliament, the High Court of Tynwald, in festivities attended by the Queen. 1979 is chosen arbitrarily as the year to celebrate, as although the parliament is believed to be over 1,000 years old, no official first meeting date is recorded.

### Fastnet Yacht Race storm
*14th August 1979* The 303 yachts competing in the Fastnet Yacht Race meet with disaster as a storm in the Irish Sea decimates the competition. Force 11 gusts capsize 75 boats and nineteen people are killed, including four spectators.

### Lord Mountbatten assassinated
*27th August 1979* The Queen's beloved cousin Lord Mountbatten of Burma, his fifteen-year-old nephew, a boat boy of the same age, and the Dowager Lady Brabourne, are killed when the Provisional IRA plants a bomb onboard the family's fishing boat. The same day, eighteen British soldiers are killed at Warrenpoint in an ambush, in a year that has already seen the British ambassador to the Netherlands shot dead, and a bomb killing one person in the House of Commons car park.

### Harrier jets hit house
*21st September 1979* Two RAF Harrier jets collide in mid-air over Wisbech in Cambridgeshire, with one plane ploughing into several semi-detached houses. The pilots eject safely, but two men and a young boy are killed on the ground, leading the RAF to raise its minimum height for training exercises from 5,000 to 8,000 feet.

### J D Wetherspoons opens
The very first J D Wetherspoon pub opens in Muswell Hill. The brainchild of Sir Tim Martin, 'Wetherspoons' or simply 'Spoons' as they become known, prove popular for their cheap but cheerful fare. Martin names his pubs after 'JD', a character from *the Dukes of Hazzard*, and the surname of a teacher, Mr Wetherspoon, who had told Martin he wouldn't amount to much.

### Fourth man revealed
*15th November 1979* The 'fourth man' in the Cambridge Five spy ring scandal of the 1950s is revealed as Anthony Blunt, the art historian in charge of the Queen's Collection.

## 5 JUL 1979
The Isle of Man celebrates the 1,000th anniversary of its Parliament ('Tynwald') with a ceremony attended by the Queen.

## AUG 1979
Picture puzzle book *Masquerade* by Kit Williams is published and sparks a nationwide treasure hunt.

## 1 SEP 1979
U2 release their first record, an EP titled *U2-3*, only available in Ireland.

# 1979

## ROYALTY & POLITICS

**'Crisis? What crisis?'**
On 10th January, Prime Minister Jim Callaghan returns from sun-drenched Guadeloupe where he has been attending a summit of world leaders, and interviewed by the press at Heathrow, denies the country is in a state of mounting chaos. *The Sun* newspaper paraphrases his comments with a front page headline, 'Crisis? What Crisis?' Meanwhile, Tory leader Margaret Thatcher makes a televised party political broadcast to acknowledge the gravity of the situation.

Walkie Talkies

**Maggie gets to No. 10**
The country goes to the polls on 3rd May, electing its first woman Prime Minister (and the first female head of government in Europe) as the Tories win with a majority of 44 seats, marking the start of what will be eighteen years of Conservative government.

## FOREIGN NEWS

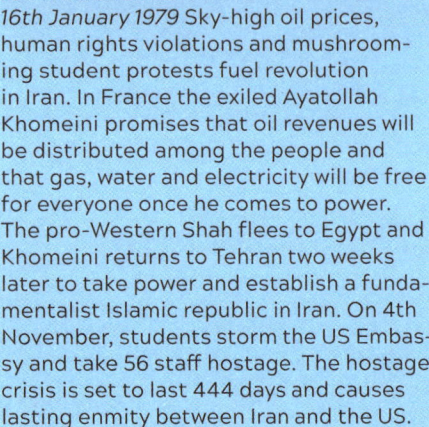

**Revolution in Iran**
*16th January 1979* Sky-high oil prices, human rights violations and mushrooming student protests fuel revolution in Iran. In France the exiled Ayatollah Khomeini promises that oil revenues will be distributed among the people and that gas, water and electricity will be free for everyone once he comes to power. The pro-Western Shah flees to Egypt and Khomeini returns to Tehran two weeks later to take power and establish a fundamentalist Islamic republic in Iran. On 4th November, students storm the US Embassy and take 56 staff hostage. The hostage crisis is set to last 444 days and causes lasting enmity between Iran and the US.

**Dictators gone**
1979 is a bad year for dictators. The Shah is expelled from Iran, guerrilla fighters put an end to the Somoza family's reign of terror in Nicaragua, rebels oust General Romero's junta in El Salvador and a democratic government comes to power for the first time in Ecuador. In Africa, the continent's cruellest dictator, Idi Amin, is deposed. Dictator Bokassa's fairy tale in the CAR also comes to an end when France supports his cousin's coup.

---

**12 OCT 1979**
Following the success of the radio series, *The Hitchhiker's Guide to the Galaxy* by Douglas Adams is published.

**22 NOV 1979**
Building societies increase mortgage rates to an all-time high of 15%.

**19 DEC 1979**
Francis Ford Coppola's *Apocalypse Now* is released in UK cinemas.

# 1979

### Three Mile Island
*28th March 1979* What nuclear energy sceptics have feared for years is happening: a meltdown at the Three Mile Island nuclear power plant in Harrisburg, Pennsylvania. An explosion is avoided but the disaster galvanises opponents of nuclear energy to organise large-scale protests around the world.

### European elections
*10th June 1979* Polling stations open throughout the European Union for three days. For the first time, citizens of the nine Member States elect their representatives to the European Parliament.

### Happy Meal
*15th June 1979* McDonald's aims a major campaign at children with a secret weapon called the Happy Meal. A colourful cardboard box contains a special children's menu with a hamburger, a small portion of fries and a drink, plus a small plastic toy.

### Communist kiss

*5th October 1979* A remarkable sight at the 30th anniversary celebrations of the German Democratic Republic: Chief of State Erich Honecker welcomes Soviet leader Leonid Brezhnev with a traditional socialist brotherly kiss on the mouth.

### Mother Teresa
*December 1979* In the 1970s, Mother Teresa's congregation has grown to encompass almost a hundred monastic homes across the world. Now she receives the Nobel Peace Prize for her work with the vulnerable and impoverished.

Telephone flip up index

### One-child policy
In China, Mao's successor Deng Xiaoping announces a drastic scheme to slow down population growth: in future, parents will be allowed to have only one child.

# 1979

## ENTERTAINMENT

**Blankety Blank**
Terry Wogan, armed with a unique, wand-like microphone, hosts *Blankety Blank*, a new game show starting 18th January in which six celebrities try to help contestants fill in the blanks. The amiable Wogan never takes things too seriously, wryly raising an eyebrow at blundering answers and good-naturedly mocking the prizes - miserly in comparison to those on rival channel ITV. The winner of the first episode of *Blankety Blank* takes home a fridge freezer. We almost hope contestants will instead leave with the underwhelming and yet strangely iconic consolation prize, the *Blankety Blank* cheque book and pen.

**Kids give up smoking**
The government launch a national anti-smoking campaign aimed at school children where Superman fights his enemy Nick O'teen and asks kids to sign an 'I'm against smoking' pledge. In tandem with this, sweet cigarettes, which come in miniature boxes and mimic real cigarettes, are renamed 'candy sticks'.

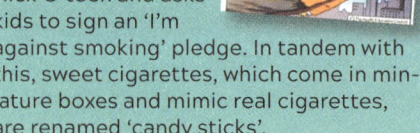

**Cash in the attic**
*Antiques Roadshow* begins on BBC1 on 18th February. Arthur Negus leads a team of ten experts as they assess various treasures brought along by members of the public. It's a format that changes little through the years, and although it occupies the cosy early evening slot on Sundays, there is always a frisson of tension as everyone awaits the valuation of each item.

**Sony Walkman launched**
*1st July 1979* The Sony Walkman is a simple yet revolutionary idea: a battery-operated cassette tape-playing machine with earphones, small and lightweight enough to take anywhere. Now consumers can hear the music of their choice wherever they go. It's the first step in the reorientation of audio from communal to personalised listening.

**Tricks on TV**
'You'll like this. Not a lot, but you'll like it.' Middlesbrough conjurer Paul Daniels becomes the UK's magical top dog with *The Paul Daniels Magic Show* which begins on 9th June. Soon accompanied by his assistant, 'the lovely Debbie McGee', Daniels blends sleight of hand tricks with larger set pieces, invites celebrity guests to become part of his illusions, and debunks magic myths in the 'Bunco Booth'. *The Paul Daniels Magic Show* continues until 1994.

# 1979

**Nanu nanu**
Mork (Robin Williams) comes from the planet Ork and is sent to Earth, where humour is forbidden, to observe human behaviour; Mindy (Pam Dawber) befriends him, invites him to live with her and teaches him about the American way of life. *Mork and Mindy* begins on ITV in December 1978 but by 1979, everyone is adopting the typical Orkan greeting, 'Nanu nanu'.

**Is *Life of Brian* blasphemous?**
'He's not the Messiah. He's a very naughty boy!' The Pythons unite for another smash-hit film, this time with a controversial parody of the New Testament directed by Terry Jones. Graham Chapman is Brian, who, through a case of mistaken identity, is proclaimed the Messiah, in a story that pokes fun at organised religion and factious radical politics. Nervous about its potential to offend, EMI Films pulls the plug on finance, but the production is saved by George Harrison who sets up Handmade Films in order to fund it. Italy, Ireland and Norway bans it (allowing the Pythons to gleefully print 'So funny they banned it in Norway' on the film posters for Sweden) as do several town councils around the UK.

**Sapphire and Steel**
The lack of any budget for special effects in *Sapphire and Steel*, which starts on ITV on 10th July, forces the show's creator, Peter J. Hammond, to be inventive with locations, lighting, and sound effects. The result is a surprisingly tense and claustrophobic sci-fi drama in which Joanna Lumley as Sapphire and ex-*Man from U.N.C.L.E.* David McCullum as Steel investigate strange events and anomalies in time and space.

**G-Force - Guardians of the Galaxy**
*Battle of the Planets*, which is first shown in the UK on 3rd September, is an American adaptation of the Japanese animation, *Science Ninja Team Gatchaman*. The series is not only dubbed in English but is edited to remove scenes of violence and any profanities. The group of five protect Earth from attacks by the planet Spectra and its evil mastermind, Zoltar.

**Stone Age superhero**
'Set free by the Teen Angels from his prehistoric block of glacial ice, comes the world's first superhero... Captain Caaaaaaaavvve-ma-aa-aaaaaan!' Cavey, a walking ball of hair with a club that propels him through the air, and transforms into various gadgets, first appears on BBC1 on 28th June. He's the secret weapon of the Teen Angels, whenever Dee Dee, Brenda and Taffy are on a mystery-solving mission.

# 1979

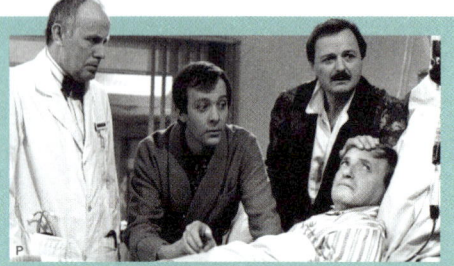

### Laughter is the best medicine
In *Only When I Laugh*, which is shown for the first time on ITV on 29th October, Roy Figgis (James Bolam), Archie Glover (Peter Bowles) and Norman Binns (Christopher Strauli) are the in-patients of a men's hospital ward, under the care of sardonic surgical consultant Mr Thorpe (Richard Wilson). Its popularity leads to three more series. Very much of its time, the patients in *Only When I Laugh* regularly puff away on cigarettes.

### Flambards
K. M. Peyton's trilogy of novels, set before and during the First World War, are the basis for this thirteen-part series in which an orphaned heiress, Christina Parsons, goes to live with her uncle and his two sons at their crumbling country pile, Flambards. It's a picture-perfect Edwardian family saga, with love affairs, class division and war shaping the characters' destinies.

### Moonraker
The Star Wars effect leads Bond producers to send 007 into space in *Moonraker*, the eleventh Bond film, and fourth featuring Roger Moore. The production budget is double that of 1977's *The Spy Who Loved Me* with the special effects nominated for an Academy Award. Opening at the Odeon Leicester Square on 26th June, *Moonraker* becomes the most financially successful Bond escapade to date.

### Mod-ern times
The Mod movement of the mid-1960s is recreated in *Quadrophenia*, released on 29th October and based on the Who's 1973 rock opera album. Phil Daniels dons a parka and hops on his scooter, supported by a cast that includes Phil Davis, Lesley Ash, Sting and Toyah. *Quadrophenia* captures the rebellious mood and tribalism of 1960s youth, while a carefully curated selection of additional songs on the soundtrack such as *Louie Louie* by The Kingsmen and *Green Onions* by Booker T and the M.G.s further enhance the period atmosphere.

### Rock on Tommy
Two ex-welders from Oldham, comedy duo Tommy Cannon and the impish Bobby Ball, appear on various variety programmes until this year, they get their own ITV show, which begins on 28th July. Tommy is the straight man, and Bobby, with his catchphrase, 'Rock on, Tommy!' accompanied by a twanging of his braces, is cheeky and excitable. It's a combination made for family viewing, and they become a staple of Saturday night entertainment as the show runs for the next nine years.

# 1979

## MUSIC

### Oh so Chic
*1st January 1979* Bass-driven dance track sensation *Le Freak* tops the US chart for Chic, the band formed by producers Nile Rodgers and Bernard Edwards. Replacing mechanised disco rhythms with sumptuous guitar and bass riffs, they end the decade as the most in-demand producers around.

### Monday blues
*29th January 1979* In San Diego, California, teenager Brenda Spencer goes on a shooting spree in her school playground. Asked why, she explains 'I don't like Mondays'. The incident leads Bob Geldof of Irish new wavers the Boomtown Rats to write *I Don't Like Mondays*, a UK No. 1 in late July that many US radio stations decline to play.

### Village People
*6th January 1979* The first ever openly gay group to top the UK chart are the Village People, four men from New York City brought together by Moroccan Jacques Morali and launched with the irresistible disco track *YMCA*. After they introduce the famous hand gestures spelling out the letters on TV's *American Bandstand*, the *YMCA* dance becomes an overnight sensation.

### Vicious death
*2nd February 1979* Former Sex Pistol Sid Vicious is found dead from an overdose in New York, having been released on bail the day before ahead of his trial for the murder of girlfriend Nancy Spungen.

### Punk meets disco
*3rd February 1979* Having brought sex, glamour and catchy tunes to punk rock, Blondie and producer Mike Chapman - one of the godfathers of glam-rock in the early 70s - ally it to the synthesised dance rhythms heard on disco tracks. Acquiring a Roland drum machine, they create *Heart Of Glass* - a brilliant first-time marriage of new wave sensibility with disco that shapes the electro-pop of the 1980s.

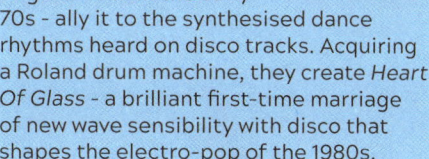

### Earth, Wind and Fire
*9th January 1979* Starring at the Music for UNICEF concert at the UN in New York is the fabulous multi-member Earth, Wind and Fire, whose eye-popping costumes reflect leader Maurice White's passion for Egyptology and mysticism. They close their set with *Boogie Wonderland*.

# 1979

### She will survive
*17th March 1979* No. 1 on both sides of the Atlantic is a true feminist-cum-gay anthem - *I Will Survive* by New Jersey singer Gloria Gaynor. As a song of resilience, it's the exact opposite in sentiment to Gloria's previous big seller, *Never Can Say Goodbye*. Originally intended only as a B-side, the song was 'flipped' at Gloria's insistence.

### Music with a message
*3rd April 1979* The 2 Tone label, bearing the distinctive black and white logo designed by owner Jerry Dammers, is launched in Coventry as a vehicle for his multi-racial, seven-man group the Special AKA (known to all as the Specials). Debuting with *Gangsters*, they deliver anti-racist and anti-authority lyrics to a classic 1960s ska backing. They're the ultimate dance band with a message.

### A brick for Christmas
*15th December 1979* The most unlikely of all Christmas No. 1s is *Another Brick in the Wall* from progressive rock royalty Pink Floyd, who usually never bother to release singles. It's from their latest album *The Wall* and features a choir of children from Islington Green School.

## MY FIRST 18 YEARS
## TOP 10 — 1979

1. Hit Me with Your Rhythm Stick *Ian Dury*
2. Sunday Girl *Blondie*
3. Message in a Bottle *The Police*
4. Gangsters *The Special AKA*
5. Good Times *Chic*
6. I'm Every Woman *Chaka Khan*
7. Oliver's Army *Elvis Costello & The Attractions*
8. Sultans of Swing *Dire Straits*
9. Off the Wall *Michael Jackson*
10. London Calling *The Clash*

Open | Search | Scan

### Off the Wall
*10th August 1979* Michael Jackson has been a hitmaker for nine years but his new *Off the Wall* album, his first with producer Quincy Jones, shows the former child star maturing into one of the most creative and free-thinking musicians in contemporary music.

### Rap in the chart
*1st December 1979* Rap music makes its very first appearance in the US record chart. *Rapper's Delight* by the Sugarhill Gang features a spoken rap over the rhythm track of *Good Times* by Chic.

### Video killing
*20th October 1979* With perfect timing comes *Video Killed the Radio Star* by Buggles, otherwise known as Trevor Horn and Geoff Downes. It's a comment on the growing importance of video exposure over radio airplay. After a spell with progressive rockers Yes, Horn goes into full-time record production for Frankie Goes to Hollywood and Downes joins the supergroup Asia.

---

PHOTO CREDITS Copyright 2024, TDM Rights BV.
Photos: **A** Bettmann - Getty Images / **B** Evening Standard - Hulton Archive - Getty Images / **C** Hulton Archive - Getty Images / **D** Fox Photos - Hulton Archive - Getty Images / **E** Anwar Hussein - WireImage - Getty Images / **F** Tim Graham - Corbis Historical - Getty Images / **G** Bettmann - Getty Images / **H** Bettmann - Getty Images / **I** Regis Bossu - Sygma - Getty Images / **J** Tim Graham - Corbis Historical - Getty Images / **K** BBC - AF Archive - Mary Evans / **L** George Wilkes Archive - Hulton Archive - Getty Images / **M** Mark Sennet - Archive Photos - Getty Images / **N** AF Archive - Mary Evans / **O** Hanna Barbera - AF Archives - Mary Evans / **P** Yorkshire Television - AF Archive - Mary Evans / **Q** Polytel Who Films - Ronald Grant Archives - Mary Evans / **R** Yorkshire Television - AF Archive - Mary Evans / **S** Ronald Grant Archive - Mary Evans / **T** Michael Ochs Archives - Getty Images / **U** GAB Archive - Redferns - Getty Images / **V** Images Press - Archive Photos - Getty Images.

# 1980 — MY FIRST 18 YEARS

## SPORT

### Ice dream
Bristol-born figure skater Robin Cousins has the year of his sporting life when he takes the gold medal at the Winter Olympics at Lake Placid, New York, on 23rd February, skating a routine of artistic brilliance.

### Gold rush for GB
With many countries, including the USA, boycotting the Olympic Games in Moscow in protest at the USSR's invasion of Afghanistan, there are claims that British athletes have greater opportunities in track and field events. Speedy Scot, Allan Wells scoops gold in the 100 metres final, with a time of 10:25, but proves any doubters wrong at a meeting in Cologne less than a fortnight later, where he beats the Americans Carl Lewis and Harvey Glance in the 100 metres with a time of 10:19 seconds. Elsewhere, Daley Thompson wins gold in the decathlon, a medal indicative of his dominance in the event during this period, regardless of who else is competing.

### Clash of the tennis titans
The atmosphere on Centre Court is electric at Wimbledon on 5th July as Swedish ice man Bjorn Borg hopes to achieve a fifth, record-breaking men's singles title in a meeting with American 'Superbrat' John McEnroe. The confrontation, between two polar opposites, lasts for five nail-biting sets, including a fourth set tie-break that goes to 16-17, but Borg eventually triumphs and falls to his knees in his now familiar champion's ritual. The match feels like the apogee of tennis's golden era; two genius players with their wooden racquets and their headbands, playing at the height of their powers.

### Brute force
British boxer Alan Minter faces Vito Antuofermo in a boxing match for the World Middleweight title, at Caesar's Palace, Las Vegas on 16th March. The pair go the full fifteen rounds, with a split decision result, in Minter's favour. Minter proves his supremacy on 28th June in a bloody rematch from which he emerges undisputed World Middleweight Champion but loses the title to Marvin Hagler later in the year.

## 18 JAN 1980
Sir Cecil Beaton, photographer, illustrator, and diarist, dies at the age of 76.

## 25 FEB 1980
Political comedy, *Yes, Minister* with Paul Eddington and Nigel Hawthorne, begins on BBC1.

## 19 MAR 1980
MV *Mi Amigo*, the ship from which pirate station, Radio Caroline broadcasts, runs aground and sinks in the Thames estuary.

# 1980

## Middle-distance duels
Great Britain's prowess in middle-distance running during this period is embodied by the legendary rivalry of Sebastian Coe and Steve Ovett, two runners who break and counter-break each other's records, but whose actual meetings on the track are few and far between; until, that is, the Olympic final of the 800 metres in the Lenin Stadium in Moscow on 26th July. In a race Coe is widely expected to win, Ovett barges to the front of the pack to power down the final 100 metres and win gold (photo). Coe, suffering from what he later describes as a tactical disaster, settles for silver, but four days later, finds the form of his life to win gold in the 1500 metres. Ovett finishes with a bronze.

## Naturist beaches
*1st April 1980* Britain gets its first official naturist beach in Brighton. Despite shocking some, the idea proves popular, and soon others open across the country.

## Iranian Embassy siege
*5th May 1980* A horrified nation watches live on television as the SAS storm the Iranian Embassy in London, ending a six-day occupation of the building by the Democratic Revolutionary Front for the Liberation of Arabistan. Television captures the moment the SAS enter through an upper-storey window to attempt a rescue. Two hostages and five of the six terrorists are killed, the rest of the captives are rescued safely.

## DOMESTIC NEWS

## British Steel strike
*2nd January 1980* The Iron and Steel Trades Confederation call their 90,000 members at British Steel out on strike. The action ends in April with an agreed 16% pay rise, but not before the industry is rocked by the announcement that the Corby plant will close with the loss of over 11,000 jobs. This was in addition to the already advertised 4,500 job closure at Consett in September.

### 29 APR 1980
Death of Alfred Hitchcock, aged 88, British director with a string of suspenseful movies to his name.

### 21 MAY 1980
*Star Wars Episode V - The Empire Strikes Back* opens at cinemas.

### 13 JUN 1980
he UN calls for South Africa to free Nelson Mandela.

# 1980

## Sixpence withdrawn
**30th June 1980** The pre-decimal sixpence, or 'tanner', is withdrawn from circulation. It had survived the initial decimalisation process, with a value equivalent to 2.5 new pennies, but is now set to be withdrawn as the country has adapted to the new currency.

## Denmark Place fire
**16th August 1980** Tragedy strikes London's Denmark Place, as petty criminal John Thompson seeks revenge for a disagreement with a barman in the Spanish Rooms. Thompson pours two gallons of petrol into the establishment and sets it on fire, killing 37 people in the bar and its neighbouring salsa club Rodo's. Thompson is sentenced to life imprisonment.

## Alexandra Palace fire
**10th July 1980** Alexandra Palace, or 'Ally Pally', is gutted by fire. The fire destroys half the building and only the outer walls and parts of the former BBC studios are preserved.

## Unemployment highs
**28th August 1980** Figures released throughout the year show that unemployment is rising quickly across the country. By August unemployment is at 2 million, the highest since 1935, with estimates that it will reach 2.5 million by the end of the year. Inflation also rises to 21.8%.

## Third-gen Escort
**1st September 1980** Ford launch the third generation of their ever-popular Ford Escort, a model which goes on to become the country's best-selling car of the decade.

## Hercules the bear
**20th August 1980** Hercules the bear goes missing on the island of Benbecula in the Outer Hebrides. The bear, owned by wrestler Andy Robin, is there to shoot a Kleenex commercial when he manages to escape. Missing for 24 days, when he is recaptured, it is discovered that he has almost starved rather than kill any animals on the island, leading to Kleenex's 'Big Softie' campaign.

## Right to buy scheme
**3rd October 1980** The new Housing Act becomes law, meaning that tenants of council-owned houses, who have lived there for three or more years, now have the right to buy their homes. These homes are sold at a large discount on market rates and are part of an aspirational policy hoping to see a rise in home ownership across the UK.

### 27 JUL 1980
England fans riot during England's opening European Championship match in Turin leading police to use tear gas.

### 1 AUG 1980
Buttevant rail disaster kills 18 and injures dozens of train passengers in Ireland.

### 3 SEP 1980
Jill Barklem's delightful, illustrated books about country mice, *Spring*, *Summer*, *Autumn* and *Winter Story* are published this month.

# 1980

### Marlborough diamond stolen
*11th September 1980* The Graff jewellery shop in Knightsbridge is robbed by thieves who take the £400,000 'Marlborough' diamond and several other jewels from the window display. A brave shop assistant follows them to their car and notes the registration, and the following day the thieves are arrested in Chicago. The diamond is never recovered.

### Foot comes first for Labour
James Callaghan resigns as Labour leader, and despite the British media believing Dennis Healey will become next leader, it is instead Michael Foot (illustration) following a vote on 10th November. Despite his far-left views, Foot is a leader who many believe can unite the party.

### Rendlesham Forest Incident
*26th & 28th December 1980* Servicemen at RAF Woodbridge are puzzled by the sight of unexplained lights descending into the nearby Rendlesham Forest. These lights, along with rumours of higher-than-average radiation readings and the panic of local farm animals, become one of the most well-known UFO events in Britain.

### The Queen Mum at 80
The Queen Mother celebrates her 80th birthday this year and on 15th July sets off with Prince Charles in the 1902 State Landau to attend a service of thanksgiving at St. Paul's Cathedral. On 4th August, her actual birthday, she greets crowds who gather outside the gates of her home in Clarence House.

## ROYALTY & POLITICS

### Shy Di
The relationship between Prince Charles and Lady Diana Spencer becomes public knowledge in September, after Diana is spotted watching the Prince fish on the Balmoral estate. An invite to the Queen's Highland retreat is widely known to be a signifier of something more serious and the following months see press intrusion reach new heights as 'shy Di', who works at a kindergarten, is pursued relentlessly by photographers.

---

**3 OCT 1980**
The Housing Act allows council housing tenants to buy their own home.

**12 NOV 1980**
Voyager 1 space probe reaches Saturn and sends back photographs of its rings of orange and yellow clouds.

**14 DEC 1980**
Thousands hold a vigil for Joh Lennon in Liverpool following his murder in New York.

# 1980

### No U-turn for the Iron Lady
Margaret Thatcher makes one of the defining speeches of her career at the Conservative Party conference on 10th October, standing firm against calls from others within her party to make a U-turn on her policy of economic liberalisation in the face of rising unemployment and recession. 'You can turn if you want to,' she says, 'The lady's not for turning.' The powerful phrase is one of Thatcher's most memorable.

### Note this
*1st April 1980* American Art Fry has had enough: his bookmark keeps falling out of his choir book. He comes up with a way to stick the bookmark to the page with a self-adhesive strip and experiments with the yellow pieces of paper on the notepad at the 3M office. Ultimately, 3M successfully markets the Post-it note.

### Tito is dead
*4th May 1980* Three days before his 88th birthday, Josip Broz, alias Tito, dies. The founder and President of Yugoslavia, who has long advocated a 'Third Way' between the bickering East and West, will receive the largest state funeral the world has ever seen.

## FOREIGN NEWS

### Street art
Art is for everyone and not just for the elite, is Keith Haring's motto. In New York he discovered graffiti, which he developed into his very own style. He makes chalk drawings on empty billboards in the subway, draws on the street and becomes known far beyond the national borders. Haring makes paintings, sculptures, paints pieces of canvas, applies decorations to vases and t-shirts. In 1985 he decorated the body of singer Grace Jones and contributed to her video *I'm Not Perfect*.

### Solidarity recognised
*14th August 1980* The protest against layoffs and inflation at the Lenin Shipyard in Gdańsk, Poland, marks the end of communism in the region. The strikers no longer demand 'a bigger sandwich' but solidarity and the recognition of trade unions. On 31st August, the anti-communist trade union Solidarność of Lech Wałęsa is recognised as the first independent trade union in the Eastern Bloc. One year after its founding, one in four Poles is a member, and the political consequences of this breakthrough are immense.

DO YOU REMEMBER THIS?
Ghetto blaster

# 1980

**Reagan is President**
4th November 1980 In the US presidential election, Americans send the incumbent President Jimmy Carter back home to Georgia. The Republican candidate, former Hollywood film actor Ronald Reagan, will become the next President.

ENTERTAINMENT

**Morning campers!**
Hi-de-Hi, set in a 1950s holiday camp, begins on 1st January on BBC1. Written by Dad's Army creators Jimmy Perry and David Croft, the staff at Maplins are Yellowcoats (inspired by Butlin's real-life Redcoats) and it is a yellow coat that scatterbrained chambermaid Peggy (Su Pollard) covets, but she never seems to quite make it. Instead, she is Cinderella to the entertainment staff (led by Paul Shane's Ted), kept in her place by self-important senior Yellowcoat Gladys (Ruth Madoc) whose xylophone tannoy announcements keep Maplins running like clockwork and whose seductive wiles make manager Jeffrey Fairbrother (Simon Cadell) hot under the collar.

**Walkies!**
Barbara Woodhouse has been training dogs and horses for decades, with occasional spots on television and radio, but the ten-part series, Training Dogs the Woodhouse Way, which begins on BBC1 on 7th January, makes her a household name at the age of 70. Woodhouse has a natural confidence on-screen, bossing around dog owners and teaching the dogs how to 'Si-T' and how to go for 'Walkies!' nicely. A true original, Barbara Woodhouse becomes a television sensation.

**Higher or lower?**
ITV launches two new game shows to bring cheer to the winter months. Family Fortunes hosted by the smooth-talking Bob Monkhouse (photo) begins on ITV on 6th January, while Bruce Forsyth fronts Play Your Card Right from 6th February. Play Your Cards Right is another winner for Brucie (even though actually winning is more to do with luck than any skill).

# 1980

### Metal Mickey
Metal Mickey, a cute, five-foot-tall, eager to please robot, first appears on *The Saturday Banana* in 1978 before becoming the title character in a new kids' comedy show on ITV, starting 6th September. The versatile Mickey, whose favourite phrase is, 'Boogie, boogie' goes on to release several hit singles in addition to his TV success.

### Game to geek out on
Seasoned BBC producer Patrick Dowling devises *The Adventure Game*, and the first of twenty-two episodes airs on 24th May. It's a melting pot of Dowling's interests in early computer adventure games, Dungeons and Dragons and Douglas Adams's *Hitchhiker's Guide to the Galaxy*.

### The Elephant Man
David Lynch directs this heart-wrenching story of Joseph Merrick, whose life-limiting deformities made him an object of ridicule and curiosity in Victorian England. John Hurt plays Merrick and Anthony Hopkins is Sir Frederick Treves, the doctor who takes him in at the London Hospital and introduces him to high society.

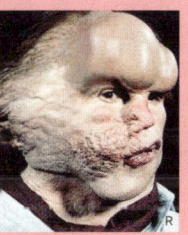

### Diff'rent Strokes
The American sitcom *Diff'rent Strokes* begins on ITV on 24th November. A wealthy New York widower adopts two Harlem boys after the death of their mother.

### Pac-Man premieres
*22nd May 1980* Launching today is a Japanese-originated video game destined to become one of the best loved and biggest selling in history. Developed by Namco with a design inspired by a pizza with a slice removed, Pac-Man is the first successful attempt to create a video game with to appeal to children and women as well as young adult males. Within two years, Pac-Man attracts over more than 50 million players across the world and inspires a whole new genre of chase-in-a-maze games.

### Airplane!
If the 1970s was the decade of disaster movies, then the 1980s is the decade to parody them, and *Airplane!* starring Leslie Nielsen, Peter Graves and Lloyd Bridges is among the first and the best, inspired by films such as *Airport* and *Airport '75* and in particular 1957's *Zero Hour!* It's non-stop jokes and slapstick all the way.

### It's a fair cop
Police dramas have been seriously lacking strong female characters, until this year when, like buses, two come along at once. On 11th April, Jill Gascoine is Detective Inspector Maggie Forbes in ITV's *The Gentle Touch* (photo). And on 30th August, BBC1 launch *Juliet Bravo*, with Stephanie Turner as Chief Inspector Jean Darblay, who must fight the prejudice of a male-dominated police force as well as criminals. Both series become hugely popular.

# 1980

### Who Shot J.R.?
On 22nd November, 21.5 million UK viewers tune in to *Dallas* on BBC1 to discover the answer to the whodunnit of the decade. 'Who Shot J.R.?' becomes the question on everybody's lips. Four episodes into season 4, the culprit is finally revealed. It's Kristin Shepard, J.R.'s sister-in-law and mistress, who gunned him down in a fit of pique.

### Button Moon
*Button Moon*, which begins on ITV on 8th December, encourages its pre-school audience to follow Mr and Mrs Spoon as they travel to the big yellow button in the sky every episode. Everything on *Button Moon* is created from household objects including the Spoon family's space rocket, which is a converted washing-up liquid bottle.

### Flash Gordon
*Flash Gordon* captures the comic-strip camp of the science-fiction adventure, and is turbo charged by a rollicking soundtrack from rock band Queen thumping along in the background as Flash only has 'fourteen hours to save the Earth' from Max von Sydow's Ming the Merciless. Eminently quotable lines include Brian Blessed's Prince Vultan roaring, 'Gordon's alive!'

### Pennysavers
Fine Fare, the UK's third largest supermarket, launches a no-frills economy range, with plain white packaging stamped with tea chest-style font.

## MUSIC

### World Police
*20th January 1980* After conquering the UK in 1979 with a masterly fusion of power pop and reggae epitomised by the Sting compositions *Message in a Bottle* and *Walking on the Moon*, the Police take off on their first world tour of 37 cities in nineteen countries.

### Sheer Madness
*January 1980* Having taken their porkpie-hatted nuttiness from 2-Tone to the Stiff label, Camden Town band Madness begin a decade of chart dominance with *My Girl*, the first of a long stream of comic but faintly melancholy observations of North London life. *Baggy Trousers* follows, a look back at schooldays, while *Embarrassment* dissects the impact of a mixed-race relationship on a close family and their fear of what the neighbours will say.

# 1980

### AC/DC death
*19th February 1980* Bon Scott, singer with Australian band AC/DC, dies in London aged 33. Cause of death is given as acute alcohol poisoning. Brian Johnson is named lead singer in his place in April.

### Led Zeppelin disband
*25th September 1980* Led Zeppelin drummer John Bonham is found dead by bandmate John Paul Jones at Robert Plant's house near Windsor. He was 32 and had choked in his sleep after a drinking session. The band decide not to continue and make the announcement in December.

### Ireland wins Eurovision
*19th April 1980* Johnny Logan wins the Eurovision Song Contest for Ireland with the song *What's Another Year*.

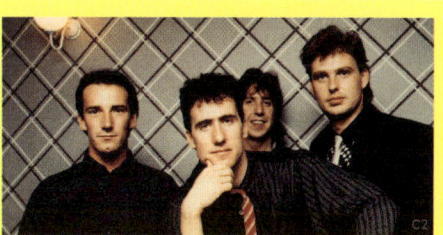

### Northern echoes
Echoing the early 1960s, the north west of England is once again a hive of music making. Out of Liverpool's club scene - notably Eric's on Matthew Street - come the Teardrop Explodes and the Mighty Wah! while Manchester's Factory record label is a nursery for the likes of the Fall, Joy Division and A Certain Ratio. Another Factory band, Orchestral Manoeuvres in the Dark (photo), quickly sign with Virgin and make an immediate impression with *Enola Gay*, titled after the plane that dropped the atomic bomb on Hiroshima in 1945.

### Ian Curtis suicide
*18th May 1980* On the eve of Joy Division's first tour of the US, singer Ian Curtis commits suicide. Rather than disband, the rest of the group elect to re-form as New Order with new member Gillian Gilbert on keyboards. The new line-up plays its first gig in Manchester in October.

### Super troupers
*15th November 1980* Abba's seventh album, *Super Trouper*, sets a record for the most pre-orders (one million) ever received for a UK LP. Fans notice a darker tone to their songs, notably the break-up song The Winner Takes it All. Bjorn and Agnetha are now divorced and Benny and Anni-Frid's separation is not yet announced.

### Sheena hits the big time
*2nd July 1980* Scottish teacher and would-be performer Sheena Easton takes part in BBC TV show *The Big Time*, in which she is groomed for a pop career. The exposure boosts the resulting single, *Modern Girl*, and gives her a first hit. US success and a James Bond theme, *For Your Eyes Only*, follow in 1981.

# 1980

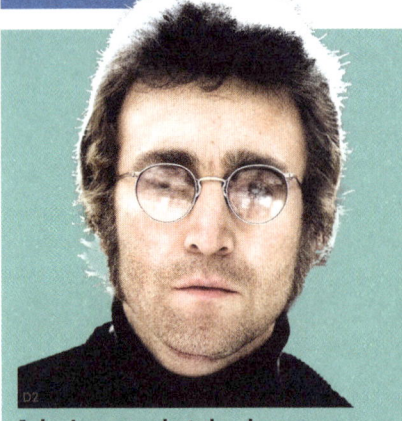

### John Lennon shot dead
*8th December 1980* John Lennon is shot four times by a smiling fan, Mark Chapman, as he arrives home at Dakota Flats, Manhattan, from a recording session at the Hit Factory. He dies in hospital half an hour later. He had recently released his first album for four years, *Double Fantasy*, and had been undertaking press interviews to promote it. Lennon had celebrated his 40th birthday in October. The shock felt around the world is palpable. Exactly a week after his death, Yoko Ono asks people all over the world to join in a silent vigil in his memory.

## MY FIRST 18 YEARS — TOP 10 — 1980

1. **Brass in Pocket** *The Pretenders*
2. **Private Life** *Grace Jones*
3. **One Day I'll Fly Away** *Randy Crawford*
4. **To Cut a Long Story Short** *Spandau Ballet*
5. **Don't Stand So Close to Me** *The Police*
6. **Games Without Frontiers** *Peter Gabriel*
7. **Three Minute Hero** *Selecter*
8. **It's Different for Girls** *Joe Jackson*
9. **Let's Get Serious** *Jermaine Jackson*
10. **On the Radio** *Donna Summer*

### The other Elvis
Despite a chip-on-the-shoulder stroppiness that made him enemies in the US during 1979, Elvis Costello is proving one of the most influential artists of the post-punk period. His albums *Armed Forces* and *Get Happy!* are classic angry young man fare with accusing lyrics and rapid-fire delivery, while his production work for the Specials and Squeeze has helped both bands get established.

### Industry troubles
The pointers are not great for music as the 1980s begin. Two of the biggest names in global music fall victim to takeover, EMI merging with Thorn Electronics and Decca joining the Polygram roster. Rising oil prices increase the cost of vinyl and prompt record companies to cut back on investment. Blank cassette sales soar while record sales drop, leading the music industry to launch a 'home taping is killing music' campaign.

# 1981

## MY FIRST 18 YEARS

## SPORT

### You cannot be serious?
Living up to his nickname of Superbrat, John McEnroe's furious outburst at umpire Edward James during a first-round match at Wimbledon on 22nd June makes headlines around the world. McEnroe disputes James's call that his serve was out and in full meltdown screams, 'You cannot be serious!?'. It's an incident that confirms McEnroe's hot-tempered notoriety and goes down in the annals of sporting history. Despite the tantrum, McEnroe's genius takes him all the way to the final where he finally unseats five-times champion Bjorn Borg. Borg, despite winning at the French Open this year, acknowledges there is a new king of centre court and announces his retirement early in 1983 at the age of 26.

### Botham's Ashes
During the 51st Ashes series of Test matches between Australia and England, the talismanic all-rounder Ian Botham scores a breathtaking 149 not out during the 3rd Test at Headingley on 16th July, setting Australia a target of 130. Bob Willis then bowls a fearsome spell of 8 for 43 to dismiss Australia for 111. Botham also takes 5-11 in the 4th Test and hits 118 from 102 balls in the 5th. England retain the Ashes 3-1 in what becomes known, quite rightly, as 'Botham's Ashes'.

### Rowing revolution
22-year-old Susan Brown, a biochemistry student, becomes the first woman cox in the history of the Oxford-Cambridge boat race when she steers her crew to victory on 4th April.

### Davis pots to the top
Steve Davis wins his first World Snooker Championship title at the Crucible Theatre in Sheffield, beating the defending champion Cliff Thorburn in the semi-final and Doug Mountjoy in the final on 20th April by 18 frames to 12. It is the first of eight world championships Davis will win during a decade in which he dominates the sport.

### Marathon men
The first London Marathon takes place on 29th March. 6,747 Runners take part with 6,255 crossing the finish line on Constitution Hill.

### 27 JAN 1981
Rupert Murdoch is permitted to buy The Times without the usual investigation by the Monopolies Commission.

### 10 FEB 1981
The Coal Board announces plans to close 50 pits employing 30,000 miners.

### 1 MAR 1981
IRA prisoner, Bobby Sands begins a hunger strike at the Maze prison. He dies on 5th May.

# 1981

## DOMESTIC NEWS

**Yorkshire ripper arrested**
*5th January 1981* Police arrest 34-year-old lorry driver Peter Sutcliffe on suspicion of being the serial killer known as the Yorkshire Ripper. Sutcliffe has killed thirteen women and attacked seven more. He is found guilty and sentenced to life imprisonment.

**The Troubles**
1981 sees a continuation of violence associated with the Troubles in Northern Ireland. In the UK there are two major bombings, one at RAF Uxbridge, which is successfully evacuated, and one at the Chelsea Barracks in London which kills two people. A parcel bomb addressed to the Prime Minister is intercepted and defused, and a coal ship, the *Nellie M,* is bombed and sunk by the Provisional IRA. January sees the murders of former MP Sir Norman Stronge and his son James, and an attack on civil rights campaigner MP Bernadette McAliskey who is shot nine time in her home.'

**ZX81 computer launches**
*5th March 1981* The ZX81 is launched by Sinclair Research, intended to provide an affordable at-home computer to the public. It is small and simple and connects to a television set rather than coming with its own screen, with a cheaper cost for those who are prepared to assemble it themselves. 1.5 million devices are sold.

**March for jobs**
*30th May 1981* London plays host to over 100,000 people from across the country as they come together to protest unemployment and economic deprivation in the 'March for Jobs', organised by the Trade Union Congress.

**New Cross house fire**
*18th January 1981* A party at a house in New Cross ends in tragedy as a fire claims the lives of thirteen young people aged 14-22. The victims are black, and many believe the fire to be a case of arson. Moved by the tragedy, 20,000 people take to the streets.

**Humber Bridge opens**
*17th July 1981* Her Majesty Queen Elizabeth II arrives in Hessle for the opening of the Humber Bridge. The longest of its type in the world, the bridge connects Barton-upon-Humber in the south, with Hessle in the north, allowing traffic to flow across the Humber estuary.

**27 APR 1981**
Paul McCartney's band Wings breaks-up.

**8 MAY 1981**
Ken Livingstone is elected leader of the Greater London Council (GLC).

**11 JUN 1981**
The Queen opens Europe's tallest building - the Natwest Tower in the City of London.

# 1981

## Penlee lifeboat disaster
**19th December 1981** A rescue mission off the coast of Cornwall goes badly wrong when the lifeboat RNLB *Solomon Browne* is dispatched to rescue the crew of the MV *Union Star*. Despite reaching the vessel and evacuating some of the men, both ships are soon overcome by the Force 12 gales, and the sixteen men on board are lost. The volunteers aboard the lifeboat all receive posthumous medals for bravery and a devastated community raises £3 million for their village.

## A year of riots
1981 sees a wave of riots sweep the country, mostly associated with rising racial tensions. In April the Brixton riots see clashes between the police and black youths which injure 300 people and cause serious damage to property, with riots following in Finsbury Park and Ealing. June sees clashes in Coventry at a National Front march and riots in Peckham, before rioting in Southall follows the deaths of an Asian Muslim family killed by arson in Walthamstow. Riots in Toxteth, Liverpool, and Moss Side, Manchester, are the most prominent across fifteen days of violence that sweep the country.

## Moira reads the news
The BBC's Moira Stuart becomes the first black woman newsreader on television this year. Born in London to Caribbean parents, Stuart is known for her calm, poise, and silken voice.

## ROYALTY & POLITICS

### End of an era
Princess Alice, Countess of Athlone, the last surviving grandchild of Queen Victoria, dies on 3rd January at Kensington Palace at the age of 97 years and 313 days.

### Shots fired at Queen
On 13th June, the Queen is riding her horse, Burmese, at the annual Trooping of the Colour ceremony, when Marcus Sarjeant fires six blank shots at her. The Queen calmly settles Burmese who is momentarily startled while Sarjeant is apprehended and later charged under the 1842 Treason Act. He is sentenced to five years in prison.

### Charles pops the question
After months of intense speculation, Buckingham Palace announces the engagement of Prince Charles and Lady Diana Spencer on February 24th. The couple pose for the press with Diana wearing a blue skirt suit from Harrods to set off her sapphire engagement ring.

**13 JUL 1981**
Martin Hurson is the sixth IRA hunger striker to die.

**5 AUG 1981**
After touring depressed areas of Merseyside, Michael Heseltine announces a series of measures to help alleviate problems.

**10 SEP 1981**
Start of Day of the Triffids on BBC1, based on the 1951 science-fiction novel by John Wyndham.

# 1981

**Charles and Di say 'I do'**
After six months of frenzied anticipation with the nation in the grip of royal wedding fever, Prince Charles and Lady Diana Spencer marry at St. Paul's Cathedral on 29th July. The 750 million viewers who tune in to watch the wedding finally get their first glimpse of the much-discussed wedding dress, a style which launches a thousand meringue gowns and appears to need a good iron. Nevertheless, it is a glorious spectacle, with all the pomp and pageantry expected and when during the vows a radiant but understandably nervous Diana stumbles over the order of her husband's Christian names, it makes the world love her even more.

**Gang of Four**
William Rodgers, David Owen, Roy Jenkins and Shirley Williams announce a break from the Labour party with their formation of the Council for Social Democracy on 25th January, the prototype of a new party intended to fight for social justice. The so-called Gang of Four form the SDP and on 16th June announce an alliance with David Steel's Liberal party to fight the next general election as a single organisation.

## FOREIGN NEWS

**Anne Frank's diary**
*1st January 1981* Five months after the death of Anne's father Otto Frank, Anne Frank's original diary is released.

**Hostages returned**
*11h January 1981* The day after Ronald Reagan is sworn in as the 40th President of the US, Iran releases the 52 hostages it has been holding since the storming of the US embassy in 1979. They are set free in return for nearly eight billion dollars of Iranian assets frozen in American banks.

**Reagan shot**
*30th March 1981* Ronald Reagan and four others are shot outside the Hilton Hotel in Washington DC by John Hinckley Jr. A bullet punctures the President's lung and he is close to death on arrival at hospital. Prompt action saves his life.

Kenner Star Wars figures

---

**12 OCT 1981**
A report finds that the traditional nuclear family is beginning to fragment as one in eight children live in a single-parent family.

**26 NOV 1981**
Shirley Williams wins the by-election at Crosby, Merseyside, overturning a Conservative majority of 19,272.

**8 DEC 1981**
Arthur Scargill is elected president of the National Union of Mineworkers.

# 1981

## Space shuttle
*12th April 1981* Six years after the famous handshake between the US and the Soviet Union in space and twenty years to the day since Yuri Gagarin became the first human in space, NASA launches the first space shuttle. This is a reusable spacecraft designed to efficiently transport people and cargo into space. Columbia flies 36 laps around the Earth and lands in California 54.5 hours later.

## Attempt on the Pope
*13th May 1981* Pope John Paul II is shot twice as he enters St Peter's Square in Vatican City. He survives the assassination attempt by a Turkish gunman, Mehmet Ali Agca, who Pope John Paul II will meet two years later in jail.

## AIDS identified
*5th June 1981* General practitioner Joel Weisman encounters a number of homosexual young men in his practice, all of whom suffer from a reduced number of white blood cells. A few months later, Weisman publishes a report for the US Centers for Disease Control with immunologist Michael Gottlieb concerning a disease which will soon be known by the acronym AIDS (acquired immunodeficiency syndrome).

## Fast and invisible
*18th June 1981* The F-117 Nighthawk, the newest American fighter aircraft, is a precision bomber with a remarkably futuristic, angular appearance designed to be difficult to detect with radar. This first aircraft with so-called stealth properties is almost invisible to the enemy.

## Sadat assassinated
*6th October 1981* Egyptian President Anwar Sadat is assassinated in an attack by the Islamic Jihad during a military parade. It follows a failed coup in June after which he ordered a mass round-up of his Islamist opponents. Vice-President Hosni Mubarak is wounded but takes office as Sadat's successor.

## TGV in service
*27th September 1981* The first paying passengers board the brand new TGV at Gare de Lyon station in Paris. This *train à grande vitesse* takes travellers at top speeds of around 300 km/h.

# ENTERTAINMENT

## Nanny
The series *Nanny* starts on BBC1 on 10th January with Wendy Craig as Barbara Gray, a divorcee and new nanny whose itinerant career sees her moving around, taking positions with a succession of dysfunctional upper-class families where she works her Mary Poppins magic on her charges.

# 1981

### De Niro is a knockout
Robert de Niro fully commits to his leading role in Martin Scorsese's masterpiece, *Raging Bull*, the story of the rise and fall of boxer Jake LaMotta. He takes up boxing, becoming a serious contender, and in order to authentically portray LaMotta's post-boxing descent into a bloated has-been, goes on a gastronomic tour of France and Italy to gain weight. His efforts are not in vain, and he wins the Academy Award for best actor this year.

### Time Bandits
Terry Gilliam invites fellow Pythons, John Cleese and Michael Palin, to join him as he directs this time travel fantasy, in which a boy finds himself slipping through time and space in the company of a gang of dwarfs who are using a stolen map to steal treasures. They bump into Robin Hood, Agamemnon, and Napoleon along the way.

### Thinking aloud
*Think Again*, presented by Johnny Ball, begins on 16th January and is billed in the *Radio Times* as 'an entertaining excursion into an aspect of everyday life that you might be taking for granted'. *Think Again* tackles a wide range of subjects, explaining how everything works from the publishing industry and financial markets to the national grid with Ball managing to be both upbeat and jokey, but also clear and concise; a true leading light of factual entertainment.

### Raiders of the Lost Ark
Harrison Ford, his stock high following two stints as Han Solo in *Star Wars*, takes on the role of archaeologist-adventurer Indiana Jones in *Raiders of the Lost Ark* which opens in UK cinemas on 30th July. Armed with his fedora and bullwhip, Indy is on a quest to find the Lost Ark of the Covenant before the Nazis do and has to negotiate various obstacles on the way: a pit of vipers, unfriendly bandits and a rumbling boulder relentlessly pursuing him through a cavern.

### The Art of Darts
Darts game show Bullseye begins on ITV on 28th September, with Jim Bowen as host. With audiences of 20 million *Bullseye* serves up many a head-in-hands moment.

### Postman Pat
Everyone's favourite postman makes his screen debut on 16th September. As well as delivering mail to the residents of Greendale, the community-minded *Postman Pat* helps to solve their daily dilemmas and problems, ably assisted by his faithful black and white cat, Jess.

# 1981

**Language, Timothy!**
The BBC1 sitcom *Sorry!*, first broadcasts on 12th March, with diminutive Ronnie Corbett as Timothy Lumsden, a mild-mannered librarian in his forties, browbeaten by his domineering mother (Barbara Lott) into permanently living at home. Timothy's attempts to find a girlfriend and make a life for himself are repeatedly thwarted by mummy while his father, equally under the thumb, occasionally issues a stern, 'Language, Timothy!' from behind his newspaper, usually as a result of mis-hearing his son. *Sorry!* continues for seven series and by the final episode in 1988, when Timothy finally finds happiness with girlfriend Pippa, Corbett is fifty-seven years old!

**Donkey Kong**
Nintendo release the arcade game *Donkey Kong* in July. After Nintendo's *Radar Scope* (their answer to Space Invaders) failed, it is the firm's first global success and rescues them from financial ruin.

**Chariots of Fire**
'The British are coming' announces Colin Welland in his acceptance speech after winning the best screenplay Oscar for *Chariots of Fire*. The film wins four Academy Awards in total, including best picture and best soundtrack for Vangelis's unforgettable, swelling electronic theme song. A true story of two remarkable men and their rivalry at the 1924 Paris Olympics, this uplifting piece of period perfection is guaranteed to bring a lump to your throat.

**Impulse buy**
Impulse body spray, available in five different fragrances including 'Gipsy' and 'Hint of Musk', launches a memorable UK TV commercial this year, with a woman pursued through the streets by a man desperate to present her with a hastily purchased bunch of flowers, having caught a whiff of her magnetic scent, it's all because 'Men can't help acting on impulse.'

**Ken and Deirdre get spliced**
Jumping on the royal wedding bandwagon, Ken Barlow and Deirdre Langton say 'I do' on *Coronation Street*, on 27th July, two days before Charles and Di. Viewers, all 21 million of them, are amazed to see Deirdre without her trademark saucer-sized specs for once.

**Cats opens in West End**
Andrew Lloyd Webber's (photo) musical, *Cats*, based on T. S. Eliot's *Old Possum's Book of Practical Cats*, opens at the New London Theatre on 11th May. The musical is revolutionary; it's sung-through, and performed partly in the round with a hidden orchestra so the audience are part of an immersive experience. Lloyd Webber mortgages his house to help fund the venture, a risk worth taking as *Cats* runs for 8,949 performances until 2002; a benchmark for a new brand of blockbuster musical.

**The Fizz come first at Eurovision**
The Eurovision Song Contest takes place in Dublin on 4th April with a win for the United Kingdom thanks to Bucks Fizz, and the song *Making Your Mind Up*.

# 1981

**Noele reaches a career crossroads**
Noele Gordon has played Meg Richardson in ITV's *Crossroads* since it first began in 1964. When Central TV take over the franchise from ATV, they plan a revamp which includes ridding the show of Meg. When the announcement is made in June there is public outrage; Gordon has been voted favourite female personality by *TV Times* readers no fewer than eight times. She makes her final appearance on 12th November.

**Stately homes and teddy bears**
The adaptation of Evelyn Waugh's 1945 novel, *Brideshead Revisited* on 12th October is one of the year's television events. Jeremy Irons is Charles Ryder who while at Oxford befriends Lord Sebastian Flyte played by Anthony Andrews. Invited to stay at Sebastian's palatial family pile, Brideshead Castle, Charles is dazzled and seduced by the Flyte family and finds his life interwoven with theirs over the coming years. Filming the seven two-hour episodes took forty-two weeks in total.

## MUSIC

**Collins goes solo**
*9th February 1981* Genesis singer-drummer and all-round workaholic Phil Collins releases his first album, *Face Value*, so beginning a phenomenal solo career running parallel with the band. Intensely personal and melancholic in tone, most of the album's songs concern his recent divorce from his wife Andrea.

**Lennon tribute**
*7th February 1981* The shock waves from John Lennon's murder continue. Written by John for his *Imagine* album in 1971, *Jealous Guy* is the song that the re-formed Roxy Music choose when asked to honour Lennon on a German TV show. Liking the result, they release the track and achieve Roxy's first and only UK No. 1 during March.

**Antmusic**
*9th May 1981* Adam and the Ants confirm their status as the pop sensations of the moment with *Stand and Deliver*, a No. 1 for five weeks. Adam is art student Stuart Goddard who dresses in pirate gear and Native American face paint and has a signature sound combining tribal drums and Gary Glitter-like hollers. It's a potent mix adored by the colour-rich teen pop magazines like *Smash Hits* now starting to appear in newsagents.

# 1981

## MTV opens
**1st August 1981** A media revolution begins in the US with the launch of cable channel Music Television (MTV), devoted to playing music. It's a whole new marketing medium for the music industry but the channel is at first almost wholly reliant on UK record companies for material, as US labels aren't yet attuned to the potential of the promo video. The result is a new 'British invasion' of acts who break through in the US on the basis of their videos.

## Ross sets a record
**14th May 1981** After saying goodbye to Motown Records by duetting with Lionel Richie on the film theme *Endless Love*, Diana Ross ends her 21-year association with the label by signing for RCA in a deal worth twenty million dollars - an industry record. The move pays an immediate dividend with a No. 4 UK placing for a revival of Frankie Lymon's *Why Do Fools Fall in Love*.

## Ghost Town
**11th July 1981** Never has a record been more chillingly timed than the Specials' *Ghost Town*, which reaches No. 1 just as widespread rioting adds to the all-round malaise that pervades early 1980s Britain. It's the last record that the Specials will make in the band's current form: Neville Staples, Lynval Golding and Terry Hall are poised to form the Fun Boy Three. In the chart at the same time is another Midlands band with a Jamaican sound and a sharp political message: Birmingham's UB40 with *One in Ten*, about the ten per cent who now make up the unemployed in the UK.

## Marley is dead
**11th May 1981** Bob Marley, the great creative force in contemporary reggae and a peacemaker between warring factions in his native Jamaica, dies of cancer aged 36. After being diagnosed with a melanoma in his right foot he refused to have it amputated because of his Rastafarian beliefs. The cancer spread to his brain, lungs and liver. He is given a state funeral in Jamaica on 21st May.

## Ballet spruce
**16th August 1981** Out of the Blitz club in Covent Garden come Spandau Ballet, formed by brothers Gary and Martin Kemp. A feature on TV's *20th Century Box* launches them as a 'new romantic' band, as important for the styles they wear - anything from kilts to loin cloths - as the synth-led dance music they play. With Tony Hadley's trained voice giving them real distinction, the Spandaus reject punk gloom and embrace the lure of fantasy and dressing up. The funky *Chant No. 1* cements the band's rise.

# 1981

**Whole lotta Shakin' goin' on**
*28th March 1981* For many years Shakin' Stevens and his band the Sunsets were the hottest draw on the UK's rock'n'roll revival circuit playing Elvis. Now the Cardiff-born singer is at No. 1 with a brilliant rockabilly-style re-creation of the 1950s Rosemary Clooney hit *This Ole House*.

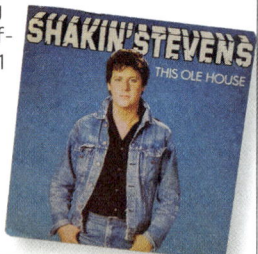

**Electro magnets**
For a long time synthesisers were just a prog rock thing, but cheaper technology and the advent of the Roland drum machine in particular have changed the game. Allied to a showy 'new romantic' look, the electro sound is everywhere in the early 80s, whether in the hands of singer-plus-synth duos like Soft Cell (*Tainted Love*), Tears for Fears (*Mad World*) and Yazoo (*Only You*) or bands with a more art school bent like Sheffield's Heaven 17 and Human League. Some like ABC and Depeche Mode (photo) embrace the whole pop experience while others like Ultravox remain a bit aloof. The failure of the latter's somewhat pompous *Vienna* to shift Joe Dolce's novelty hit *Shaddup Your Face* from No. 1 is treated in some quarters like a national scandal.

## MY FIRST 18 YEARS — TOP 10 — 1981

1. **Labelled with Love** *Squeeze*
2. **New Life** *Depeche Mode*
3. **Don't You Want Me** *Human League*
4. **In the Air Tonight** *Phil Collins*
5. **Being with You** *Smokey Robinson*
6. **Celebration** *Kool and the Gang*
7. **Bette Davis Eyes** *Kim Carnes*
8. **Kids in America** *Kim Wilde*
9. **I Go to Sleep** *The Pretenders*
10. **Once in a Lifetime** *Talking Heads*

**Julio on the ball**
*5th December 1981* Once a promising young goalkeeper for Real Madrid, Julio Iglesias turned to singing when a car accident ended his football career. He now brings a whiff of old style tuxedo-and-bow-tie glamour to the UK chart with an ice-cream smooth chart-topping version of *Begin the Beguine*, written by Cole Porter in 1935.

**League of their own**
*11th December 1981* Human League score the year's top-selling single and a Christmas No. 1 with *Don't You Want Me*, a really clever combination of a great pop break-up pop song, a synth-led soundtrack and a film noir-style video.

# 1982

## MY FIRST 18 YEARS

## SPORT

**Streaking for England**
On 2nd January, during an international rugby match between England and Australia at Twickenham, Erika Roe runs onto the pitch and strips off her top and bra, much to the appreciation of the half-time crowd. Hustled off by police who cover her assets with a flag and helmet, the incident - described by the BBC as 'perhaps the most famous of all streaks' - makes front-page news.

**Disappearance of Mark Thatcher**
*12th January 1982* Mark Thatcher, son of Prime Minster Margaret Thatcher, is officially declared missing after a four-day loss of contact during the Paris-Dakar Rally. Missing somewhere in the Sahara alongside his driver and mechanic, a large search is launched by the Algerian military who finally locate him two days later, 31 miles off course.

**Rebels suffer cricket ban**
Fifteen English cricket players are banned from international cricket for three years, as a penalty for a 'rebel' tour of South Africa currently in progress.

**Feel the burn**
*Jane Fonda's Workout video* sparks a new craze for aerobics, women's fitness - and legwarmers - as Jane takes a rapidly growing fan base of keep fit devotees through routines to tone and hone, telling us to 'Feel the burn' and 'No pain, no gain'.

## ESPAÑA 82

**'The Best England Team That Never Won'?**
England arrive at the World Cup in Spain with a line-up that includes Bryan Robson, Ray Wilkins, Kevin Keegan, Terry Butcher and Trevor Francis. England look like the team to watch during the group stages, beating France 3-1 in an inspired first match. They win the group but are next drawn against title holders West Germany and then Spain. Both matches are a draw; a missed header from Keegan against Spain is blamed on his perm softening the power of his attack. Despite scoring six goals in the tournament, conceding just one and not losing a match, England are knocked out and head home.

### 26 JAN 1982
UK unemployment figures reach 3,000,000 for the first time since the 1930s.

### 12 FEB 1982
George Davis opens the first Next clothing store. By the end of July, there are 70 branches around the country.

### 4 MAR 1982
The Barbican Centre is opened by the Queen after 11 years of construction and budget-blowing £153 million.

# 1982

**Watson wins Open double**
American golfer Tom Watson becomes only the fifth man to win both the US and British Opens in the same year amongst the challenging bunkers at Royal Troon on 19th July.

**A golden Commonwealth Games**
The Commonwealth Games take place in Brisbane from 30th September to 9th October. Great Britain's gold medal tally is 38, one behind Australia.

**First papal visit to UK**
*28th May 1982* Pope John Paul II becomes the first reigning Pope to visit the UK. Drawing crowds of thousands, his 'Pope-mobile' transports him around nine cities where he delivers speeches and open-air Masses.

## DOMESTIC NEWS

VHS video recorder

**Collapse of Laker Airways**
*5th February 1982* Laker Airways succumbs to increased competition and strategic behaviour in the aviation industry when it collapses leaving 6,000 passengers stranded. The airline's owner, Freddie Laker, sues 12 airlines for conspiracy, reaching an out of court settlement of $50 million.

**Israeli ambassador shot**
*3rd June 1982* The 1982 Lebanon War breaks out after the attempted assassination of Israel's ambassador to the UK, Shlomo Argov. Attending a banquet at the Dorchester Hotel, Argov is seriously injured. He never fully recovers, remaining in hospital until his death in 2003.

**Falklands War**
*2nd April 1982* War breaks out after the invasion of the Falkland Islands by Argentine forces. The British Falkland Islands government surrenders and the British surprise many from around the world by immediately dispatching a Royal Navy task force to recover the islands. Over the next the three months the public are gripped by events such as the sinking of the *General Belgrano*, HMS *Sheffield*, and HMS *Coventry*, and the *Battle of Goose Green*. The war lasts 74 days and ends with the surrender of Argentine forces at Port Stanley. 255 British and 649 Argentine lives are lost in the conflict.

**2 APR** 1982
Britain breaks off diplomatic relations with Argentina.

**12 MAY** 1982
The *QE2* leaves for the Falkland Islands

**30 JUN** 1982
*Crimewatch* begins on BBC1, aiming to highlight unsolved crimes and enlist the help of the public by asking for information.

# 1982

## 20 pence coin introduced
*9th June 1982* Further changes to the currency are made when the new 20 pence coin is introduced with 740 million minted in the first issue. The new coin is a heptagon, and features a crowned Tudor rose on the reverse.

## Hyde and Regent's Park bombs
*20th July 1982* Two bombs planted by the Provisional IRA explode in central London. One bomb, in Hyde Park, targets mounted soldiers of the Household Cavalry regiment the 'Blues and Royals'. Four soldiers and seven horses are killed when a car bomb explodes as the soldiers ride past. Two hours later, a second bomb in Regent's Park explodes beneath a bandstand where the band of the Royal Green Jackets are performing to a large crowd. Seven bandsmen are killed, and across both attacks a further 51 people are injured.

## Last telegrams sent
*30th September 1982* The closure of the UK Inland Telegram Service means the UK says goodbye to the telegram, a mode of communication in use for over 100 years.

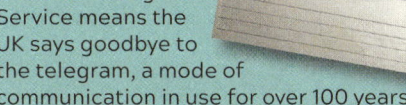

## Mary Rose raised
*11th October 1982* The wreck of Henry VIII's flagship, the *Mary Rose*, is raised from the Solent after its discovery in 1971. The wreck is moved to a dry dock at the Portsmouth Historic Dockyard; a special museum opens to display the extraordinary artefacts discovered with it.

## Droppin Well bombing
*6th December 1982* A bomb planted by the Irish National Liberation Army explodes at a disco known as Droppin Well in Ballykelly. Many people are wounded and seventeen are killed, eleven of them British soldiers from the nearby barracks who were known to frequent the disco.

## ROYALTY & POLITICS

### Riding with Reagan
The Queen invites US President Ronald Reagan and First Lady Nancy Reagan to stay at Windsor Castle. Reagan and Her Majesty go riding together in Windsor Home Park on the morning of 8th June; it is clear they have bonded over their shared love of horses.

### Stranger danger
Early in the morning of 9th July, an unemployed North London labourer manages to break into Buckingham Palace and find his way to the Queen's bedroom undetected, where he appears with a bottle of wine found in the royal cellar. The Queen keeps calm and talks to the intruder until a maid and her page discover the situation and are able to raise the alarm.

---

**19 JUL 1982**
After admitting to a homosexual affair, the Queen's bodyguard, Michael Trestrail, resigns.

**30 AUG 1982**
St. David's Hall opens in the heart of Cardiff as a national concert hall for Wales.

**22 SEP 1982**
Prime Minister Margaret Thatcher arrives in China for talks over the future of Hong Kong.

# 1982

## A midsummer prince is born
On 21st June, Prince Charles drives his wife to the Lindo Wing of St. Mary's Hospital where at 9:30pm she gives birth to a 7lb 1 ½ oz baby boy. Emerging from the hospital, Charles is greeted by chants of 'For He's a Jolly Good Fellow' and tells waiting reporters that he and Diana were still discussing names. Prince William Arthur Philip Louis, who is second in line to the throne, is christened at Buckingham Palace on 4th August.

## Pope stabbed
*12th May 1982* Less than a year since the last attempt on his life, Pope John Paul II is the intended victim of another attack. At the shrine at Fatima, a Spanish priest opposed to the Pope's reforms stabs him with a bayonet and is overcome by guards. The Pope is slightly injured but not in mortal danger. The priest is jailed for three years and excommunicated.

## A new music medium
*17th August 1982* Soon after the first commercially available compact disc player, the Sony CDP-101, is launched, the first CD goes on sale. It is a 1979 recording of Chopin waltzes played by the Chilean pianist Claudio Arrau.

## Commodore 64
With more than ten million copies sold, the Commodore 64 is the best-selling personal computer in history. The computer consists of a thick keyboard with 64 kilobytes of RAM underneath and a cassette port for loading games and professional software. It surpasses many more expensive competitors with its flexible hardware and great sound.

## FOREIGN NEWS

### Climate change
*1st January 1982* An alarming report by US researchers Atkins and Epstein shows that sea levels have risen by eleven centimetres since 1940. The reason: in the same time, 50,000 cubic kilometres of ice have melted at the North and South Poles. Sea level rise provides hard evidence that the Earth is warming.

### Computer virus
*30th January 1982* The first computer virus is found on a private PC. The Elk Cloner Virus is written during a winter vacation by fifteen-year-old student Richard Skrenta. It embeds itself via the floppy into the operating system, from where it copies itself onto every floppy inserted in the floppy drive.

## 2 OCT 1982
Popular Birmingham comic, Jasper Carrott, moves to the BBC with a new, live show called *Carrott's Lib*.

## NOV 1982
The government announce that 400,000 houses have been purchased under its right-to-buy scheme.

## 15 DEC 1982
Gibraltar's border with Spain is opened after thirteen years.

# 1982

## ENTERTAINMENT

**Diet Coke**
According to Coca-Cola, women drink too little of its brand, so the soft drink giant devises an attractive variant for those who are thinking about dieting: Diet Coke. The light version comes a full eighteen years after rival Pepsi launched Diet Pepsi and contains the sweetener aspartame instead of sugar, good for only thirteen instead of 142 kilocalories per can.

**Princess Grace dies**
*13th September 1982* Princess Grace of Monaco, the former movie actress Grace Kelly, suffers a stroke while driving near her home. She dies in hospital the next day, aged 52. Over 100 dignitaries attend her funeral including Diana, Princess of Wales.

**:-)**
*19th September 1982* At Carnegie Mellon University in Pittsburgh, a student prank prompts discussion about the limits of jokes. Computer scientist Scott Fahlman proposes labelling all messages on the digital notice board. If something is intended as a joke, you mark your message with :-). If the remark is meant to be serious, you add :-( to your message. The first emoticons are born.

**Andropov replaces Brezhnev**
*10th November 1982* The death of Soviet leader Leonid Brezhnev is announced. His successor is KGB head Yuri Andropov who remains in post for fifteen months before his own death paves the way for Mikhail Gorbachev to take over.

**Bling *Dynasty***
Shoulder pads at the ready. *Dynasty* first airs on BBC1 on 1st May. The super-rich Carringtons of Denver, Colorado, headed by patriarch Blake Carrington (John Forsythe) have made their money in oil. Sound familiar? ABC creates the Aaron Spelling-produced *Dynasty* as a direct response to the success of CBS's *Dallas*, serving up supersize helpings of glitz, glamour, feuding, cat fights, bed hopping and preposterous storylines. The soap has moderate success in its first season, but the dramatic entrance of Joan Collins as Blake's first wife, Alexis, gives Dynasty a boost and by the mid-80s, it's a ratings winner. Despite the camp and melodrama, this is a show that puts older women centre stage, all while dressed to the nines by Nolan Miller. Quite simply, *Dynasty* is the show that defines the excess of the 1980s.

***Bladerunner* - beautiful dystopia**
Widely recognised as a masterpiece of science-fiction cinema, *Blade Runner*, directed by Ridley Scott, is first shown in the UK at the Edinburgh International Film Festival in August. Set in a dystopian Los Angeles of 2019, Harrison Ford is detective Rick Deckard, searching out 'replicants' - androids masquerading as humans - while unwittingly falling for one (Sean Young). Scott's jaw-dropping sets show a future that is bleak but also beautiful.

# 1982

**Dear Diary**
*The Secret Diary of Adrian Mole aged 13 and ¾* by Sue Townsend is published on 7th October. Adrian's daily ruminations not only reveal his innermost thoughts about his love for posh Pandora, his parents' marriage breakdown or the pain of trying to cover his Noddy wallpaper with black paint, but also act as an amusing guide to the early 1980s as he shares his views on the royal wedding, the Falklands War, Margaret Thatcher and Selina Scott.

**Feeling blue**
*The Smurfs*, the little blue people in Phyrgian caps created by Belgian artist Pierre 'Peyo' Culliford, have become a global phenomenon, with the film, *Smurfs and the Magic Flute* released in the UK in 1979, a hit song with Father Abraham in 1977 and 32 million collectible figures sold in 1981 alone.

*Fame*
'Fame costs, and right here's where you start paying - with sweat.' So goes the stern warning from Debbie Allan in the opening credits of *Fame*, the TV series based on the 1980 film in which Allan played dance teacher Lydia Grant. First broadcast on BBC1 on 17th June, for several years in the 1980s, thousands of UK teenagers wish they were students at the New York School of Performing Arts alongside Leroy, Doris, Bruno et al, where spontaneously breaking out into dance routines or belting out a heart-rending ballad at the piano seem a natural part of the daily timetable.

*Rambo*
Vietnam veteran John J. Rambo is on the run from the law and fighting his demons in *Rambo: First Blood*. Sylvester Stallone, pumped up and oiled, co-writes and stars in this box office smash, which inspires one of the easiest fancy dress outfits of the 1980s. Headband, check. Sweaty vest, check, A toy machine gun and round of ammo check. *Rambo* opens at UK cinemas on 16th December.

**Gizza job**
At the time *Boys from the Black Stuff* is shown on BBC2 between 10th October and 12th November, there are three million unemployed in Britain, making Alan Bleasdale's powerful drama a timely parable on the human cost of economic policy under Margaret Thatcher. A group of men, once part of a tarmac crew ('the black stuff') return to a Liverpool in the grip of industrial decline, to find the only jobs available are illegal and cash in hand.

# 1982

## Channel 4 launches
On 2nd November Channel 4 launches, with an ambitious menu of programmes. Quiz show *Countdown* (photo) has the honour of opening proceedings and continues as a mainstay of the channel for the next 40 years. A new soap, *Brookside*, set in a cul-de-sac of a modern housing estate in Liverpool, promises juicy, issue-led storylines considering it's the creation of Phil Redmond, best-known for *Grange Hill*, and on 5th November, a young bunch of comedians star in an Enid Blyton spoof, *Five Go Mad In Dorset*, under the name, *The Comic Strip Presents...*, among them Dawn French and Jennifer Saunders.

## Scumbag students
Alternative comedy explodes onto screens on 9th November on BBC2 with *The Young Ones*. Written by Ben Elton, Rik Mayall and Lise Mayer, the action is set in the squalid flat of four Scumbag College students, violent punk Vyvyan, downtrodden hippy Neil, a self-important Rik (who worships Cliff Richard) and cool, calm Mike. It's a sitcom in the most anarchic, surreal and often puerile sense of the word.

## The Tube
Anarchic music programme *The Tube* broadcasts live from Tyne Tees studio in Newcastle for the first time on 5th November. Jools Holland, who is lead presenter with Paula Yates, later recalls of their audition, 'The TV people said we were hopeless but they couldn't stop watching us.' It's chaotic but cool, with an eclectic line-up every week from big names to new acts.

## Gandhi
Richard Attenborough's twenty-year quest to tell the on-screen story of Mohandas Kharamchand Gandhi finally comes to fruition with the release of *Gandhi* in cinemas on 3rd December. Ben Kingsley went full method in taking on the lead role; losing weight, and even learning to spin cotton. Attenborough too cut no corners in this epic, three-hour long film that uses authentic historical locations and hundreds of thousands of extras. *Gandhi* wins eight Academy Awards including Best Picture, Best Director for Attenborough and Best Actor for Kingsley.

# 1982

**The Sloane Ranger Handbook**

*The Official Sloane Ranger Handbook* by Peter York and Ann Barr of *Harper's & Queen* magazine becomes a bestseller this year. Mildly self-deprecating but hugely amusing, the manual offers rules for wannabe and established Sloanes, an upper-class species found roaming around Chelsea and Fulham or at home counties shooting parties. They're the types that wear pie crust collars, pearls, and Hunter wellies; who consider a crash in the Land Rover to be a mere prang, but the wrong shade of blue on a Tuesday to be an utter disaster. High priestess of this cult is Princess Diana, who features front and centre on the cover of this arch observation on a peculiarly British phenomenon.

**A Touch of Glass**

In the 2nd December episode of *Only Fools & Horses*, Delboy and Rodney take on a job in a country house cleaning chandeliers. Nothing ever goes smoothly where the Trotters are concerned, and this is no exception. The smashing climax becomes one of the sitcom's best-loved moments.

**Walking in the Air**

A Christmas tradition is born on Boxing Day this year when Raymond Briggs's 1978 illustrated book *The Snowman* is brought to life in an animation directed by Dianne Jackson for Channel 4. The combination of Briggs' illustrations together with a score by Howard Blake (including *Walking in the Air* sung by St. Paul's Cathedral choir boy Peter Auty) makes *The Snowman* one of television's most timeless and magical festive treats. The following year, *The Snowman* has the added cachet of an introduction by none other than David Bowie.

**Quatro**

Fruity canned fizzy drink Quatro is launched this year claiming its place as a soft drink to define the decade with a TV advert where the tropical beverage is formulated in an arcade game-style vending machine, operated by a dude with a mullet. Quatro's fizz goes flat eventually, and it is discontinued in the UK in 1989.

**E.T. phone home**

E.T.'s strange but appealing appearance was apparently created by superimposing the eyes and forehead of Einstein onto a baby's face. Steven Spielberg's sweet extra-terrestrial proves not all aliens are out to get us in this charming film, released 13th August, which has the world repeating E.T.'s plaintive request, 'E.T. phone home.'

# 1982

## MUSIC

### Ozzy's year
*20th January 1982* Assuming it's made of rubber, Ozzy Osbourne bites into a live bat thrown from the audience at a gig in Des Moines, Iowa. But it's not the worst thing to happen to him this year: in March, a light aircraft in which his lead guitarist Randy Rhoads is a passenger, clips Ozzy's tour bus and crashes. Rhoads, his pilot and another passenger are killed. More happily, Ozzy marries Sharon Arden in Hawaii on 4th July.

### Olivia gets *Physical*
*23rd January 1982* Olivia Newton-John's *Physical* spends the last of ten weeks at No. 1 in the US - the longest chart-topping run since Elvis Presley's *Hound Dog* in 1956. It's a big switch of pace for the singer whose fame went up another level with the film *Grease* in 1978. A change of image sees her dressed in Jane Fonda-type aerobics gear (dig those legwarmers) in a curve-accentuating video and singing of, well, physical pleasures.

### Goodbye to the Monk
*17th February 1982* Jazz piano legend Thelonious Monk, known as the High Priest of Bebop, dies in New Jersey aged 64. His compositions included *Round Midnight* and *Straight, No Chaser*. His most famous saying was 'The piano ain't got no wrong notes.'

### Doobies disband
*31st March 1982* The Doobie Brothers, America's leading west coast band after the Eagles, announce their break-up. Formed in 1970, their *Listen to the Music* and *What a Fool Believes* remain all-time radio classics.

### Rocking the Casbah
*24th May 1982* One of the few original punk bands still espousing radical politics, the Clash release *Combat Rock* just as Topper Headon leaves the band and Joe Strummer returns from a mystery disappearance. It includes Clash classics *Rock the Casbah* and *Should I Stay or Should I Go*.

### Get the Message
*1st July 1982* Released today, *The Message* by Grandmaster Flash and the Furious Five is a genuine milestone. One of the first true hip hop records from a genius of the turntables, it breaks new ground with a portrait of inner-city life that's full of tension and fury.

### Celtic soul
*7th August 1982* Dexy's Midnight Runners lead man Kevin Rowland fashions a complete change of image - all dungarees and sandals - for the band to tie in with the release of new album *Too-Rye-Ay*. The single *Come On Eileen* harks back to Rowland's Belfast roots while the music is a hybrid that he calls 'Celtic soul', mixing blues rhythms and highly non-trendy folk instrumentation. Can anyone remember the last time an old-fashioned fiddle was heard on a No. 1 single?

# 1982

### Mad about the Boy
*23rd September 1982* For UK parents, the sight of Boy George singing *Do You Really Want to Hurt Me* with Culture Club on *Top of the Pops* is one of those classic 'Is it a girl or a boy?' moments. Playing in a reggae-cum-soul style, Culture Club is another band to emerge from the Blitz club, the cradle of London's 'new romantic' scene. George explains that the band's name reflects its mixture of cultures - a gay Irishman on lead vocals, a black Londoner on bass, a white Englishman on keyboards and a Jewish drummer.

## MY FIRST 18 YEARS
## TOP 10 — 1982

1. **I Don't Wanna Dance** Eddy Grant
2. **Fame** Irene Cara
3. **House of Fun** Madness
4. **A Town Called Malice** The Jam
5. **Love Plus One** Haircut 100
6. **Planet Rock** Afrika Bambaataa
7. **Poison Arrow** ABC
8. **Centerfold** J. Geils Band
9. **Save a Prayer** Duran Duran
10. **The Model** Kraftwerk

### Pass the... what?
*2nd October 1982* How did a song about passing round a marijuana joint make it to No. 1 - and in the hands of Musical Youth, a five-piece band from Birmingham whose members are all under eighteen years old? The answer is that they changed the letter 'k' in *Pass the Kutchie* to 'd' and explained to the press that a 'dutchie' was a Jamaican serving dish.

### Marvin reborn
*20th November 1982* After leaving Motown and moving to Belgium for tax reasons, Marvin Gaye emerges rejuvenated with *Sexual Healing* from the album *Midnight Love*. Returning to the erotic themes of his *Let's Get it On* period, he jump starts his career and wins his first Grammy award.

### Jackson heights
*1st December 1982* Michael Jackson's *Thriller* hits the stores. Continuing his collaboration with producer Quincy Jones and songwriter Rod Temperton, it is set to top the chart in every country of the world and will become the biggest selling album of all time - 45 million copies and counting by 2024. No fewer than seven singles will be extracted from it including the title track, which is supported by a thirteen minute video directed by John Landis and featuring a red jacketed Michael dancing with a horde of zombies.

### Weller splits the Jam
*11th December 1982* The Jam play their final gig at Brighton Conference Centre, then disband. It is Paul Weller's decision and bassist Bruce Foxton will not speak to him for twenty years. The band bow out with a last No. 1, *Beat Surrender*.

PHOTO CREDITS Copyright 2024, TDM Rights BV.
Photos: **A** PA Images - Getty Images / **B** PA Images - Getty Images / **C** David Levenson - Getty Images Europe - Getty Images / **D** PA Images - Getty Images / **E** Terence Laheney - Hulton Archive - Getty Images / **F** Tim Graham - Tim Graham Photo Library - Getty Images / **G** Anwar Hussein - WireImage - Getty Images / **H** Science & Society Picture Library - SSPL - Getty Images / **I** Cheryl Chenet - Corbis Historical - Getty Images / **J** Bettmann - Getty Images / **K** Aaron Spelling Productions - Ronald Grant Archive - Mary Evans / **L** Sunset Boulevard - Corbis Historical - Getty Images / **M** BBC - Ronald Grant Archive - Mary Evans / **N** AF Archive - MGM - Mary Evans / **O** Ronald Grant Archive - Mary Evans / **P** RB - Redferns - Getty Images / **Q** Comic Relief - Getty Images Europe - Getty Images / **R** Ronald Grant Archive - Mary Evans / **S** Sunset Boulevard - Corbis Historical - Getty Images / **T** AF - Archive BBC - Mary Evans / **U** Murakami-Wolf Productions - Ronald Grant Archive - Mary Evans / **V** Fin Costello - Redferns - Getty Images / **W** Michael Ochs Archives - Getty Images / **X** Allan Tannenbaum - Archive Photos - Getty Images / **Y** Steve Rapport - Hulton Archive - Getty Images / **Z** Rob Verhorst - Redferns - Getty Images / **A2** Ron Galella - Ron Galella Collection - Getty Images.

# 1983

## MY FIRST 18 YEARS

## SPORT

### Dev digs deep
In the Cricket World Cup at the Nevill Ground, Tunbridge Wells, India's Kapil Dev gives an incredible individual performance during a group match against Zimbabwe. India have just 17 for 5 when Dev smashes a breathtaking 175 runs off 138 balls; an innings that includes sixteen boundaries and six sixes. Buoyed up by his brilliant performance, India proceed to defeat England and Australia, to reach the final at Lord's where they topple the mighty West Indies by 43 runs.

### Corbiere a winner
Corbiere wins the Grand National on 9th April, the first winner of the legendary steeplechase to be trained by a woman, Jenny Pitman.

### World Championships in Helsinki
British athletes prove their worth on the world stage at the World Athletics Championship in Helsinki which has its final day on 14th August. Steve Cram emerges from the shadow of Ovett and Coe to take gold in the 1500m, while Daley Thompson seals victory in the decathlon. Elsewhere, American multi-discipline maestro Carl Lewis (photo) wins gold in the 100m, long jump and 4 x 100m relay.

### Jennings reaches 1,000 goal
Arsenal and Northern Ireland goalkeeper Pat Jennings becomes the first footballer in the English league to make one thousand senior appearances, at a match against West Bromwich Albion on 26th February, which, fortunately, is goalless!

### England defeat the All Blacks
The All Blacks' rugby union tour of England and Scotland reaches its climax at Twickenham on 19th November, when a New Zealand team depleted of more experienced members, but still dangerous, meet England, who have not beaten them on home turf since 1936. In a rough match, beset by injury on both sides, England manage to hold off New Zealand to seal a 15-9 win, thanks in part to a try from Maurice Colclough.

### 8 JAN 1983
Margaret Thatcher arrives in the Falkland Islands for a four-day visit to British troops.

### 15 FEB 1983
The Austin Metro is Britain's best-selling car.

### 15 MAR 1983
The Budget raises tax thresholds, effectively cutting taxes by £2 billion.

# 1983

## DOMESTIC NEWS

### Police drown in Blackpool
*5th January 1983* Tragedy strikes Blackpool as three members of the police force, two men and a woman, drown whilst attempting to rescue a man from the sea. The man had gone into the water after his Jack Russell terrier and cannot be saved despite best efforts.

### Shooting of Stephen Waldorf
*14th January 1983* 26-year-old Stephen Waldorf is shot and seriously injured by armed policemen whilst travelling through London in the passenger seat of a friend's car. The police had mistaken Waldorf for an escaped prisoner, David Martin, who would be rearrested two weeks later.

Double deck cassette recorder

### Seatbelts mandatory
*31st January 1983* The wearing of seatbelts becomes mandatory across the UK. Seat belts have been essential safety components in cars since 1972, but compliance has been low. This next step of legislation leads to a 30% reduction in fatal injuries of front seat passengers.

### Muswell Hill murderer
*11th February 1983* Dennis Nielson is arrested and charged with murder after human remains are discovered at his Muswell Hill flat. As the investigation progresses, he is revealed to have murdered at least twelve young men and boys since 1978.

### New £1 coin
*21st April 1983* A new £1 coin is introduced to replace the £1 note, a feature of the British currency since 1797. The new coin features the Queen's portrait on the front, and a different reverse image is issued every year, starting with the royal coat of arms, and followed by emblems reflecting the different nations of the UK.

### British Airways S-61 crash
*16th July 1983* A British Airways helicopter flight is downed in heavy fog over the Celtic Sea. Twenty people on board are killed, while six are rescued by a lifeboat.

### Maze Prison escape
*25th September 1983* 20 guards are injured, and one dies of a heart attack, when 38 IRA prisoners escape from HM Prison Maze in Northern Ireland. The prisoners escape using guns, smuggled into the prison, to hijack a lorry in what becomes the biggest prison break in British history.

**23 APR 1983**
The People's March for Jobs sets off from Glasgow, reaching London in early June.

**11 MAY 1983**
Aberdeen win the European Cup Winner's cup against Real Madrid 2-1.

**23 JUN 1983**
Monty Python's The Meaning of Life is released, the final film for the Python gang.

# 1983

## ROYALTY & POLITICS

**Thrust 2 land speed record**
*4th October 1983* Scottish entrepreneur Richard Noble breaks the land speed record in jet-powered car Thrust 2. Racing over a course in the Black Rock Desert in Nevada, he sets a speed of 634.051 miles per hour.

**Thatcher wins second term in office**
On June 10th, the Conservatives win a landslide victory in the General Election, with a 144 majority. The decisive victory leads to the resignation of Labour leader Michael Foot and the SDP's Roy Jenkins. On 2nd October, Labour elects 41-year-old Welsh left-winger Neil Kinnock as party leader, with the more moderate Roy Hattersley as deputy leader.

**Brink's-Mat robbery**
*26th November 1983* A robbery at Heathrow International Trading Estate sees six thieves break into the Brink's-Mat warehouse. Described as the 'crime of the century', the men make away with 6,800 gold bars, diamonds, and cash, in total worth nearly £26 million. Whilst two men are arrested and convicted, most of the stolen goods are never recovered.

**Tory scandal - Cecil Parkinson resigns**
Cecil Parkinson, Secretary for Trade and Industry and mastermind of the Tory election campaign, admits to his long-term affair with his former secretary, who is pregnant with his child. Parkinson announces he will not be resigning, and has decided to stay with his wife. But Sara Keays gives an interview to *The Times*, and her revelations force Parkinson, Mrs Thatcher's golden boy (photo), to resign in disgrace. He is replaced by Norman Tebbit.

**Harrods bombing**
*17th December 1983* A car bomb planted by the Provisional IRA explodes outside Harrods department store in London. Despite a warning being received, the area is not evacuated in time and six people are killed alongside 90 injured. Eight days later, on Christmas Day, another bomb explodes on Oxford Street with no casualties.

## 26 JUL 1983
Mother of 10, Victoria Gillick, loses a court case against the DHSS to prevent the distribution of contraceptives to under-16s.

## 1 AUG 1983
Sales of new cars receive a boost as A-prefix car registration plates are introduced.

## 5 SEP 1983
Adventure cartoon *He-Man and the Masters of the Universe* has its world premiere on Children's ITV.

# 1983

## Queen presents honour
The Queen presents the Order of Merit to Mother Teresa of Calcutta in a ceremony in the grounds of the Presidential Palace in New Delhi.

## FOREIGN NEWS

## Switched on
*1st January 1983* A switch is turned at the American Advanced Research Projects Agency. The switch marks the beginning of the internet as we know it.

## Black holes
*1st January 1983* Scientists discovered the first black hole - formed when a star implodes at the end of its existence - in 1971. Now an article appears about a second black hole, 170,000 light-years from Earth. It is smaller than Scotland, but weighs ten times as much as the Sun.

## Fake Hitler diaries
*30th January 1983* Fifty years after Adolf Hitler came to power, 62 of his diaries are found in Germany. The Führer describes his experiences from 1932 until the day before his death. Then master forger Konrad Kujau confesses that he wrote the diaries himself and that he received 2.5 million marks from the Der Stern journalist who supposedly 'discovered' them. The blunder marks a new low in European journalism.

## Ice cold
*21st July 1983* At the Vostok station in Antarctica, in the middle of the polar cap, the polar station measures a temperature of -89.2°C. It is the lowest reliably measured temperature ever recorded on Earth.

## Korean Air Flight 007
*1st September 1983* When Korean Air Flight 007 en route from New York to Seoul ends up in a restricted part of Soviet airspace due to a navigation error, the Boeing 747 is shot down 55 kilometres from Moneron Island. All 269 people on board are killed. It is another low point in the Cold War and sends a shiver across the world.

## 27 OCT 1983
A memorial service is held for much-loved actor and raconteur David Niven who had died on 30th July.

## 18 NOV 1983
Janet Walton from Liverpool gives birth to six baby girls after taking fertility drugs. The sextuplets become national celebrities.

## 3 DEC 1983
As part of an ongoing peace campaign, women protestors break into RAF Greenham Common in Berkshire.

# 1983

## Word and Lotus 1-2-3

*1st October 1983* Microsoft releases the first version of the word processing programme Word, which allows computer users to format typed text with line breaks and bold and italic letters. Multi-Tool Word, as it is called, comes free with *PC World magazine*. Users find the interface strange and WordStar and WordPerfect prove more popular. How different things will be with Lotus 1-2-3, now ready for launch. Many businesses buy the IBM computer specifically for it, to create clear spreadsheets, graphs and databases.

## US invades Grenada

*25th October 1983* The Caribbean island of Grenada, a member of the British Commonwealth, is invaded by US forces aiming to prevent communist rule there. For virtually the only time in Ronald Reagan's presidency, Margaret Thatcher expresses private disapproval of US action, especially over the fact that the UK was not consulted.

## Nuclear false alarms

As cruise missiles arrive in Europe for stationing in NATO countries, two major nuclear scares bring the world momentarily to the brink of catastrophe. On 26th September, Soviet officer Stanislav Petrov correctly identifies a warning of a US missIle attack as a false alarm. On 7th November, a NATO exercise is misinterpreted by Soviet officials as cover for a nuclear attack and Warsaw Pact forces are placed on full alert. The danger passes with the conclusion of the exercise four days later.

# ENTERTAINMENT

## The Roly Polys

Dance troupe The Roly Polys, seven generously proportioned ladies, led by 4' 11" Mo Moreland, tap and shimmy their way onto screens for the first time on *The Les Dawson Show* on 15th January.

## The Machine Gunners

The first episode of the TV adaptation of Robert Westall's 1975 Carnegie medal-winning children's novel, *The Machine Gunners*, is aired on 23rd February. The Second World War drama set in a north-east coastal town in February 1941 centres on Chas McGill and his friends who discover a crashed German plane, complete with machine gun and ammunition.

## Home video surges

New figures show that 10% of UK households now own a video recorder - and that the vast majority of those prefer VHS to Betamax, its technically superior but more expensive rival format. Home video is a revolutionary new medium that enables recording and playback of television programmes, gives users the opportunity to make videos of their own, and makes movies old and new available for home viewing. By the end of the decade, more than half of households in the UK will own a VCR.

137

# 1983

### Let's act
Nagisa Oshima's *Merry Christmas, Mr. Lawrence* is released on 25th August. Based on Laurens van der Post's memoirs about his experiences in a Japanese POW camp in Java during the Second World War, Bowie is the rebellious Major Jack Culliers opposite Tom Conti and Ryuichi Sakamoto. Oshima cast Bowie in the role after seeing him perform in the play *The Elephant Man* on Broadway in 1980.

### Wake up and smell... a rat?
Early risers can enjoy telly with their cornflakes from 17th January, when *Breakfast Time* launches on BBC1. Hot on its heels is ITV's morning offering, *TV-am*, beginning on 1st February. *TV-am's* early weeks are beset by problems and viewing figures flag but the introduction of puppet rodent Roland Rat on 1st April helps to revive its fortunes.

### Fan-dabi-dozee!
After years on the cabaret circuit, Wee Jimmy Krankie and his sensible, grown-up sidekick, Ian Krankie, have become TV favourites through appearances on *Crackerjack*. Their star has risen to such heights that they get their own show this year; *The Krankies Klub* begins on BBC1 on 10th September. Much loved by a generation of kids, who adore cheeky Jimmy Krankie's mischievous antics and his catchphrase, 'Fan-dabi-dozee', the eventual realisation that Jimmy is in real life Janette Krankie, a woman in her thirties who is married to Ian, comes as a shock, second only to finding out Father Christmas doesn't really exist.

### Corrie love triangle
*Coronation Street* fans are gripped during its 21st February episode when Ken Barlow discovers his wife Deirdre has been having an affair with Mike Baldwin who Ken describes as a 'spiv' and 'little creep'. It's an emotional scene full of high drama with the usually mild-mannered Ken losing his cool and almost throttling Deirdre when Mike arrives at their door.

DO YOU REMEMBER THIS?

Donkey Kong game

### The Dark Crystal
Chief Muppeteer Jim Henson taps into the vogue for fantasy films, working with Frank Oz on *The Dark Crystal*, first shown in UK cinemas on 17th February. Five years in the making, it is essentially a tale of good versus evil, with the vulture-like Skeksis pitted against the gentle Mystics. In a plot that borrows liberally from Tolkein, two elfin Gelflings are tasked with spiriting the powerful Dark Crystal away from the Skeksis before the alignment of three suns.

# 1983

### Cabbage Patch craziness
Harrods is swamped with shoppers on 1st December, as they descend on the store to grab this festive season's must-have toy - a Cabbage Patch doll. Despite their strange, pudgy faces, which everyone, even the buyers, agree are rather ugly, the Cabbage Patch phenomenon has caused violent riots among shoppers in the US.

### Just Seventeen
On 20th October, comes the launch of *Just Seventeen* magazine, a fresh new title aimed at teenage girls, heavy on fashion, heartthrobs and pithy advice, and light on the soppy romance photo-stories which magazines like *My Guy* peddle. *J-17* doesn't patronise its readers, has some great cover giveaways and feels like the ideal read for any sophisticated 1980s teen.

### Tootsie
*Tootsie* steals the hearts of UK audiences when it opens on 28th April. Sydney Pollack's direction and Dustin Hoffman's entertaining turn as a difficult, out-of-work actor who lands a plum role in a primetime soap by becoming 'Dorothy Michaels', brings the screwball comedy of the 1930s bang up to date. There's an underlying message about gender and male privilege, but it's delivered without losing any of its sparkle. As she becomes an unlikely standard bearer for feminism, 'Dorothy' falls in love with his/her co-star played by Jessica Lange, who won an Oscar for Best Actress. A dragged-up delight.

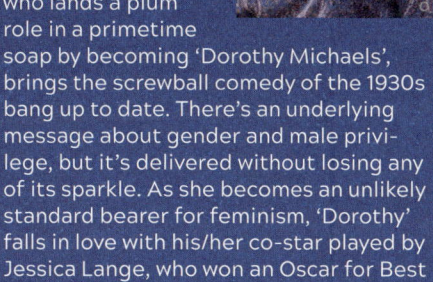

### I'll have a 'P' please, Bob
*Blockbusters*, a quiz game for sixth-formers hosted by Bob Holness, first airs on ITV on 29th August. More intellectually rigorous than the majority of teatime quiz shows, one solo player battles a team of two as they make their way across a board of interlocked hexagons by answering general knowledge questions linked to the letter on each hexagon. The winner goes on to try their luck at the Gold Run, with a chance to stay and defend their champion status each week.

### Cheers to that
Channel 4 builds a reputation for sniffing out great American sitcoms, beginning with *Cheers* which it presents for the first time on 4th February. Set in a Boston bar where 'everybody knows your name', the wisecracks flow as freely as the beer.

### Tweenyboppers
*Minipops* airs for the first time on Channel 4 on 8th February. Featuring pre-teen children impersonating current pop stars and singing along to chart hits, the appearance of these mini-me popstrels with crimped hair and eyeliner is controversial to say the least and after one season, the ill-judged *Minipops* is dropped.

139

# 1983

**The A Team**
On the run from the US government, 'for a crime they didn't commit', ex-commandos The A-Team become the action-adventure sensation of 1983. First screened on ITV on 22nd July, it's the de facto star, the muscular Mr T as B.A. Baracus, with his acres of gold chains, surly countenance and magical, mechanical know-how, who becomes a cult figure. Of course, nobody's perfect and B.A.'s Achilles heel is his fear of flying; 'I ain't getting on no plane' becomes one of the show's memorable catchphrases.

**Tucker's Luck**
The first episode of Tucker's Luck, a Grange Hill spin-off series, begins on BBC2 on 10th March. Featuring one of the most popular characters from Grange Hill's original cast, it follows the teenage Peter 'Tucker' Jenkins (Todd Carty) as he negotiates life, work (or lack of it) and girls after leaving school.

**Blue Peter's sunken garden vandalised**
The decline of civilisation can perhaps be pinpointed to the moment in November 1983 when Blue Peter's Italian sunken garden is vandalised. Viewers are horrified as Janet Ellis confirms that the upturned sundial, ripped-up plants and oil on the pond are due to senseless vandalism. Percy Thrower finds it hard to hold back the tears and in a moment of political incorrectness, suggests the perpetrators are 'mentally ill'.

**Thrills and chills**
The golden age of the music video has truly arrived when Michael Jackson's Thriller is screened at the ungodly hour of 1:05am on Channel 4, introduced by Jools Holland of The Tube. Zombies, teen movie schtick and gobsmacking dance routines combine to make this a major multimedia event, at a time Jackson is reaching the peak of his solo success.

**Swatch out**
Swatch watches are launched on 1st March, Switzerland's riposte to the growing dominance of digital watches from Asia. Swatches are analogue, quartz time pieces, but they're also affordable and their colourful, simple design make them a classic 1980s accessory.

**Caped crusaders**
Early October sees the advent of two animated superheroes. On 3rd October, the lantern-jawed, fruit-fuelled Bananaman, who originated in the comic Nutty, comes to life on BBC1, voiced by members of The Goodies. Superted airs a day later, also on BBC1, almost a year after he had first been shown on Welsh TV channel, S4C. Originally created by Mike Young as a series of books, written to help cure his young son's fear of the dark, Superted, a toy factory reject, is brought to life by a visiting alien from the Planet Spot and given superpowers.

# MUSIC

### Blue Monday
**19th March 1983** Breaking new ground musically, technically and commercially is *Blue Monday* by New Order. It uses a synth bassline, a sequencer and a drum machine. Sampling Kraftwerk's *Uranium* and echoing Donna Summer's *Our Love* and the soundtrack of *The Good, the Bad and the Ugly*, it's an extraordinary amalgam of sound and voice that is a hit twice during 1983, in twelve-inch and standard format versions.

### Wizards of Oz
Men at Work lead a succession of Australasian bands to big success in the UK and US. With its ironic articulation of Antipodean clichés, their *Down Under* becomes almost a second Australian anthem, while 1983 sees Michael Hutchence's INXS (photo) debut in New York and Icehouse build their reputation by supporting David Bowie on tour. Nick Cave and the Bad Seeds emerge from the ashes of the much-admired Birthday Party, while Rick Springfield and the Little River Band each have a strong run of hits in more conventional soft rock mode in the US. Uncompromising and politically active, long-timers Midnight Oil are on the cusp of an international breakthrough as the year ends.

### Pink Floyd on hiatus
**21st March 1983** After releasing *The Final Cut*, which is largely the work of Roger Waters, Pink Floyd dissolve into acrimony. For the next four years the members will focus on solo work and dealing with legal action around the right to use the Pink Floyd name.

### Duran Duran
**26th March 1983** Hitting No. 1 for the first time - and doing so just one week after the single's release - are new romantic pin-up boys Duran Duran with *Is There Something I Should Know*. Thanks to their super-glamorous and very MTV-friendly videos, Simon Le Bon and friends are the hottest UK property in the US at the moment, where audience hysteria is likened to Beatlemania. They are named after a character in the 1964 sci-fi film *Barbarella* starring Jane Fonda.

### Billy's innocent
The album of the year has to be Billy Joel's multi-platinum *An Innocent Man*, on which Long Island's finest pays homage to the singers and groups who influenced him. The songs brilliantly capture the styles, characteristics and qualities of the Drifters (the title track), Motown (*Tell Her About It*), doo wop (*The Longest Time*) and the Four Seasons (*Uptown Girl*). More than a tribute, it's a series of loving re-creations with nostalgically choreographed videos to match.

# 1983

### Bowie and Nile

*9th April 1983* It's a marriage made in heaven – David Bowie teaming up with ex-Chic guitarist and producer Nile Rodgers for a chart-topping album and single, both called *Let's Dance*, that do not pretend to be anything more than solid slices of ultra-funky contemporary dance music. *China Girl* and *Modern Love* are also hits from the same album, the warm reception to which encourages Bowie to tour for the first time in five years.

## MY FIRST 18 YEARS
### TOP 10 — 1983

1. **Billie Jean** Michael Jackson
2. **War Baby** Tom Robinson
3. **Lovecats** The Cure
4. **Karma Chameleon** Culture Club
5. **Every Breath You Take** The Police
6. **IOU** Freeez
7. **Islands in the Stream** Dolly Parton, Kenny Rogers
8. **Come Dancing** The Kinks
9. **Back on the Chain Gang** The Pretenders
10. **Heartache Avenue** The Maisonettes

### Soul brothers

Young white soul boys are in their element in UK pop in the 1980s. Paul Weller launches the Style Council with Mick Talbot to create the Otis Redding/Curtis Mayfield style soul he adored as a teenager. Spandau Ballet swap outrageous new romantic get-ups for a smart-suited new look and storm the chart with *True*. And Paul Young (photo), has the temerity to cover a hallowed Marvin Gaye classic, *Wherever I Lay My Hat (That's My Home)*, and take it No. 1.

### Pointed politics

Politics is part of the pop mix in 1983. Written in the wake of the Falklands War, two of the most pointed songs of the year both originate on Elvis Costello's *Punch the Clock* album – *Shipbuilding* and *Pills and Soap*. Beautifully covered in deadpan style by Robert Wyatt, once of Soft Machine, *Shipbuilding* is a swipe at the prospect of a closed-down British industry being revived for making battleships, told from the conflicted perspective of an unemployed man.

### Thrashing it out

*25th July 1983* The thrash metal genre arrives with a vengeance with *Kill 'Em All* by Metallica, a four-piece formed in 1981 by Lars Ulrich and influenced by the UK bands who comprised the 'new wave of heavy metal' at the time. Metallica combine speed and energy with a Zeppelin-esque density of sound and soon find themselves one of the big four of the metal scene alongside Anthrax, Slayer and a band formed by ex-member Dave Mustaine, Megadeth.

---

PHOTO CREDITS Copyright 2024, TDM Rights BV.
Photos: **A** Getty Images - Hulton Archive - Getty Images / **B** Mirrorpix - Getty Images / **C** Tony Duffy - Getty Images / **D** PA Images - Getty Images / **E** PA Images - Getty Images / **F** Brownie Harris - Corbis Historical - Getty Images / **G** Mirrorpix - Getty Images / **H** Anwar Hussein - Getty Images Europe - Getty Images / **I** Heritage Images - Hulton Archive - Getty Images / **J** Ullstein Bild - Getty Images / **K** Denver Post - Getty Images / **L** Avalon - Hulton Archive - Getty Images / **M** Ronald Grant Archive - Mary Evans / **N** AF Archive - Universal Pictures - Mary Evans / **O** Art Zelin - Archive Photos - Getty Images / **P** Ronald Grant Archive - Mary Evans / **Q** Ronald Grant Archive - Mary Evans / **R** Avalon - Hulton Archive - Getty Images / **S** AF Archive - Mary Evans / **T** Jean-Louis URLI - Gamma-Rapho - Getty Images / **U** Fin Costello - Redferns - Getty Images / **V** Michael Putland - Hulton Archive - Getty Images / **W** Krasner Trebitz - Redferns - Getty Images.

# 1984

## SPORT

**Torvill and Dean's golden moment**
One of the most iconic moments in sporting history takes place at the Winter Olympics in Sarajevo, appropriately on 14th February. The United Kingdom's Jane Torvill and Christopher Dean skate a risky routine of fluid grace and breathtaking romance to Ravel's Bolero in the free dance competition, earning them an unprecedented perfect score of 6.0 from every judge for artistic impression. The routine is watched by 23 million Britons at home.

**The fall**
South African athlete Zola Budd, who breaks American Mary Decker's 5000m world record in January, controversially gains a British passport on 6th April allowing her to compete at the Olympic Games in Los Angeles. When Budd (who runs barefoot) and Decker meet in the 3000m Olympic final more controversy follows. Budd makes her way to the front of the pack and Decker, pinned behind, trips over Budd's heel, and falls on her hip. Decker fails to finish the race and Budd comes seventh.

**Lewis leads the way at the Olympics**
Carl Lewis equals Jesse Owens' Olympic tally of 1936 by winning four gold medals, in the 100m, 200m, 4x100m relay and long jump. Seb Coe overcomes a period of injury and equals his own medal tally, by once again winning gold in the 1500m and silver in the 800m. Tessa Sanderson gains gold for Great Britain in the javelin, as does Daley Thompson in the decathlon. Steve Redgrave gets the first of his five rowing gold medals in the men's coxless fours. The LA Olympics has been a ritzy, glitzy affair, and one that shows hosting the Games can be a commercial success.

**West Indies overwhelm England's cricketers**
A majestic West Indies side under Clive Lloyd thrashes David Gower's England 5-0 in the summer Test series; the only instance where England have suffered such a resounding whitewash at home.

### 6 JAN 1984
The British turn their backs on cigarettes as anti-smoking group ASH say two million have given up in the last two years.

### 9 FEB 1984
As open civil war erupts in Beirut, 400 Britons are evacuated from the city.

### 28 MAR 1984
Nissan select the north-east town of Washington, near Sunderland, as the location for its new UK car plant.

# 1984

**Turnaround for the Toffees**
Everton end a fourteen-year trophy drought and emerge from the shadow of their Merseyside sibling, Liverpool, by winning the FA Cup Final, beating Watford 2-0 on 19th May. It's a pivotal moment for manager Howard Kendall and his team signalling the beginning of purple patch of success.

**Olympic boycott**
*8th May 1984* In retaliation for the decision of the US to boycott the Olympic Games in Moscow in 1980, the Soviet National Olympic Committee boycotts the Los Angeles Olympic Games. All Eastern Bloc countries with the exception of Romania also confirm their non-participation.

## DOMESTIC NEWS

**Halfpenny withdrawn**
*1st February 1984* The government announces that the halfpenny is to be withdrawn from circulation at the end of the year. Whilst the new decimal version of the coin has only been in circulation since 1971, the country has had halfpennies since 1672.

**Miners' strikes**
*12th March 1984* The National Union of Mineworkers go out on strike in protest at government plans that will see the closure of most of Britain's remaining coal pits. Clashes between police and miners in April and May continue into June, when the 'Battle of Orgreave' results in over 120 injuries and 95 arrests in one of the most violent incidents of the dispute. A mass lobby by miners at the Houses of Parliament ends in violence and 120 arrests, and in September the strike is ruled unlawful.

**Chatham Dockyard closes**
*31st March 1984* The Medway in Kent witnesses an end to over 400 years of shipbuilding at the Chatham Dockyard, as it is closed for the final time. 84 acres of the Dockyard is preserved as a heritage attraction, telling the story of shipbuilding on the site since the reign of Elizabeth I.

**WPC Yvonne Fletcher**
*17th April 1984* A gunman inside the Libyan Embassy shoots and kills WPC Yvonne Fletcher and wounds 11 others during peaceful protests outside. Following the shooting, armed police lay siege to the building, and Britain severs diplomatic ties with Libya.

**21 APR 1984**
Return of the groundbreaking US series *Cagney and Lacey* to BBC1.

**19 MAY 1984**
Poet and protector of Britain's building heritage, Sir John Betjaman dies at his Cornish home, aged 78.

**22 JUN 1984**
The first Virgin Atlantic flight to New York takes off from Gatwick, with fares costing £99.

# 1984

**Thames Barrier opened**
8th May 1984 The Queen formally opens the Thames Barrier, a new system designed to protect London from flooding. High tides and storm surges have threatened the capital since the Roman period, and this new barrier will allow authorities to close the 520m width of the river when the city is in danger.

**Abbeystead disaster**
23rd May 1984 An explosion at a waterworks' valve house in Abbeystead, Lancashire, kills sixteen people. The explosion is caused by a build-up of methane gas that investigators determine has seeped into the pipes from nearby coal deposits, igniting when the valves were opened.

**Hong Kong agreement**
19th December 1984 After months of negotiations, Britain and China sign the Sino-British Joint Declaration, which agrees the return of the British Overseas Territory of Hong Kong to Chinese control.

**York Minster fire**
9th July 1984 The country watches on in horror as a fire breaks out in the early hours of the morning at York Minster. Quick-thinking firefighters choose to collapse the roof of the South Transept, where the fire has started, in a successful attempt to prevent the fire from spreading, and the rest of the medieval building is saved.

**Brighton hotel bombing**
12th October 1984 The entire cabinet are the intended targets of a Provisional IRA bomb planted in the Grand Hotel in Brighton. The hotel is hosting the Conservative Party conference, and the explosion is intended to strike after Prime Minister Margaret Thatcher and her fellow ministers have arrived. Five people, including MP Anthony Berry, are killed and several more are seriously injured and trapped in the rubble.

**BT privatised**
20th November 1984 Shares in British Telecom go on sale after plans for the privatisation of the company were unveiled in 1982. The government retain 50% of the shares, whilst over two million members of the public choose to invest, amounting to approximately 5% of the population.

## 12 JUL 1984
Robert Maxwell acquires Mirror Group newspapers and states his editors will be 'free to produce the news without interference'.

## 4 AUG 1984
The BBC continues its coverage of the Los Angeles Olympics until 4am each day, and supplements this with Ceefax Olympics AM.

## 29 SEP 1984
A huge IRA arms cache is discovered on board an Irish trawler sailing off the southwest coast of Britain.

# 1984

**Gorbachev Visits UK**
16th December 1984 The UK welcomes Soviet politburo member Mikhail Gorbachev on a week-long semi-official tour of the country. Gorbachev meets government ministers and politicians, and tours factories and cities, meeting with Prime Minister Margaret Thatcher at Chequers. Her verdict that 'we can do business together' proves prophetic as he shows himself to be a reformer seeking closer ties with the West.

## FOREIGN NEWS

**First compact computer**
24th January 1984 Apple launches the first compact computer with the Apple Macintosh 128k. The Macintosh has 128 kilobytes of RAM and its own operating system, Mac OS. The computer has no hard drive, and to keep the device as quiet as possible, Steve Jobs insists that no fan be built in.

**CIA chief kidnapped**
16th March 1984 The ongoing war in Lebanon claims another high-profile victim. The CIA's station chief in Beirut, Willliam Buckley, is kidnapped by the Islamic Jihad and dies in captivity.

## ROYALTY & POLITICS

**Birth of Prince Harry**
The Princess of Wales gives birth to a second son on 15th September. The following day it is announced the new baby prince will be given the names Henry Charles Albert David, although he quickly becomes known as Prince Harry.

**Sony markets the Discman**
19th November 1984 Just as its original Walkman design boosted sales of cassettes to unprecedented levels, so Sony's Discman is set to do exactly the same for the new compact disc format. More robust and user friendly than the Walkman, the Discman is the ultimate aid to personalised music listening.

### 1 OCT 1984
Dr. David Jenkins, the outspoken Bishop of Durham, makes a public attack on Margaret Thatcher's social policies.

### 20 NOV 1984
McDonald's makes its 50 billionth hamburger.

### 19 DEC 1984
Mrs. Thatcher signs the Sino-British Declaration handing Hong Kong to China, ending 155 years of British rule in the colony.

# 1984

### HIV positive
*23rd April 1984* US Department of Health and Human Services Secretary Margaret Heckler announces that the cause of AIDS - the HIV virus - has been discovered by Dr Robert Gallo and colleagues at the National Cancer Institute. She reveals the development of a diagnostic blood test to identify infection and holds out the hope that a vaccine against AIDS will be produced within two years.

### Reagan re-elected
*6th November 1984* Ronald Reagan secures a second term as US President with a landslide win over his Democrat opponent Walter Mondale. Reagan achieves nearly 70 per cent of the popular vote and wins all the states except Washington DC and Mondale's home state of Minnesota.

### Bhopal
*3rd December 1984* Methyl isocyanate escapes from a Union Carbide factory in the Indian city of Bhopal. In a short time, this poisonous gas cloud kills more than 8,000 people outright and affects over half a million people. The final death toll is estimated at over 20,000. It is the worst industrial accident in history and results in criminal prosecutions against Union Carbide and individuals running the factory.

## ENTERTAINMENT

### Hartbeat
Tony Hart has been the go-to man for art on children's TV for twenty years, first with *Vision On*, and then *Take Hart*. *Hartbeat* is the latest iteration, airing for the first time on 14th September. It retains all the familiar aspects of previous programmes, including his plasticine sidekick, Morph, and The Gallery segment where viewers send in their own artwork. But there are updates too. The set is jazzier, Tony has female co-presenters and occasionally he invites a graphic designer onto the programme to show how to create designs on a computer.

DO YOU REMEMBER THIS?

Water ring game

### Consumer trends
While McDonald's proclaims the consumption of its 50 billionth hamburger, new global business launches in 1984 include Papa John's Pizza, Dell Computers and LA Fitness. Wrist watch calculators are the must-have gadgets of the year. In the fast rising world of video games, Commodore International founder Jack Tramiel founds Tramel Technology, buys the consumer assets of Atari Inc from Warner Communications and renames the company Atari. The biggest selling toys on the planet are Hasbro's Transformers, cleverly promoted via a cartoon TV series. The Cambridge Diet is launched in Europe and Blue Nun white wine with its distinctive dark bottle and blue labelling enjoys its best year for sales since launching in the 1920s. It's also a peak year for Filofax sales and power dressing as yuppie culture takes hold.

# 1984

### The Box of Delights
*The Box of Delights*, BBC1's adaptation of the 1935 fantasy novel for children by John Masefield, broadcasts between 21st November and 24th December. At a cost of £1 million, it is the most expensive children's production the BBC has ever undertaken and wins several awards for its special effects. A landmark moment in children's television drama, *The Box of Delights* quite literally lives up to its name.

### Mousse mania
First developed by L'Oréal in France, hair mousse becomes the favoured product to give your bonce the necessary 'bouff' as hair styles become progressively voluminous. L'Oréal's Studio Line range, with geometric, primary coloured packaging, is aimed at a younger customer; whereas its Freestyle product promises soft, sculpted waves for a sophisticated look.

### Just like that
On 15th April, comedian and magician Tommy Cooper has a heart attack and collapses on stage at Her Majesty's Theatre during a live television broadcast to an audience of 12 million. He dies soon afterwards in Westminster Hospital. The following month, on 28th May, Eric Morecambe also dies after suffering a heart attack following a performance at a charity event at the Roses Theatre in Tewkesbury the day before.

### Tales of the River Bank
Following a successful film in 1983, a stop-animation TV series based on Kenneth Grahame's *Wind in the Willows* begins on ITV on 27th April. Produced by the Manchester-based Cosgrove Hall, already with well-established successes such as *Danger Mouse, Chorlton and the Wheelies* and *Jamie and the Magic Torch*, the *Wind in the Willows* characters are voiced by British acting's finest including Peter Sallis as Ratty, David Jason as Mr Toad and the recently knighted Sir Michael Hordern as Badger.

### Pranks a lot
*Game for a Laugh* first appeared on screens in 1981, dreamt up by ITV as a light entertainment rival to BBC1's *The Generation Game*. Hosted by a quartet of presenters perched on high stools, Henry Kelly, Matthew Kelly, Sarah Kennedy and Jeremy Beadle offer a mixed buffet of practical jokes, candid camera-style 'gotcha' moments and some of Britain's most bizarre eccentrics. The series continues until 1985 and on 25th August this year, a *GFAL* special 'Best of' programme is aired.

# 1984

## 'Listen very carefully, I shall zay this only once'

René Artois is a French café owner, who simply wants a quiet life, but what with his nagging wife, complicated affairs with his waitresses, his involvement with the French resistance, the permanently suspicious occupying Nazis, a policeman prone to malapropisms ('Good moaning'), some stranded British airmen and the whereabouts of a painting of 'The Fallen Madonna with the Big Boobies', there is never a dull moment in 'Allo 'Allo, which begins on BBC1 on 7th September. 'Allo 'Allo is farcical fun, awash with exaggerated accents, national stereotypes and catchphrases. It runs for nine series and eighty-five episodes until 1992.

## A new old Bill

The uniformed officers and detectives of Sun Hill police station make their debut on ITV on 16th October following a successful one-off 1983 drama called *Woodentop*. *The Bill* remains on screens for the next 26 years, the UK's longest-running police drama.

## Spitting Image

British satire is alive and well and finds a new outlet in the form of puppetry when *Spitting Image* first broadcasts on ITV on 26th February. Lampooning politicians, the royal family and various public figures and celebrities, *Spitting Image* puppets includes Margaret Thatcher as a cigar-smoking tyrant in a pin-striped suit, a gin-swilling Queen Mother and a bumbling Ronald Reagan, the nuclear button unnervingly close to his bedside.

## Body conscious

The Body Shop, originally a single shop founded by Anita Roddick in Brighton in 1976, has rolled out across the country by the mid-1980s, tempting shoppers with a whole new experience in beauty retail. The environmentally friendly products and the company's ethical practices are part of the appeal, but the shops are an Aladdin's Cave of novel smells and magical potions, with glass pipettes inviting us to sniff the various perfume oils and bottles bearing the brand's distinctive green labels. Fruit glycerine soaps, bath pearls, Japanese washing grains, cucumber cleansing milk, White Musk and Dewberry are just some of the tempting products concocted by this revolutionary retailer.

## Gremlins and Ghosties

Comedy, horror, action, and special effects combine in two of this year's biggest movie blockbusters when *Gremlins* and *Ghostbusters* are both released on 7th December. *Gremlins* is given a 15 rating after American parents who had taken small children to see the film in the summer discovered that cute furry Gizmo actually spawns a marauding bunch of reptilian imps who go on a gruesome murder spree. *Ghostbusters* (given a PG rating) has the odd terrifying moment too but it's all very tongue-in-cheek and carried along by Ray Parker Jr.'s bouncing soundtrack. Who you gonna call?

# 1984

**This is Spinal Tap**
Mocumentary rockumentary *This is Spinal Tap* follows the rise and rapid descent (mostly the latter) of the English metal band Spinal Tap, whose past members of whom have perished in the most ludicrous circumstances, as these rock losers try to tour their latest album, *Smell the Glove*, around the US to a rapidly diminishing fanbase. Treading a genius line between subtlety and stupidity, *This is Spinal Tap* sets the standard for all future on-screen spoofs, in time becomes nothing short of a cult sensation.

**Mini-series addicts**
British viewers can't get enough of American mini-series and this year sees a TV blockbuster based on a literary bonkbuster. Richard Chamberlain is sexy priest Father Ralph and Rachel Ward is Meggie in *The Thorn Birds*, based on Colleen McCullough's sprawling tale of forbidden love.

**Nineteen-eighty-score**
George Orwell's dystopian vision *1984* is ably transferred to the big screen by writer and director Michael Radford, with John Hurt as Winston Smith and Richard Burton playing O'Brien, his last screen role. The film is overshadowed by a row over the soundtrack. Radford wants a classical score. However, Virgin Films, who have provided finance for the movie, insist on a score of pop electronica by Eurythmics and release an album which includes the band's top 10 hit *Sex Crime* (1984).

***Crackerjack* the last broadcast**
*Crackerjack* has been a stalwart of the BBC's children's programming since 1955, during which time it has been hosted by Eamonn Andrews, Leslie Crowther, Michael Aspel, Ed 'Stewpot' Stewart and Stu 'Crush a Grape' Francis. It blends comedy sketches and music acts with the long-running 'Double or Drop', a quiz where kids have to keep a grip on a mounting pile of prizes, as well as cabbages given for wrong answers.

**United Colours of Benetton**
Oliviero Toscani, creative director of Benetton, photographs the first multiracial advertisement for the clothing brand, which is at the height of its desirability. As the decade progresses, the provocative nature of the Italian brand's campaigns continues to be a talking point.

# MUSIC

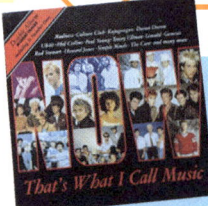

**The time is Now**
*17th January 1984* At No. 1 in the album chart is the very first compilation album in the hugely popular *Now That's What I Call Music* series. It comprises a whopping total of 30 current hits and is heavily promoted by television advertising. The series runs to 116 individual releases and lasts for four decades.

# 1984

### Elton marries
*14th February 1984* Elton John bemuses friends, fans and the gay community by marrying recording engineer Renate Blauel. The couple divorce four years later.

### Marvin shot dead
*1st April 1984* Now living at his parents' home in Los Angeles because they fear he is suicidal, Marvin Gaye is shot dead by his father during a violent family row. Marvin Gaye Sr receives five years for voluntary manslaughter.

### Frankie say…
*13th January 1984* Dominating 1984 are Liverpool club band Frankie Goes to Hollywood. They're a phenomenon through the brilliance of record label ZTT's promotion campaign, not to mention those iconic 'Frankie say' T-shirts. They court controversy from the start: *Relax*, backed by a video that is famously banned by the BBC yet still stays at No. 1 for nine weeks and on the chart for almost the whole year. The nuclear war-themed *Two Tribes* has a spoken section advising what to do in the event of an attack. From here, however, it is all downhill, as the US largely ignores them and MTV won't touch their videos.

### Starlight Express
*Starlight Express*, the train engine musical with music by Andrew Lloyd Webber and lyrics by Richard Stilgoe, opens at the Victoria Palace Theatre on 27th March. Arlene Phillips choreographs the cast who perform entirely on roller skates.

### George in a whisper
Youth unemployment is rising and, for some, now is the time to form a band and turn being on the dole to productive use. That's the idea behind Wham! - best pals George Michael and Andrew Ridgley - and it's the philosophy behind *Wham Rap* that launches the boys in 1982. Two years on, they're ruling the pop roost with such hymns to hedonism as *Wake Me Up Before You Go-Go* and *Club Tropicana*. But the ambitious George surprises all and sundry with *Careless Whisper*, a cutting, mature break-up ballad that's full of self-recrimination and regret. Released under his own name rather than Wham!, it's one of the records of the decade.

### All hail Madonna
*27th January 1984* Is the UK ready for Madonna? A singer-dancer from Detroit with a brilliant grasp of look, fashion and choreography, she makes an arousing *Top of the Pops* debut with *Holiday*. Back in the US she films *Desperately Seeking Susan*, marries actor Sean Penn and closes the year with the image-defining *Like a Virgin*, produced by Nile Rodgers.

# 1984

### Tina is back
No comeback is more deserved than Tina Turner's. She left husband Ike in 1978 after over a decade of abuse and has spent much of her time since playing nostalgia shows. Asked to guest on records by Sheffield electro band Heaven 17 and boosted by David Bowie's verbal support, she re-launches her career in astonishing style with the UK-made *Private Dancer* album and singles *Let's Stay Together* and *What's Love Got to Do with It*.

### Prince of sales
*7th July 1984* Prince Rogers Nelson, known to all as Prince, is an icon in the US but has been awaiting a UK breakthrough for years. Now it comes via the rock-soul hybrid *When Doves Cry* from his semi-autobiographical movie *Purple Rain*, the soundtrack of which sells over 20 million albums and sits atop the US chart for 24 weeks. He writes, produces and plays every instrument on the track but - curiously for a dance record, and in typically perverse Prince fashion - he omits a bassline.

## MY FIRST 18 YEARS
## TOP 10 — 1984

1. **Careless Whisper** *George Michael*
2. **Radio Gaga** *Queen*
3. **Girls Just Wanna Have Fun** *Cyndi Lauper*
4. **White Lines** *Grandmaster Flash & Mel Melle*
5. **I Feel for You** *Chaka Khan*
6. **Smalltown Boy** *Bronski Beat*
7. **Nightshift** *The Commodores*
8. **Move Closer** *Phyllis Nelson*
9. **Last Christmas** *Wham!*
10. **Let's Stay Together** *Tina Turner*

Open | Search | Scan

### Band Aid
*25th November 1984* Following a distressing BBC TV news report about the famine in Ethiopia, Bob Geldof of the Boomtown Rats has an idea. He calls Midge Ure of Ultravox and together they write a song, *Do They Know It's Christmas*, to raise money for relief charities. They call on all the music stars they know to join them for the recording at Trevor Horn's studio - and dutifully, early on a Sunday morning, most of the biggest names in UK pop music turn up including George Michael, Paul Young, Sting, Status Quo, Spandau Ballet, Duran Duran, Bananarama, Bono and - hotfooting it late from New York on Concorde - Boy George. The record is pressed and on sale within ten days and by mid-December it's at No. 1. By the time Christmas 1985 rolls around, Band Aid's single will have raised £8 million and inspired a US counterpart, *We Are the World*, and the most famous concert in music history - Live Aid.

# 1985

## MY FIRST 18 YEARS

## SPORT

**Everton denied treble**
18th May 1985 Manchester United beat Everton 1-0 at Wembley to win the FA Cup, denying Everton 'the Treble'. Having already secured victory in the Football League for the first time in fifteen years, Everton's hopes of a historic treble had been raised after their victory in the European Cup Winners' Cup just three days before the Wembley final.

**Heysel Stadium disaster**
29th May 1985 39 football fans are killed, and hundreds injured, as Juventus beat Liverpool in the European Cup. The victims are mostly Juventus fans who get crushed against a wall which then collapses, whilst fleeing a confrontation with Liverpool fans. An increasing culture of football hooliganism is blamed, and both the FA and UEFA impose bans on English teams playing in Europe. seventeen Liverpool fans are found guilty of manslaughter.

**Becker wins Wimbledon**
7th July 1985 Unseeded seventeen-year-old Boris Becker stuns the tennis world by beating Kevin Curren to become Wimbledon champion. It is the first time a player from Germany has won the championship, and Becker soon becomes an iconic figure in tennis, going on to win 64 titles. The women's event is won for the sixth time by Martina Navratilova in her fourth consecutive Wimbledon final.

**Davis vs Taylor**
27-28th April 1985 Steve Davis and Dennis Taylor meet in the World Snooker Championship Final, in what is considered by many to be the greatest snooker match of all time. With Davis having led for most of the sessions, the Championship comes down to the potting of the final black ball. Both players miss the shot several times before Taylor pulls off a surprise victory. The match is often credited with reviving the sport in the 80s and 90s.

**JAN 1985**
Vodafone launch the first UK mobile phone network.

**9 FEB 1985**
Madonna releases album *Like a Virgin*.

**3 MAR 1985**
UK Miner's Strike ends after a year of industrial action and violent clashes.

# 1985

### England regain ashes
*2nd September 1985* The Australian cricket team's six-Test tour of England is won by the hosts in the final Test. England are victorious after a more than 350-run batting partnership between Graham Gooch and David Gower, which sees them win the final Test by 94 runs and an innings.

### Newry mortar attack
*28 February 1985* A Royal Ulster Constabulary police station in Newry, County Down, is struck by mortar shells fired by the Provisional IRA; nine officers aged 19-41 are killed. Over 30 people are injured, including civilians, and the day is dubbed 'Bloody Thursday' by the British press.

## DOMESTIC NEWS

### Bradford City Stadium fire
*11th May 1985* Horror unfurls at a Third Division football match between Bradford City and Lincoln City when a fire starts in the main stand. Multiple fire hazards within the stadium, combined with windy weather, mean the whole stand is engulfed in less than four minutes, claiming the lives of 56 fans, and injuring over 260 more. Dramatic photos of the fire transfix a grieving nation, and calls are made for changes to safety regulations when it is revealed that exits were padlocked, barring escape routes.

### Sinclair launches C5
*10th January 1985* Sir Clive Sinclair launches his iconic but short-lived Sinclair C5, an electrified, one-person tricycle able to travel 20 miles before it needs a charge. Sinclair hopes the C5 will prove a popular mode of transport and replace petrol engines in the future, but sadly, despite proving a lot of fun, the product sells only 17,000 units and ceases production in August.

### Red telephone boxes
*17th January 1985* The newly privatised British Telecom announce that they will phase out their iconic red telephone boxes. A huge campaign is launched to save them, but BT insist that they are rarely used and are expensive to clean and maintain. In response many local authorities give their phone boxes protected status, and over 2,000 are listed.

## 11 APR 1985
An eighteen-month-old baby becomes the youngest person in the UK to die in the AIDS epidemic.

## 22 MAY 1985
James Bond film, *A View to a Kill* permieres, it's the last to star Roger Moore.

## 23 JUN 1985
An Air India Boeing 747 disappears off the Irish coast after a bomb detonates killing all 325 people onboard.

# 1985

### Hole in the ozone
*16th May 1985* Three scientists associated with the British Antarctic Survey, Joe Farman, Brian Gardiner and Jonathan Shanklin, discover a hole in the planet's ozone layer over Antarctica. Their research suggests that a group of chemicals known as chlorofluorocarbons are to blame.

### White House Farm murders
*7th August 1985* Grandparents Nevill and June Bamber, their daughter Sheila, and her six-year-old twin children are found shot dead in their home in a killing that horrifies the country. The investigation soon focuses on the Bambers' other child, Jeremy, who had claimed to be away from home at the time. Jeremy is found guilty of murder and sentenced to life in prison.

### Manchester air disaster
*22nd August 1985* 55 people are killed when a British Airtours flight from Manchester to Corfu suffers damage to an engine and abandons take off. The accident causes a fire in one of the plane's underwing fuel tanks, and issues with the plane's emergency exits mean that only 80 of the 135 people on board make it off safely.

### Broadwater Farm riot
*6th October 1985* The death of a 49-year-old black woman, Cynthia Jarrett, who dies of heart failure during a police search, leads to a riot on the Broadwater Farm council estate in Tottenham. With tensions already enflamed following the Brixton riots a few days before, the violence leads to the murder of PC Keith Blakelock, who trips and falls whilst attempting to protect the London Fire Brigade from attack. He is set upon by a crowd armed with knives and other weapons.

### Comic Relief launched
*25th December 1985* Comedians Richard Curtis and Sir Lenny Henry found charity Comic Relief in response to the Ethiopian famine. Whilst Live Aid and Band Aid are the talk of the summer, Comic Relief proves to have much more longevity as it begins a biennial fundraising event, the first of which takes place in 1986. Becoming enormously popular for showing famous people doing silly things, the event becomes 'Red Nose Day' in 1988.

### Titanic located
*1st September 1985* The wreck of famous ocean liner the RMS *Titanic* is discovered by a joint French and American expedition, 3,700 metres below the surface of the North Atlantic. A few days later, the explorers take the very first photographs and footage of the wreck, showing it in two pieces rather than intact as had previously been believed.

---

**6 JUL 1985**
At Wimbledon, Martina Navratilova beats Chris Evert in 3 sets in the women's singles final.

**22 AUG 1985**
A terrible month for air travel sees three disasters across the globe claim the lives of 711 people.

**19 SEP 1985**
A magnitude 8 earthquake strikes Mexico City, killing over 5000 people.

# 1985

## ROYALTY & POLITICS

**Queen tours Caribbean**
*9th October 1985* The Queen embarks on a royal tour of the Caribbean. Flying in to Belize, she will spend almost a month on board the Royal Yacht *Britannia* with Prince Philip, as they visit Belize, Bermuda, the Bahamas, St Kitts and Nevis, Dominica, St Lucia, St Vincent and the Grenadines, Grenada and Trinidad.

**First black council leader**
*30th April 1985* The country gains its first black council leader, when Bernie Grant is elected leader of Haringey Council in London. Born in Guyana, he is a member of the Labour Party, and later becomes MP for Tottenham.

**Anglo-Irish agreement signed**
*15th November 1985* Prime Minister Margaret Thatcher and Irish Taoiseach Garret FitzGerald sign the Anglo-Irish Agreement at Hillsborough Castle. The agreement gives the Irish government an advisory role in Northern Ireland in a move that it is hoped will lessen the violence of the Troubles.

## FOREIGN NEWS

**Angel of Death**
*June 6 1985* The skeleton of Josef Mengele turns up in a grave near São Paulo in Brazil, proof that the 'Angel of Death' is no longer alive. Mengele is responsible for the deaths of hundreds of thousands of Jews in the Auschwitz concentration camp during World War II.

**DO YOU REMEMBER THIS?**

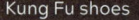

Kung Fu shoes

---

**9 OCT 1985**
Strawberry Fields memorial to John Lennon is revealed in Central Park, NYC.

**21 NOV 1985**
Soviet Leader Mikhail Gorbachev and US President Ronald Reagan hold productive meetings in Geneva in what Reagan calls a 'fresh start'.

**9 DEC 1985**
Argentinian Junta leaders Jorge Videla and Emilio Massera are sentenced to life imprisonment.

# 1985

## Apostle of peace
*April 7 1985* The new leader of the Russian Communist Party, Mikhail Gorbachev, announces a unilateral moratorium on the deployment of the SS-20 medium-range missiles in Europe, valid until the end of November. Gorbachev indicates that he is looking for peace. With a five-year plan, he hopes to save the Soviet Union, which is in decline due to a very expensive war in Afghanistan and economic malaise. 'Uskorenie' (accelerated economic development), 'perestroika' (thorough reforms), and 'glasnost' (openness and transparency) are the main lines of his policy.

## Schengen
*June 14 1985* On a boat on the Moselle near the Luxembourg village of Schengen, the heads of government of the Benelux nations, West Germany and France agree that border controls between those countries will gradually disappear. This creates a 'Schengen area' without internal border controls on persons and goods.

## Rainbow Warrior
The Greenpeace flagship, the Dutch *Rainbow Warrior*, sails to New Zealand for a demonstration against French nuclear tests. But things don't get that far, because in the port of Auckland, agents of the French intelligence service DGSE commit an attack on the ship with the blessing of French President Mitterrand. The *Rainbow Warrior* is sunk with mines secretly attached to the boat by divers. A Dutch photographer is killed in the attack. 'Opération Satanique' causes a major diplomatic row.

## AIDS wave
*October 2 1985* When American film star Rock Hudson dies of AIDS, his suffering and death make a deep impression. The masses now realize what AIDS is and the damage the disease causes. New statistics show that the number of AIDS patients in Europe has tripled in one year, to 1,126 registered cases.

# ENTERTAINMENT

## We are sailing
*Howard's Way*, a saga of yachts and yuppy types, begins on BBC1 on 1st September. It's a sort of British *Dynasty*, but set on the Hampshire coast instead of Colorado, and with deck shoes and jumpers casually tied round the shoulders instead of sequins and shoulder pads.

# 1985

## Victoria Wood As Seen on TV
The Beeb lures multi-talented comedian Victoria Wood away from ITV, and the result is *Victoria Wood As Seen on TV*, which first airs on BBC2 on 11th January. Wood, who writes all sketches, is given a decent budget, creative freedom and comes up with comedy gold. The show is bursting with what quickly become some of television's finest moments, from spoof soap *Acorn Antiques* to Julie Walters as a doddery waitress in the 'Two Soups' sketch; Wood as Ena Sharples in a 1960s episode of *Coronation Street* grimly predicting the endings of numerous characters, to musical numbers like the uproarious *Ballad of Barry and Freda - Let's Do It* where the line 'Beat me on the bottom with a *Woman's Weekly*' encapsulates her down-to-earth genius.

## No Limits
A programme that combines pop music clips with young presenters roaming the country to share the best bits of the UK's different regions, *No Limits* is the brainchild of Jonathan King, who has been doing much the same thing with his own show *Entertainment USA*. *No Limits* begins on BBC2 on 30th July, presented by Jeremy Legg and Lisa Maxwell, who are later replaced with jokey pair Tony Baker and Jenny Powell.

## The Broom Cupboard
As part of an overhaul of Children's BBC, Phillip Schofield appears from a control desk called 'The Broom Cupboard' on 9th September, where he provides links between programmes with the help of a furry friend called Gordon the Gopher. When Schofield begins presenting Saturday morning show *Going Live!*, Gordon goes with him, and The Broom Cupboard is occupied by Andy Crane and Edd the Duck. Andi Peters and Zoe Ball are two more who cut their presenting teeth in the country's best-known confined space.

## Looking for love
Cilla Black plays cupid as host of ITV's new Saturday night fixture, Blind Date, which begins 30th November. With three possible dates hidden behind a screen, a contestant must decide which one they'd like to go on a date with according to how promising their answers are to three questions. After a round-up from 'Our Graham' (the voice of Graham Skidmore) the pair see each other for the first time as the screen falls back, and then learn whether they're going to the Caribbean or Clacton for their date.

## I'll be back
Ex-body builder Arnold Schwarzenegger's wooden acting and deadpan delivery is just what director James Cameron needs for the cyborg assassin - *The Terminator* - sent from the future to destroy the mother of the boy who will grow up to lead a human resistance against Skynet's machines. Arnie's monotone promise 'I'll be back' proves propitious as *The Terminator* franchise goes on for five sequels.

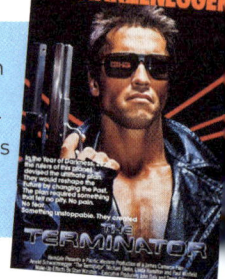

# 1985

### Eastenders

13 million viewers tune in on 19th February to watch the first episode of BBC1's brand new soap, *Eastenders*. Set in the fictional borough of Walford in east London, the residents live in the characterful Albert Square, where, for some reason, London's soaring house prices are never discussed and local boozer the Queen Vic acts as a stage for feuds, punch-ups, scandals, revelations and even murder. The first episode sets the tone for a soap where trouble and strife are rarely far away. *Eastenders*, pitched to compete with ITV's *Coronation Street*, provides drama and characters to equal those of the Street, and soon its tropes and famous lines become part of soap opera lore, whether that's the inevitable black cab, hailed to spirit away departing characters, or Barbara Windsor's Peggy Mitchell screaming, 'Get outta my pub!'

### Back to the Future

In *Back to the Future*, Michael J. Fox stars as Marty McFly, the high school kid who time travels back to 1955 in a bid to keep his parents together so that he can be born. Already a heartthrob thanks to his role in the US sitcom *Family Ties*, *Back to the Future* turns Fox into a movie megastar.

### Girls on Top

Dawn French, Jennifer Saunders, Tracy Ullmann and Ruby Wax are four mismatched flat mates in *Girls on Top*, a female riff on *The Young Ones* format, first shown on ITV on 23rd October. Wax plays to type as a loud, brash American, French is a militant feminist who works at *Spare Cheek* (a skit on *Spare Rib*), Saunders is her doltish school friend, Ullmann a manipulative nymphomaniac, while veteran actress Joan Greenwood plays their eccentric landlady. Ullman departs after the first series to find stardom in the US, and after a second series in 1986, the cast are killed off allowing French and Saunders to tread their own paths, right to the top.

### Levi's 5 'Oh!' 1

A new advertising campaign for Levi's 501, the 'original shrink-to-fit' jeans, has TV viewers looking as stunned as the ladies in the 1950s laundromat who watch in awe as Nick Kamen strips down to his boxers to wash his favourite jeans, to the strains of Marvin Gaye's hit, *I Heard it Through the Grapevine*. The commercial is a sensation; it leads to rocketing sales of 501 jeans. Gaye's song takes to the charts and Kamen, with his demi-god looks, has his own moment of pop stardom.

# 1985

### Cute + cuddly = cash
The cuddly Care Bears are first created by artist Elena Kucharik for American Greetings in 1981. Each one's tummy bears the insignia of a special emotion, and they live in the clouds in the faraway realm of Care-a-lot (aah). *A Care Bears* cartoon series for television and *The Care Bears Movie* this year guarantee the plush toy Care Bears are a money-spinner.

### To the barricades
The Royal Shakespeare Company English-language production of Schönberg and Boublil's musical adaptation of Victor Hugo's novel, *Les Misérables*, opens at the Barbican Centre on 8th October and transfers to the Palace Theatre on 4th December. At the time of writing it is estimated that 132 million around the world have seen *Les Mis*, and it is the second-longest West End show after *The Mousetrap*.

### Brat Pack's *Breakfast Club*
Arguably the ultimate teen flick. *The Breakfast Club* director and producer John Hughes assembles a group of young actors who become part of a set the media dub 'The Brat Pack'. Forced to endure a weekend detention at school in each other's company, a group of teenagers begin the morning as strangers but as they reveal their hopes, fears and frailties, depart united by their shared experience. The film relies largely on sharp dialogue rather than action, and with the talented cast and an 80s soundtrack led by Simple Minds' *Don't You Forget About Me*, it's a surprisingly emotive piece of cinema.

### Rock me Amadeus
Tom Hulce brings some rock-star swagger to the role of the eighteenth century's musical prodigy in the film version of Peter Shaffer's play about Mozart which has its UK theatrical release on 17th January. F. Murray Abraham is the embittered court composer Salieri, whose consuming jealousy of the clownish Mozart's genius sours his entire career. *Amadeus* wins eight Academy Awards including Best Picture.

## MUSIC

### USA for Africa
*28th January 1985* Prompted by the UK Band Aid charity single, dozens of US music stars pool their talents to record an American equivalent – *We Are the World*, written by Michael Jackson and Lionel Richie and released under the name USA for Africa. Performers include Ray Charles, Billy Joel, Bob Dylan, Smokey Robinson, Kenny Rogers, Diana Ross, Tina Turner and Bruce Springsteen. The record raises $50 million for famine relief.

### Red Wedge
*21st March 1985* A spine-tingling moment on *Top of the Pops* as Billy Bragg performs his unequivocally pro-miners and anti-Thatcher song, *Between the Wars*. Billy goes on to form the Labour Party-supporting musicians' collective Red Wedge with Paul Weller and Jimmy Somerville. Gigs and tours follow but, with as many critics on the left as on the right, it is wound up in 1990.

# 1985

### Going digital
*13th May 1985* Led by guitarist brothers Mark and David Knopfler, Dire Straits are trailblazers for the new compact disc era with *Brothers in Arms*, one of the first to be recorded digitally rather than on analogue magnetic tape. It is the first album to sell more via the CD format than on vinyl and includes the self-deprecating *Money for Nothing*.

### Springsteen fever
*3rd July 1985* A month after his marriage to Julianne Phillips in Oregon and in the middle of an exhilarating 156-date world tour to promote his *Born in the USA* album, Bruce Springsteen plays three epic dates at Wembley Stadium. Such is the Springsteen fever overwhelming the UK this summer that his previous six albums all enter the chart on re-release.

### Tipper's crusade
*13th May 1985* Tipper Gore, wife of Senator Al Gore, forms the Parents Music Resource Center (PMRC) with three other 'Washington wives' to combat what they see as excessive reference to sex, violence, drugs and the occult in rock lyrics. Although much derided, they succeed in persuading the music industry to add 'parental advisory' stickers to products deemed likely to cause offence.

### Live Aid
*13th July 1985* With wall-to-wall live television coverage, the momentous Live Aid concert takes place in Wembley Stadium and JFK Stadium in Philadelphia. Thanks to Concorde, Phil Collins performs at both. Status Quo open the London show with *Rockin' All Over the World*, with Queen, the Who, U2, Elton John and David Bowie all following. In Philadelphia, performers include the Beach Boys, the Pretenders, Santana, Neil Young, Duran Duran and a specially re-formed Led Zeppelin, who hate their performance so much they remove it from the official video. The total amount raised by both concerts is estimated at $150 million.

### In Dublin's fair city
*29th June 1985* Currently the top band on the planet thanks to their *The Unforgettable Fire* album, U2 come home to Dublin to play to a 55,000-strong audience at Croke Park. It is their biggest concert in their homeland to date.

### Beatles publishing sold
*6th September 1985* An unamused Paul McCartney discovers that the Northern Songs publishing catalogue containing most of the songs he composed with John Lennon has been sold to Michael Jackson.

# 1985

**Angels and sisters**
*27th July 1985* Eurythmics - the oldest, canniest and most musically interesting of all the UK's many UK electro duos - miss out on Live Aid because of Annie Lennox's throat problems but top the UK chart with *There Must Be An Angel*, featuring Stevie Wonder on harmonica. Three months later they collaborate once more with soul music royalty - Queen of Soul Aretha Franklin - on the anthemic *Sisters Are Doin' It for Themselves*.

## MY FIRST 18 YEARS
## TOP 10 — 1985

1. **Material Girl** Madonna
2. **Dancing in the Street** Mick Jagger & David Bowie
3. **Saving All My Love for You** Whitney Houston
4. **Between the Wars** Billy Bragg
5. **Would I Lie to You** Eurythmics
6. **Nightshift** The Commodores
7. **Frankie** Sister Sledge
8. **Running Up That Hill** Kate Bush
9. **A New England** Kirsty MacColl
10. **Glory Days** Bruce Springsteen

**Norway's year**
*19th October 1985* Dedication pays off in the end. That's the lesson of Norwegian trio A-Ha's *Take On Me*, which has just been released for the third time in two years. Promoted this time by an award winning pencil-drawn animated video, it helps A-ha become the first Norwegian act ever to top the US chart.

**Lionel makes history**
*9th November 1985* Four years after leaving the Commodores (photo), Lionel Richie is now the leading solo act in the US. He moves on from steering the USA for Africa project to create history with *Say You Say Me* from the movie *White Nights*. He is the only composer ever to have written nine No. 1s in nine consecutive years. Now planning his next album and single, *Dancing on the Ceiling*.

PHOTO CREDITS Copyright 2024, TDM Rights BV.
Photos: **A** Mark Leech - Offside - Getty Images / **B** Matthew Ashton - Corbis Sport - Getty Images / **C** Bongarts - Getty Images / **D** Adrian Murrell - Getty Images Europe - Getty Images / **E** David Levenson - Hulton Archive - Getty Images / **F** Keystone - Hulton Archive - Getty Images / **G** Riorita - Getty Images / **H** NOAA Institute for Exploration - University of Rhode Island - / **I** Steve Rapport - Hulton Archive - Getty Images / **J** John Shelley Collection Avalon - Hulton Royals Collection - Getty Images / **K** PA Images - Getty Images / **L** Bryn Colton - Hulton Archive - Getty Images / **M** 3rd Party Agents - Getty Images / **N** Ronald Grant archive - Mary Evans / **O** LWT - Ronald Grant archive - Mary Evans / **P** Mike Lawn - Hulton Archive - Getty Images / **Q** United Archives Hulton - Getty Images / **R** TV Times - Getty Images / **S** AF Archive Universal - Mary Evans / **T** Ronald Grant Archive - Mary Evans / **U** Aaron Rapoport - Corbis Historical - Getty Images / **V** Gary Gershoff - Getty Images / **W** Michaek Ochs Archives - Getty Images / **X** Lester Cohen - Archive Photos - Getty Images / **Y** Aaron Rapoport - Corbis Historical - Getty Images / **Z** Paul Harris - Archive Photos - Getty Images.

# 1986

## MY FIRST 18 YEARS

## SPORT

**Chelsea win Full Members Cup**
*23rd March 1986* Chelsea become the first winners of the new 'Full Members Cup', a competition designed to fill the scheduling gap left by UEFA's ban on English clubs playing in European competitions. The final at Wembley sees an incredible fight back from Manchester City, who at one point are 5-1 down, to set the final score at 5-4 to Chelsea.

**Argentina win World Cup**
*29th June 1986* Argentina secure victory in the 1986 FIFA world cup final in Mexico City, with a 3-2 win against West Germany. Argentinian captain Diego Maradona celebrates the win just a week after breaking English hearts with his famous 'hand of God' goal in their 2-1 defeat of England in the quarter-final.

**Birmingham Superprix**
*24th August 1986* The inaugural Birmingham Superprix kicks off in the city centre, becoming the first motorsport street race to be held in mainland Britain. Part of the Formula 3000 Championship, the race is red flagged when bad weather leads to a crash, with Spanish driver Luis Pérez-Sala taking the win.

**Liverpool victorious**
*5th May 1986* Liverpool beat Chelsea 1-0 to win the First Division title for the 16th time, a new record. Five days later they defeat local rivals Everton 3-1 to win the FA Cup in the first all-Merseyside final.

**More hooliganism**
*8th August 1986* The future of English participation in European football is placed in further doubt when violence breaks out between Manchester United and West Ham fans onboard a ferry to Amsterdam. The clubs are both due to play friendlies in the city, whilst UEFA maintain their ban on English clubs in European competitions for a second season.

### 16 JAN 1986
Police arrest 2 IRA-terrorists in Amsterdam who had escaped from the Maze prison in 1983.

### 17 FEB 1986
Single European Act signed to establish the goal of a single market by 1992.

### 31 MAR 1986
Greater London Council abolished along with several other metropolitan county councils.

# 1986

## DOMESTIC NEWS

**Channel Tunnel planned**
*12th February 1986* France and the United Kingdom sign the Franco-British Channel Fixed Link Treaty to initiate the creation of a Channel Tunnel. The idea of a permanent tunnel connecting the two countries has been around since the early 1800s, but now the idea becomes a reality as the Eurotunnel Group is formed in August to finance and build the project.

**John McCarthy kidnapped**
*17th April 1986* The Lebanon hostage crisis continues as British journalist John McCarthy (left) is kidnapped by Islamic jihadists in Beirut. In retaliation for US airstrikes in Libya, McCarthy is captured by gunmen on his way to the airport and held for over five years.

**Northern Ireland Assembly dissolved**
*24th June 1986* Attempts to restore the devolution of power to Northern Ireland fall apart as the dissolution of the Assembly is ordered by the Secretary of State. Ian Paisley and his Democratic Unionist Party members refuse to leave their seats, leading to ugly scenes as they are dragged out by the Royal Ulster Constabulary.

**New exams launched**
*September 1986* 14-year-olds across Britain begin their new 'GCSE' courses, which replace the old GCE 'O' Levels and CSEs. The first exams will be sat in 1988.

**Babes in the Wood murders**
*9th October 1986* Nine-year-old Nicola Fellows and her friend, ten-year-old Karen Hadaway, are reported missing near Brighton. The following day, their bodies are found in Wild Park. Russell Bishop, a twenty-year-old roofer, is soon arrested and charged, but thanks to errors in the investigation is acquitted, and will not be brought to justice until 2018.

**M25 opens**
*29th October 1986* The London Orbital Motorway is finally completed 11 years after the first section opened in 1975. At almost 120 miles long, it opens as the longest ring road in Europe.

**14 APR 1986**
Desmond Tutu elected Archbishop of Cape Town, South Africa.

**17 MAY 1986**
*Chicken Song* by Spitting Image becomes number one in the UK Singles Chart.

**8 JUN 1986**
Alleged Nazi Kurt Waldheim elected President of Austria.

# 1986

### Childline opens
**30th October 1986** A new telephone counselling service for children and young people launches in the UK. Childline is open 24 hours a day, 365 days a year, and is launched by Esther Rantzen at the BBC, who hopes it will help to intervene and save the lives of children in danger across the country.

### British gas privatised
**8th December 1986** Following the 'If you see Sid... tell him!' advertising campaign, 4 million people apply for shares of British Gas as it is floated on the stock exchange. The initial share offering gives the company a valuation of around £9 billion.

## ROYALTY & POLITICS

### Shetland Chinook crash
**6th November 1986** A Chinook helicopter crashes into the ocean on the approach to Sumburgh Airport on the Shetland Islands. The helicopter is acting as a shuttle, carrying workers from the nearby Brent Oilfield back to the island, and comes down with 47 people on board, only two of whom survive.

### The Westland affair
**9th January 1986** Two cabinet ministers resign over the so-called 'Westland Affair' in a debacle that comes close to unseating the Prime Minister. In a cabinet disagreement over the future of Westland Helicopters, Secretary of State for Defence Michael Heseltine resigns after claiming Margaret Thatcher will not allow a full discussion of the issue at cabinet. Trade and Industry Secretary Leon Brittan follows when it is revealed he leaked confidential letters to the press.

### AIDS crisis campaign
**21st November 1986** Amid a rising death toll and estimates that as many as 30,000 people may be infected across the country, the government launches a £20 million campaign to raise awareness of the dangers of HIV, known as the 'Don't Die of Ignorance' campaign.

### Queen hit by eggs
**February 1986** Queen Elizabeth is struck by an egg whilst touring in New Zealand. The Queen and Prince Philip are targeted by two assailants protesting an 1840 treaty made between the British Crown and New Zealand Maoris. The Queen is unharmed, and later jokes that she 'prefers her New Zealand eggs for breakfast'. She is clearly not deterred from public duty, as later in the year she becomes the first British monarch to tour China.

### UNESCO designates UK sites
**November 1986** The UK gains its first UNESCO World Heritage Sites, as places including Stonehenge, Durham Cathedral, Ironbridge Gorge and Giant's Causeway are officially recognised for their cultural significance.

---

**1 JUL 1986**
Unemployment hits a post-war high of 3,280,106 meaning almost 15% of the workforce are affected.

**19 AUG 1986**
National Bus Company privatised as Devon General bought out by management.

**8 SEP 1986**
The Oprah Winfrey Show is first broadcast in the US.

# 1986

**Prince Andrew marries**
*23th July 1986* The Queen's third child, Prince Andrew, marries Sarah Ferguson at Westminster Abbey. In honour of the event, the Queen makes the new couple the Duke and Duchess of York.

**Archer resigns**
*26th October 1986* Deputy Chairman of the Conservative Party Jeffrey Archer resigns over a *News of the World* story that claims he paid a prostitute £2,000 to leave the country.

Pogo Ball

 **FOREIGN NEWS**

**Challenger disaster**
*28th January 1986* Immediately after the launch of the Challenger space shuttle, things go horribly wrong. A sealing ring on a thruster malfunctions and gas and fuel begin to leak. After 73 seconds, the Challenger turns into a huge fireball. One of the seven-person crew is 37-year-old teacher Christa McAuliffe, who Americans had already taken to their hearts. The launch is recorded and broadcast on television with a delay. The crew compartment, human remains and other fragments from the shuttle are recovered during a three-month recovery operation. The space shuttle programme is suspended for three years.

**People power**
*25th February 1986* The twenty-year dictatorship of President Ferdinand Marcos of the Philippines ends when he is forced into exile by what is described as a 'people power' revolution and, crucially, the removal of US support. Corazon Aquino, widow of the murdered opposition leader, becomes President.

**1 OCT 1986**
'Big Bang' Day in London Stock Exchange as computerisation is introduced and foreign companies are welcomed.

**22 NOV 1986**
Mike Tyson becomes youngest heavyweight champion of the world at 20 years old.

**9 DEC 1986**
First case of bovine spongiform encephalopathy is diagnosed British cattle as the BSE crisis unfolds.

# 1986

### Iran-Contra affair
*21st November 1986* On this day, as investigations into the Iran-Contra affair continue, Lieutenant Colonel Oliver North and his secretary begin shredding documents implicating them in selling weapons to Iran and using the proceeds to fund the Contra rebels in Nicaragua. Although Iran was and remains under an arms embargo, it emerges that a secret deal to sell arms was made to try to facilitate the release of US hostages then held in Lebanon. President Reagan denies all knowledge.

### Olof Palme
*28th February 1986* Swedish Prime Minister Olof Palme and his wife are shot dead in the street in central Stockholm after a visit to the cinema. The murder of a democratically elected head of government is a huge shock in normally peaceful Sweden and far beyond.

## ENTERTAINMENT

### The Color Purple
Stephen Spielberg takes a step away from fantasy and sci-fi to direct the film version of Alice Walker's book *The Color Purple*, with newcomer Whoopi Goldberg revelatory as a wonderfully expressive Celie, and Oprah Winfrey making her screen debut as Sofia. UK audiences get to see it on 11th July.

### Chernobyl burns
*26th April 1986* The worst nuclear disaster in history unfolds. Due to human error during a safety test, explosions occur in nuclear reactor 4 of the Chernobyl nuclear power plant in Ukraine, then part of the Soviet Union. The first explosion blows away the 2,000-ton lid of the reactor vessel. The graphite blocks catch fire and the power plant continues to burn for ten days. The fire releases enormous amounts of radioactive materials into the atmosphere. Communication about the catastrophe from the Soviet authorities is slow. More than 100,000 residents from the immediate area are evacuated. Chernobyl and the larger Pripyat turn into ghost towns. The radioactive cloud spreads rapidly across Europe and Asia. Thousands of kilometres away, radioactive particles flutter down. To prevent further spread of radioactive materials, a gigantic concrete sarcophagus is built around the nuclear reactor in Chernobyl. Although the first explosion kills just 31, thousands to tens of thousands of people die due to the effects of radioactive radiation, mainly from cancer.

# 1986

## Neighbours
The inhabitants of Ramsay Street, Erinsborough are introduced to British viewers at 1:25pm on 27th October, as part of its new daytime scheduling. *Neighbours* tackles the same themes as other soaps but it has the exotic appeal of being Down Under in houses and with weather less familiar to British viewers. It's also populated by a clutch of teenage characters who soon gain thousands of British fans. The burgeoning romance of Scott and Charlene, played by Jason Donovan and Kylie Minogue, sees the show enjoy peak viewing figures when their wedding takes place in 1988, with both actors using their characters' relationship as a platform for their music career. Australia seems to be having a moment with the Poms, as film comedy *Crocodile Dundee*, starring Paul Hogan, is also released this year, on 12th December.

## Top Gun
'I feel the need, the need for speed!' Thrilling fighter jet sequences, Harley Davidsons, jukebox crooning, beach volleyball and a locker room bristling with testosterone: Tony Scott's *Top Gun* delivers a glossy, action-packed adrenalin rush which catapults Tom Cruise as 'Maverick' into Hollywood's super-league. A thundering soundtrack which includes Kenny Loggins' *Danger Zone* keeps up the pace and Berlin's *Take My Breath Away* spends four weeks at No.1 after the film's UK release on 3rd October.

## Bobby Ewing's soapy return
The makers of *Dallas* like nothing better than leaving its viewers teetering on the edge of a cliffhanger at the end of each season, and season 9 is no exception when Pam finds husband Bobby lathering himself in the shower. Barely cliffhanger material you might think, except Bobby was killed off at the end of season 8. The entirely logical explanation for Bobby's resurrection, revealed in season 10, is that Pam had dreamt the entire past 31 episodes.

## Out of Africa
'I had a farm in Africa'. So begin Karen Blixen's memoirs, translated to the screen by Sydney Pollack in a sweeping romance in which the majestic Kenyan countryside shares top billing with Meryl Streep as Blixen, and Robert Redford as the dashing adventurer, Denys Finch-Hatton, into whose arms she falls. *Out of Africa* is one of those stately, heart-swelling, must-see movies. Not only does it scoop eight Academy Awards but it leaves many wishing they too could have their hair washed by Robert Redford!

# 1986

## Merchant Ivory - a very British film partnership
Released in the UK on 18th April, *A Room with a View* cements the reputation of producer-director team Ismail Merchant and James Ivory for gorgeous, literary period films. It also thrusts Helena Bonham-Carter into the spotlight as she plays Lucy Honeychurch, the young woman whose romantic awakening takes place against picturesque Tuscan scenery. A sterling British cast including Maggie Smith, Denholm Elliott, Julian Sands and Daniel Day-Lewis lend admirable support.

## Racy *Riders*
*Riders* by Jilly Cooper, is published this year, the first book in the author's steamy Rutshire Chronicles; a racy page-turner about the rivalries and love affairs in the world of competitive showjumping.

## Lovejoy
Ian McShane is lovable rogue *Lovejoy*, an antiques dealer and part-time detective with an eye for a bargain as he tootles around the pretty Essex and Suffolk countryside wheeling and dealing. The first series begins on 10th January.

## I have a cunning plan
The first series of *Blackadder*, set in the fifteenth century, had enjoyed modest success but the arrival of his descendant, Edmund Blackadder, a suave and shrewd Elizabethan courtier, in *Blackadder II* on 9th January, makes this historical comedy, a nationwide favourite. Rowan Atkinson's wily Edmund is both supported and hampered by his loyal, turnip-eating servant Baldrick whose cunning plans to get his master out of his latest scrape are invariably rejected. The rest of the cast provide brilliant Tudor caricatures.

## Bread
The first episode of *Bread* airs on BBC1 on 1st May and introduces viewers to the Boswells, a close-knit, working-class family presided over by matriarch and staunch Catholic Nelly 'Ma' Boswell, whose disgust at her husband's mistress 'Lilo' Lill leads to her frequently spitting the line, 'She is a tart!'. Nelly's brood of four sons and a daughter, through back handers, dodgy deals and dole diddling keep the family finances afloat with the day's 'bread' (money) donated to a chicken-shaped pot every episode under the watchful eye of their indomitable mother.

## The Singing Detective
Dennis Potter's *The Singing Detective* starring Michael Gambon as the hospitalised detective Philip Marlow, reminiscing about his childhood and unravelling mysteries in his head, airs on BBC1 on 16th November. Potter suffered from the same painful skin disease as his character and was sometimes forced to write with his pen tied to his wrist, as Philip does in the final episode.

# 1986

## Casualty rates
*Casualty* begins on BBC1 on 6th September, a hospital drama set in the accident and emergency department of Holby City Hospital, in a fictional area of Bristol. Written by Jeremy Brock and Paul Unwin, who based the storylines on observations they had personally made in NHS hospitals, the show is initially planned to run for fifteen episodes. Instead, its popularity leads to it becoming a more permanent fixture and *Casualty* goes on to become the longest-running medical drama in the world.

## Fashion fix
Style mavens get a weekly fashion fix with the launch of BBC1's *The Clothes Show* on 13th October. Presented by designer Jeff Banks, who developed the idea out of the fashion slot he had on *Pebble Mill at One*, his co-host is Selina Scott, and they are later joined by fashion journalist and cool cat Caryn Franklin. Together they bring news from the catwalks, show viewers how to create budget looks at home, investigate great arbiters of style, and run a nationwide model competition.

## Trouble and strife
Tensions are high in the Queen Vic on 16th October as two of *Eastenders*' most popular characters, Den and Angie Watts (Leslie Grantham and Anita Dobson) have an entire half hour devoted to their marriage breakdown and a surprising denouement. Den wants a divorce, and to leave Walford behind to make a new life with his mistress Jan. Angie tries to distract him and reveals to Den that she has only six months to live, obliging him to promise to stay with her.

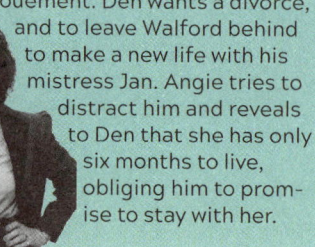

## The video age
*The Chart Show* begins on Channel 4 on 11th April, launching its first episode with the music video *What You Need* by INXS. Created to rival *Top of the Pops*, but without any cheesy DJ presenters, *The Chart Show* has in fact no presenters at all.

## The Golden Girls
*The Golden Girls* comes to Britain this year, with the first episode broadcast on Channel 4 on 1st August. The chemistry between Bea Arthur as Dorothy, Betty White as Rose, Rue McClanahan's Southern belle Blanche and Estelle Getty as Dorothy's feisty, wise-cracking mother is irresistible as the four characters rub along together in the Florida house they share.

 **MUSIC**

## West End boys
*11th January 1986* Just as the electro pop era appear to be passing, another solemn-looking pair of Brits in long coats appears. The Pet Shop Boys offer a new slant, however. A former journalist with *Smash Hits*, Neil Tennant and synth-playing partner Chris Lowe write smartly rhymed lyrics to disco rhythms and deliver them in a passionless, almost bored style. With its echoes of Grandmaster Flash and T. S. Eliot's *The Waste Land*, *West End Girls* is the first No. 1 of 1986 and announces a duo who will still be having hits nearly 40 years later.

# 1986

### Europe rocks
*6th December 1986* With an apocalyptic lyric partly inspired by David Bowie's *Space Oddity*, The Final Countdown tops the UK chart for two weeks for Swedish hard rock band Europe.

### Sister in control
*4th February 1986* Working with producer-writers Jimmy Jam and Terry Lewis, Janet Jackson emerges from brother Michael's shadow with break-through album *Control* and single *What Have You Done for Me Lately*. In a year when Michael releases no new material, Janet fills the vacuum with her own pot-pourri of funk, soul and Paula Abdul-directed choreography.

### Running the world
*June 1986* Having had to turn down an invitation to play Live Aid, UK synth duo Tears for Fears back the next Ethiopian relief fund raiser, Sport Aid, by re-recording their BRIT Award-winning *Everybody Wants to Rule the World* as *Everybody Wants to Run the World*. The song was originally featured on the album *Songs from the Big Chair*, which achieved ten million sales in 1985 and established the band as a major force in the US.

### *Chain Reaction*
*8th March 1986* After Barbra Streisand and Dionne Warwick, newly married Diana Ross is the latest music diva to benefit from the hit writing skills of Barry, Robin and Maurice Gibb. A homage to her Motown past, *Chain Reaction* tops the UK and most overseas charts but flops completely in the US.

### Arise, Sir Bob
*10th June 1986* Dublin-born Bob Geldof receives an honorary British knighthood for his work raising money for famine relief in Ethiopia.

### Last gigs
*9th August 1986* At the end of a tour promoting the *A Kind of Magic* album and single, Queen play what will turn out to be their last concert with Freddie Mercury as lead singer, at Knebworth Park in Hertfordshire. A number of other leading bands play their last concerts this year – pending reunions, of course – including Madness, Boomtown Rats, Weather Report, Wham! and the Clash, while the Smiths drift inexorably towards disbandment.

### Graceland controversy
*25th August 1986* Paul Simon's *Graceland* album is released to a barrage of criticism over his decision to record in apartheid-gripped South Africa. Simon counters by pointing out his employment of and close collaboration with black musicians who wouldn't otherwise be heard anywhere in the West.

# 1986

### Hip hop hybrid
New York hip hop kings Run-DMC didn't plan to smash genre boundaries with their take on a 1975 Aerosmith track, *Walk This Way*. With the latter's Steve Perry repeating the original's irresistible guitar riff, they create an eye-opening hybrid of rap and metal that defies US radio conventions and leads rock music into a whole new direction.

### Bangles go manic
California's all-female Bangles become the UK's favourite American band of 1986 with the 1960s-styled guitar-and-harmonies hits *Manic Monday* (written by Prince), *Going Down to Liverpool* and *Walk Like an Egyptian*.

### Blue collar rock
Maybe it's the Springsteen influence but 'blue collar rock' - rugged no-nonsense rock'n'roll aimed at a working-class audience - is in many ways the sound of 1986. Setting the standard is New Jersey boy Jon Bon Jovi and his band, whose *Slippery When Wet* album tops the US listings. The highlight is a blue collar anthem to cap them all - *Livin' on a Prayer*.

## MY FIRST 18 YEARS
## TOP 10  1986

1. **The Way it Is** Bruce Hornsby and the Range
2. **Sledgehammer** Peter Gabriel
3. **Caravan of Love** The Housemartins
4. **Addicted to Love** Robert Palmer
5. **Holding Back the Years** Simply Red
6. **Papa Don't Preach** Madonna
7. **Take My Breath Away** Berlin
8. **White Wedding** Billy Idol
9. **Kiss** Prince
10. **Word Up** Cameo

### Hull of a band
*20th December 1986* They look gawky, dance like dads at a disco and play up their roots in unfashionable Hull. But for all the Housemartins' comic veneer, *Happy Hour* delivers a strong pro-union and anti-Murdoch message. During the year-long miners' strike, Paul Heaton and friends played more gigs for miners' families than any other band in the country. A captivating album cheekily titled *London O Hull 4* is followed by an unexpected Christmas No. 1 - a lovely acapella version of the Isley Brothers' *Caravan of Love*.

# 1987

## MY FIRST 18 YEARS

## SPORT

### Football firsts
1987 sees some footballing firsts, as Aldershot FC become the first team to win promotion through the new playoff system, Arsenal win the League Cup for the first time, and Coventry become first-time winners of the FA Cup.

### First Rugby World Cup
*22nd May 1987* The very first Rugby World Cup kicks off in New Zealand with a home side victory over Italy. 16 nations battle it out, with Wales proving the best performing home nation, securing third place over joint-hosts Australia. Favourites New Zealand go on to win the tournament with a 29-9 victory over France as the Webb Ellis Cup is lifted for the first time.

### Great year for British golf
*19th July 1987* Nick Faldo wins the Open Championship by just one stroke, becoming the first Englishman to claim the title since Tony Jacklin in 1969. One week later, Laura Davies, just 23 years old, wins the US Women's Open, having won the British Open the previous year.

### Whitbread gold
*6th September 1987* British athlete Fatima Whitbread puts in a wonderful performance at the World Athletics Championships to win the country's only gold medal with an incredible 76.64 metre throw in the javelin.

### Cricket Cup and controversy
*8th November 1987* England are defeated by Australia in the final of the Cricket World Cup in Calcutta, a disappointment that is followed in December by fractious scenes on the English tour of Pakistan. During the second test, Captain Mike Gatting and umpire Shakoor Rana engage in a foul-mouthed shouting match that is broadcast worldwide. Gatting issues Rana with a written apology.

## DOMESTIC NEWS

### Naji al-Ali shot in London
*22nd July 1987* Shots ring out in London as Palestinian cartoonist Naji al-Ali is attacked outside the offices of Kuwaiti newspaper *al-Qabas*. Famed for his satirical cartoons lampooning politicians across the Middle East, his sharply critical commentaries earned him many enemies, including Yasser Arafat. His murder is still unsolved.

---

**1 JAN 1987**
British Airways is floated on the stock market ahead of its privatisation in February.

**27 FEB 1987**
The General Synod of the Church of England votes for legislation to allow the ordination of women priests.

**24 MAR 1987**
Soul Train Music Awards winners are Janet Jackson and Luther Vandross.

# 1987

### MS *Herald of Free Enterprise*
**6th March 1987** Tragedy strikes as car and passenger ferry the MS *Herald of Free Enterprise* gets into difficulty leaving the harbour of Zeebrugge in Belgium. The bow door of the ship is left open, allowing the ferry to flood with water and capsize, coming to rest on its side. Many stories of bravery emerge following the rescue attempts, but despite most of the 539 passengers and crew on board being rescued safely, 193 passengers lose their lives in the worst British maritime disaster in over 150 years.

### Knightsbridge robbery
**12th July 1987** Two men hold up the Knightsbridge Safe Deposit Centre and steal £60 million in what would prove to be one of the largest robberies in history. The mastermind, Valerio Viccei, is identified by a fingerprint at the scene and, despite having fled the country, is later arrested when he returns to pick up his Ferrari Testarossa.

### Archer wins libel case
**25th July 1987** Former Conservative deputy chairman Jeffrey Archer wins a libel case against the *Daily Star*, and the tabloid is forced to pay him £500,000 in damages. Despite this, he is found guilty of perjury in 2001 after providing a false alibi during the trial.

### The Troubles
The Provisional IRA conduct a number of attacks in 1987, including a bomb at a British Army barracks in Rheindahlen, West Germany, which injures 31. In November, the Enniskillen bombing claims the lives of 12 people at a Remembrance Day service and injures over 60 who had gathered to commemorate the war dead. The IRA themselves suffer their biggest loss of the Troubles in May, when eight members are killed by the SAS in an ambush at Loughgall, County Antrim, in which a civilian is also killed.

### *Spycatcher* causes trouble
**31st July 1987** Trouble erupts over the publication of the book *Spycatcher*, an autobiography written by former MI5 officer Peter Wright. The book, which contains many embarrassing details about the activities of the secret services, is banned from publication in the UK. Gag orders are served to several newspapers who attempt to publish details of some of the allegations made, leading many to mock and ridicule the Law Lords. The book is eventually cleared for publication in 1988.

### Hungerford massacre
**19th August 1987** Gunman Michael Ryan goes on a rampage armed with handguns and a semi-automatic rifle in the town of Hungerford, Berkshire. He kills sixteen people, including his own mother, and injures sixteen more before turning the gun on himself.

**3 APR 1987** Gorbachev offers to remove all Soviet short-range weapons from Eastern Europe.

**11 MAY 1987** British Rail rebrands its second class as 'standard class' travel.

**12 JUN 1987** Ronald Reagan challenges Mikhail Gorbachev to 'tear down' the Berlin wall.

# 1987

## The Great Storm
*15th - 16th October 1987* England is struck overnight by the 'Great Storm', hurricane force winds which cause extensive damage and claim the lives of 22 people in the UK and Normandy. An estimated 15 million trees are felled, several ships are wrecked and the whole of the National Grid South East power system is shut down. Initial weather predictions had assumed the storm would be limited to coastal areas, and BBC weatherman Michael Fish receives much criticism for appearing to downplay the severity of the approaching winds.

## No sign of Nessie!
*11th October 1987* A million-pound project to scan the entirety of Loch Ness in search of the Loch Ness Monster fails to get a glimpse of the legendary beast. Operation Deepscan deploys 24 boats with echo-sounding equipment to scan the waters, and despite encountering several unidentified objects, the results are written off as debris on the loch bottom and seals at play.

## IKEA arrives in the UK
*1st October 1987* The first IKEA store in the UK opens in Warrington, Cheshire. The Swedish store, founded in 1943, has been popular across the continent for decades and now for the first time Brits can get their hands on the reasonably priced flatpack furniture that makes the store famous.

## King's Cross fire
*18th November 1987* A terrible tragedy strikes the London Underground as a fire takes hold on an escalator at King's Cross Underground Station. The fire quickly burns out of control, filling the tunnels with noxious gases and claiming the lives of 31 people.

# ROYALTY & POLITICS

## 1987 General Election
*11th June 1987* Margaret Thatcher wins a third term in office as the Conservatives secure another landslide victory. Despite losing 21 seats Thatcher is still comfortable with 376, a majority of 102.

## SDP merges with Liberals
*6th August 1987* The Social Democratic Party votes to merge with the Liberal party in a move that sees leader Dr David Owen resign. He is replaced as leader by Robert Maclennan but founds a breakaway faction of the party to continue outside the proposed merger.

**7 JUL 1987**
Chessington Zoo reopens as a theme park, Chessington World of Adventures.

**1 AUG 1987**
MTV Europe launches; *Money For Nothing* by Dire Straits is the first video played.

**1 SEP 1987**
The Montreal Conference sees over 70 nations agree on measures to protect the ozone layer.

# 1987

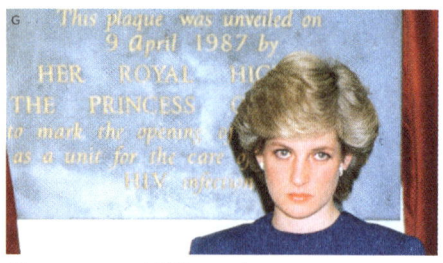

**Diana opens AIDS ward**
*9th April 1987* Princess Diana opens the Broderip Ward at the Middlesex Hospital, the first ward in the UK exclusively for the treatment of HIV and AIDS. The princess makes a stir when she shakes the hands of patients without wearing gloves, directly challenging the fear many people had of the disease.

**Andy Warhol dies**
*22nd February 1987* Pop art godfather, film maker and entrepreneur Andy Warhol dies in New York, aged 58. In his time he has elevated such everyday things such as Campbell's soup cans to art. Out of his New York City studio The Factory came a revolution that swept the art world, while Warhol also made a huge contribution to the history of rock music through sponsoring and producing the Velvet Underground.

## FOREIGN NEWS

**Political suicide**
*22nd January 1987* A bizarre scene on television in the US. R. Budd Dwyer, Pennsylvania's state treasurer, has been taking millions of dollars in kickbacks from a computer company and faces 55 years in prison. The day before the prison sentence starts, Dwyer holds a press conference. Everyone expects him to announce his resignation. But Dwyer takes a revolver from an envelope and shoots himself in the head.

**Terry Waite kidnapped**
*20th January 1987* Terry Waite, the Archbishop of Canterbury's special envoy, is in Lebanon to attempt to negotiate the release of UK hostages held there when he himself becomes a victim of kidnapping. He will remain captive until 1991.

**Waldheim banned**
*27th April 1987* The US Department of Justice declares Kurt Waldheim, former Secretary General of the UN and now the elected President of Austria, 'an undesirable alien' over his recently discovered role in Nazi persecution during the Second World War.

**Black Monday**
*19th October 1987* The global stock exchanges are turning into battlefields. After five years in which stock prices rose by an average of 350 per cent, the bubble has suddenly burst. It's Black Monday: 600 billion dollars on the Dow Jones evaporates in one day. The exact cause of the sudden stock market crash is unclear.

**30 OCT 1987**
George Michael's debut album *Faith* is released.

**18 NOV 1987**
King's Cross fire kills 31 people on the London Underground.

**1 DEC 1987**
Construction begins on the Channel Tunnel.

# 1987

**Very expensive Van Goghs**
*30th March 1987* Vincent van Gogh sets the record twice for the most expensive painting ever. A Japanese insurance company pays $39.7 million for *Vase of Fifteen Sunflowers* (1889) at an auction at Christie's in London. On 11th November, the controversial Australian businessman Alan Bond buys Van Gogh's *Irises* (1889) at Sotheby's for 49 million dollars.

**Five billion**
*11th July 1987* UN figures reveal that the world's population now stands at five billion.

**Rudolf Hess dies**
*17th August 1987* Rudolf Hess, Adolf Hitler's deputy, commits suicide at Spandau prison in West Berlin aged 93. He had been imprisoned since his conviction for crimes against peace in 1947.

**INF Treaty**
*8th December 1987* In the White House, American President Ronald Reagan and Soviet leader Mikhail Gorbachev conclude a historic agreement. The superpowers agree that both sides will no longer possess, make or test ground-launched missiles with a range of 500 to 5,000 kilometres.

**Flying stunt**
*28th May 1987* German teenager Mathias Rust performs a stunt that makes world news. The eighteen-year-old boy from Wedel rents a Cessna plane in Hamburg and flies to the Russian border via Iceland and Scandinavia. He flies on to Moscow and circles his plane a few times above the Kremlin, before landing the plane next to Red Square. He is arrested and sent to a labour camp. After fourteen months, Rust is pardoned.

# ENTERTAINMENT

**Through the Keyhole**
Nosy types tune in to *Through the Keyhole* on 3rd April, as Lloyd Grossman snoops around celebrity homes while the panellists back in the studio, guided by David Frost, try to guess 'who might live in a house like this?' It's a perfect opportunity to see how the other half live and reminds us that money doesn't necessarily buy good taste.

# 1987

### Going for Gold
Quiz show *Going for Gold*, presented by Henry Kelly, begins on BBC1 on 12th October. Seven contestants from different European countries battle it out through several rounds in a bid to make it to the grand final.

### Prime Minister's questions
Prime Minister Margaret Thatcher appears on *Saturday Superstore* on 10th January, taking part in their Pop Panel, and burying the hatchet in the career of indie band Thrashing Doves by praising their latest hit. When teenager Alison Standfast rings in and persists in asking Thatcher where she will be in the event of nuclear war, asking bluntly, 'Haven't you got a bunker or something?', things suddenly feel rather awkward. *Saturday Superstore*'s final episode is on 18th April and a new Saturday morning show, *Going Live!*, presented by Philip Schofield, begins in the autumn this year.

### It's a Royal Knockout
The Royal Family appear on the small screen this year when they take part in *The Grand Knockout Tournament* on 15th June, with a medieval tournament theme. Organised by Prince Edward, there are four teams led by himself, the Princess Royal, and the Duke and Duchess of York, each aiming to raise funds for their individual charities. In support is an eclectic mix of celebrities from Meatloaf to John Mills participating in what some see as an undignified display of royal buffoonery (apparently the Queen disapproves). Nevertheless, *It's a Royal Knockout* raises £1.5 million and has an estimated global audience of 400 million.

### Coffee?
The first TV commercial for Nescafé Gold Blend airs this year, featuring yuppy neighbours Sharon Maughan and Anthony Head who begin a flirtation over coffee. Their on-screen chemistry leads to a series of adverts over the next six years in an ongoing will they/won't they soap opera. 30 million viewers tune in to see the finale where he finally professes his love. Meanwhile, Nescafé Gold Blend sales increase by 70%.

### Bring me the finest wines
Richard E. Grant is the Withnail in *Withnail and I*, playing the hungover, loquacious libertine with boundless gusto. Withnail and Marwood (Paul McGann) are out-of-work actors who leave their squalid Camden flat for a holiday in the Lake District where they stay in a rundown cottage owned by Withnail's Uncle Monty. Full of memorable moments including the scene when Withnail strides into a Penrith tearoom and demands, 'We want the finest wines available to humanity. We want them *here*. And we want them *now*!', never has a miserable existence been quite so hilarious.

# 1987

### The Untouchables
Released 18th September, the violent underworld of Prohibition-era Chicago is the backdrop to Brian de Palma's thrilling, *The Untouchables*, with Kevin Costner as Treasury agent Eliot Ness, who assembles a team of uncorruptible law men to dismantle the power base of mob boss Al Capone and bring him to justice. As Capone, Robert de Niro takes on another role requiring him to pile on the pounds, while Sean Connery wins Best Supporting Actor Oscar for playing heroic cop Jimmy Malone.

### Thundercats - Innocence under siege
Lion-O, Cheetara, Panthro, Tygra et al thunder onto the small screen on 2nd January, a team of handsome cat-human heroes determined to save the Eye of Thundera from the Mutants of Plum-Darr and evil sorcerer, mummified Mumm-Raa. Along with other American imports like *Transformers* and *He-Man*, *Thundercats* is criticised not only for the level for violence, but also how commercially driven it is.

### Chucklevision
Paul and Barry Chuckle bring a finely-tuned blend of slapstick, jokes and vivid characters to CBBC on 26th September in *Chucklevision*. They travel around on the Chuckmobile, mess up every job they take on and coin a series of catchphrases that infiltrate the subconscious of adults as well as children. Through a staggering 293 episodes over 22 years, 'From Me...To You' and 'No slacking' become part of the national lexicon.

Treets now M&M's

### Blackadder the Third
Beginning on BBC1 on 17th September, *Blackadder the Third* transports Edmund Blackadder to the eighteenth century this time, where he is courtier and friend to Hugh Laurie's frightfully dim Prince of Wales, while Baldrick is still filthy, still stupid and still existing on a diet of turnips. Ben Elton and Richard Curtis have great fun with the Georgian references from Mrs. Miggins's Pie Shop to the episode where Baldrick accidentally burns Samuel Johnson's dictionary, obliging Edmund to re-write it in a weekend.

### Logan's Eurovision Run
Following on from his 1980 success with *What's Another Year?* on 9th May, Irish crooner Johnny Logan returns to the Eurovision Song Contest, this time held in Brussels, for another stab at glory with *Hold Me Now*. He brings the title back home to the Emerald Isle and passes into Eurovision legend as one of only two double winners in the history of the competition. He also pens Ireland's 1992 winning entry, *Why Me?*, sung by Linda Martin.

179

# 1987

## Morse code
A cerebral detective inspector who drives a Jaguar Mark 2 and has a fondness for real ale, opera and cryptic crosswords, *Inspector Morse*, first shown on ITV on 6th January, is a different animal to the traditional TV cop. In fact, Morse, who first appeared in a series of books by Colin Dexter, couldn't be more different than Jack Regan, the police character previously played by John Thaw in *The Sweeney*. The crimes are somehow more elevated too, being carried out among the dreaming spires of Oxford and surrounding countryside. Accompanied by the down-to-earth Geordie Sergeant Lewis (Kevin Whateley), Morse runs until 1993; at its peak drawing audiences of 18 million.

## Top toys
Among this year's best-selling toys are Hasbro's My Little Pony, colourful equine figures with delicious names like Applejack and Peachy, with toy sales boosted by *My Little Pony - The Movie*. And firmly entrenched as a family favourite is Trivial Pursuit, the game of general knowledge based on the famous quotation from Pope's *Rape of the Lock* - 'What mighty contests rise from trivial things.'

## Jailbirds
*Prisoner Cell Block H*, the Australian soap opera set in a women's prison, first airs on Central TV on 25th April (although Yorkshire TV has been showing it since 1984). It soon becomes a surprise, late-night ratings success.

# MUSIC

## House on fire
*24th January 1987 Jack Your Body* by Steve 'Silk' Hurley is the first record in the 'house' genre to top the UK chart. Originating in Chicago, house is a form of electronic dance music ruled by producer deejays such as Frankie Knuckles and Farley 'Jackmaster' Funk. In the UK, Beatmasters, Bomb the Bass and others are fuelling the Manchester-centred acid house boom to come.

## Smiths to split
*14th June 1987* The headline in *New Musical Express* reads 'Smiths to split'. It's premature, but it's correct: singer Morrissey and guitarist Johnny Marr are no longer talking. Marr is having much more fun working with Billy Bragg, Bryan Ferry and Talking Heads, while the opinionated, talented but difficult to like Morrissey is plotting a solo career.

# 1987

### 'Nobody puts Baby in the corner'
When Frances 'Baby' spends her summer at a holiday resort in upstate New York with her parents in 1963, she falls in love with Johnny, a dance instructor from the wrong side of the tracks whose moves and grooves are anything but polite. *Dirty Dancing*'s multi-million selling soundtrack includes the hit song, *I've Had The Time of My Life* - played during the film's climax when Baby and Johnny dance the routine they've practised and finally smash THAT lift. *Dirty Dancing* is a global sensation; UK audiences flock to see it when it opens on 16th October.

### Def Jam

*10th February 1987* Founded in 1985, producer Rick Rubin's New York based Def Jam label is the epicentre of east coast hip hop with LL Cool J, the Beastie Boys and Public Enemy on its books. The latter's debut album *Yo! Bum Rush the Show*, released today, mixes in-your-face lyrics with radical political messaging.

### Flower of Scotland
Just as the Pogues' *Fairytale of New York* is part of a venerable tradition of Irish diaspora songs, so the Proclaimers' *Letter from America* does the same for the Scottish emigration story. Twin brothers Craig and Charlie Reid are just the latest flowering of talent from Scotland.

### Beasties in Britain
*30th May 1987* Every couple of years, the UK press and publicity-seeking MPs create a media panic about some new band or style. This year their target is white hip hop trio the Beastie Boys, whose reputation follows them from the US. Tonight sees a particularly infamous gig in Liverpool including fights, missiles, a mini-riot and the arrest of Beastie Adam Horovitz, but did they really 'sneer at dying kids' as the *Daily Mirror* claims? Of course not.

### D'Arby debut
*13th July 1987* Attracting huge media attention is the debut album by Terence Trent D'Arby, R&B singer-songwriter whose rebel attitude saw him court martialled out of the Army in 1983. Entitled *Introducing the Hardline According to Terence Trent D'Arby*, it features four major hit singles including *Wishing Well*.

### Blockbusters
Three blockbuster albums dominate the sales charts in 1987. Now the world's mightiest stadium band, U2 (photo) sell fourteen million with *The Joshua Tree*, which also wins the Grammy for best album and produces two US No. 1s. Michael Jackson's *Bad*, despite uneven reviews, produces five US No. 1s - a new record for any album. Then comes the biggest selling debut album ever: *Appetite for Destruction* from new hard rock icons Guns N' Roses.

# 1987

**Family matters**
Five Star seem to have it all: a solid disco-funk sound, cross-generation appeal, great choreography and TV-friendly looks. From Romford, Deniece Pearson and her four siblings are the missing link between the Jacksons and Sister Sledge.

## MY FIRST 18 YEARS TOP 10 — 1987

1. **I Knew You Were ...** Aretha Franklin & George M.
2. **So Strong** Labi Siffre
3. **Don't Dream It's Over** Crowded House
4. **La Bamba** Los Lobos
5. **Mary's Prayer** Danny Wilson
6. **With or Without You** U2
7. **I Think We're Alone Now** Tiffany
8. **Wonderful Life** Black
9. **Build** The Housemartins
10. **Wishing Well** Terence Trent D'Arby

**Hit factory**
The studio owned by production/writing team Mike Stock, Matt Aitken and Pete Waterman is called 'the hit factory' - and no wonder. Two No. 1s - *Respectable* by Mel and Kim (photo) and *Never Gonna Give You Up* by the boyish but big-voiced Rick Astley - follow hits for Dead or Alive and Bananarama, plus a dance track called *Roadblock* that they release anonymously to fool their critics. And all this is before a certain actress arrives from Australia to discuss making a record.

**A Christmas fairytale**
*23rd November 1987* Irish punk folk band the Pogues record *Fairytale of New York* with Kirsty MacColl. Inspired by J. P. Donleavy's novel, it's a bruising but touching account of an Irish couple down on their luck in post-war Manhattan. Although a No. 2 hit, no one guesses how the song will keep coming back every Christmas and earn classic status - even if colourful language like 'scumbag', 'slut' and 'faggot' causes airplay issues in later years.

# 1987

### 'Nobody puts Baby in the corner'
When Frances 'Baby' spends her summer at a holiday resort in upstate New York with her parents in 1963, she falls in love with Johnny, a dance instructor from the wrong side of the tracks whose moves and grooves are anything but polite. *Dirty Dancing*'s multi-million selling soundtrack includes the hit song, *I've Had The Time of My Life* - played during the film's climax when Baby and Johnny dance the routine they've practised and finally smash THAT lift. *Dirty Dancing* is a global sensation; UK audiences flock to see it when it opens on 16th October.

### Def Jam
*10th February 1987* Founded in 1985, producer Rick Rubin's New York-based Def Jam label is the epicentre of east coast hip hop with LL Cool J, the Beastie Boys and Public Enemy on its books. The latter's debut album *Yo! Bum Rush the Show*, released today, mixes in-your-face lyrics with radical political messaging.

### Flower of Scotland
Just as the Pogues' *Fairytale of New York* is part of a venerable tradition of Irish diaspora songs, so the Proclaimers' *Letter from America* does the same for the Scottish emigration story. Twin brothers Craig and Charlie Reid are just the latest flowering of talent from Scotland.

### Beasties in Britain
*30th May 1987* Every couple of years, the UK press and publicity-seeking MPs create a media panic about some new band or style. This year their target is white hip hop trio the Beastie Boys, whose reputation follows them from the US. Tonight sees a particularly infamous gig in Liverpool including fights, missiles, a mini-riot and the arrest of Beastie Adam Horovitz, but did they really 'sneer at dying kids' as the *Daily Mirror* claims? Of course not.

### D'Arby debut
*13th July 1987* Attracting huge media attention is the debut album by Terence Trent D'Arby, R&B singer-songwriter whose rebel attitude saw him court martialled out of the Army in 1983. Entitled *Introducing the Hardline According to Terence Trent D'Arby*, it features four major hit singles including *Wishing Well*.

### Blockbusters
Three blockbuster albums dominate the sales charts in 1987. Now the world's mightiest stadium band, U2 (photo) sell fourteen million with *The Joshua Tree*, which also wins the Grammy for best album and produces two US No. 1s. Michael Jackson's *Bad*, despite uneven reviews, produces five US No. 1s - a new record for any album. Then comes the biggest selling debut album ever: *Appetite for Destruction* from new hard rock icons Guns N' Roses.

# 1987

## Family matters
Five Star seem to have it all: a solid disco-funk sound, cross-generation appeal, great choreography and TV-friendly looks. From Romford, Deniece Pearson and her four siblings are the missing link between the Jacksons and Sister Sledge.

### MY FIRST 18 YEARS — TOP 10 — 1987
1. I Knew You Were … *Aretha Franklin & George M.*
2. So Strong *Labi Siffre*
3. Don't Dream It's Over *Crowded House*
4. La Bamba *Los Lobos*
5. Mary's Prayer *Danny Wilson*
6. With or Without You *U2*
7. I Think We're Alone Now *Tiffany*
8. Wonderful Life *Black*
9. Build *The Housemartins*
10. Wishing Well *Terence Trent D'Arby*

## Hit factory
The studio owned by production/writing team Mike Stock, Matt Aitken and Pete Waterman is called 'the hit factory' - and no wonder. Two No. 1s - *Respectable* by Mel and Kim (photo) and *Never Gonna Give You Up* by the boyish but big-voiced Rick Astley - follow hits for Dead or Alive and Bananarama, plus a dance track called *Roadblock* that they release anonymously to fool their critics. And all this is before a certain actress arrives from Australia to discuss making a record.

## A Christmas fairytale
*23rd November 1987* Irish punk folk band the Pogues record *Fairytale of New York* with Kirsty MacColl. Inspired by J. P. Donleavy's novel, it's a bruising but touching account of an Irish couple down on their luck in post-war Manhattan. Although a No. 2 hit, no one guesses how the song will keep coming back every Christmas and earn classic status - even if colourful language like 'scumbag', 'slut' and 'faggot' causes airplay issues in later years.

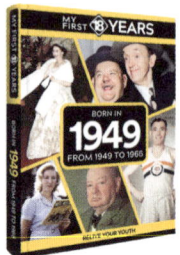 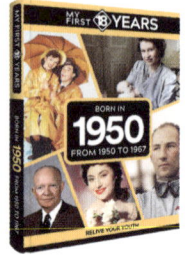 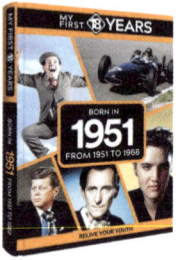 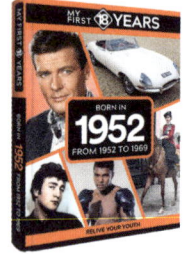
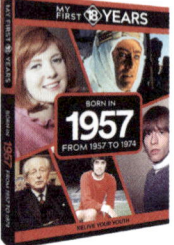 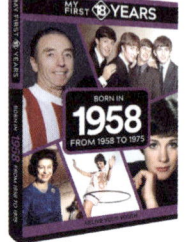 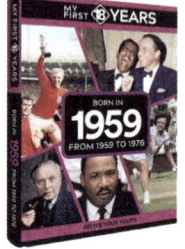 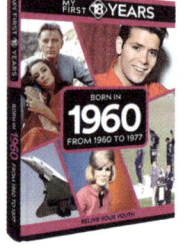
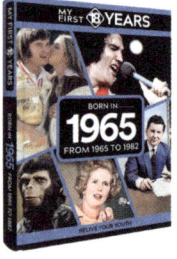  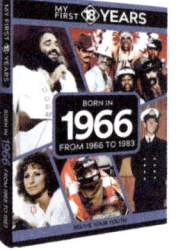
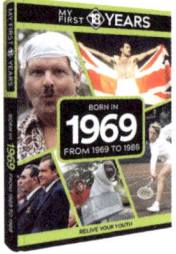   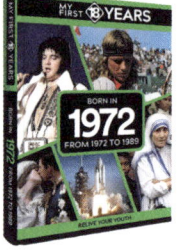
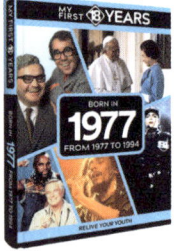 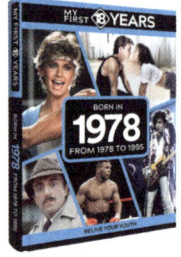 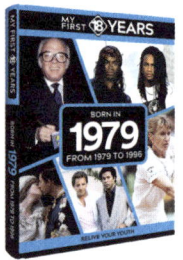 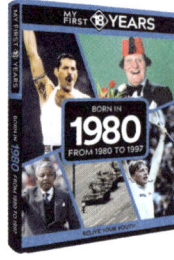